THE CYCLADES COMPUTER NETWORK

MONOGRAPH SERIES OF THE INTERNATIONAL COUNCIL FOR COMPUTER COMMUNICATIONS

Volume 2

the cyclades computer network

TOWARDS LAYERED NETWORK ARCHITECTURES

edited by

L. POUZIN

authors

Edouard André
Jean Claude Chupin
Michel Gien
Jean-Louis Grangé
Jean Le Bihan
Gérard Le Lann
Najah Naffah
Louis Pouzin
Vincent Quint
Guy Sergeant
Hubert Zimmermann

1982

NORTH-HOLLAND PUBLISHING COMPANY – AMSTERDAM · NEW YORK · OXFORD

ISBN: 0 444 86482 2

Published by:

NORTH-HOLLAND PUBLISHING COMPANY – AMSTERDAM · NEW YORK · OXFORD

Sole distributors for the U.S.A. and Canada:

ELSEVIER SCIENCE PUBLISHING COMPANY, INC.
52 Vanderbilt Avenue
New York, N.Y. 10017

Library of Congress Cataloging in Publication Data
Main entry under title:

The Cyclades computer network.

   (Monograph series of the International Council
for Computer Communications ; v. 2)
   Bibliography: p.
   1. Computer networks.   I. Pouzin, L. (Louis)
II. André, Edouard.   III. Series.
TK5105.5.C93 1982   001.64'404   82-14162
ISBN 0-444-86482-2

PRINTED IN THE NETHERLANDS

TABLE OF CONTENTS

ACKNOWLEDGEMENTS

The authors of this book are only a subset of the whole team who planned, designed, implemented or somehow contributed to the CYCLADES project. Although it is not possible to mention them all, we would like to name some of them :

J.P.	ANSART		M.	JASTRABSKY
M.	AUGER		H.	LE GOFF
J.	BOUDENANT		M.	MARTIN
J.F.	CHAMBON		A.	MARCHAND
M.	COMBES		P.	MAXIMOVITCH
D.	COMTE		G.	MEDIGUE
M.	DANET		R.	NEGARET
N.	DANG		B.	NIVELLET
K.	DANG QUOC		R.	PEDRONO
P.	DECITRE		M.	PLACE
F.	DENJEAN		J.	RASCOL
J.	DUMASLE		S.	SEDILLOT
M.	FARZA		J.	SEGUIN
R.	FOURNIER		M.	SICCO
C.	GARCIA		J.P.	TOUCHARD
R.	GARDIEN		M.	VIVINIS
M.	IRLAND		S.	WEBER

A special mention is due to the late Michel Monpetit who, at the Delegation a l'Informatique and then at IRIA, initiated and constantly supported the project even in the midst of political backwaters. Experience shows that such an individual was an unusual blessing.

Last, but not the least, we are indebted to Eric Manning's enlightening editorial contribution, which greatly contributed in putting the initial raw material in a readable form.

Louis POUZIN

CHAPTER 1

INTRODUCTION

1.1. The CYCLADES short story

The CYCLADES computer network was developed under government sponsorship (Delegation a l'Informatique) in France, between 1972 and 1975, to link about twenty heterogeneous computers located in universities, research centers and data processing centers. The goal was to set up a prototype network in order to foster experimentation in various areas, such as data communications, computer interaction, cooperative research and distributed data bases [POU72]. A particular objective was to provide access to a number of data bases available or under development within France. The network was intended to be both an object for research, and an operational tool.

In order to speed up the implementation, standard equipment was used, and modifications to operating systems were minimized. Rather, the design effort concentrated on a carefully layered architecture, allowing for a gradual insertion of specialized protocols and services tailored to specific applications and user classes [POU73c].

Network protocols were designed for simplicity and validated by simulation [LEL73]. Portable specifications were produced and implemented on several computer systems without difficulty [GAR75].

CYCLADES uses a packet-switching sub-network, which is a transparent message carrier, completely independent of host-host conventions [POU74d]. While in many ways similar to ARPANET, it presents some distinctive differences in address and message handling, intended to facilitate interconnection with other networks. In particular, addresses can have variable formats, and packets may be delivered out of sequence, so that they can flow out of the network through several gates toward an external destination.

Terminal concentrators are mini-hosts, and implement whatever services users or applications require, such as sequencing, error recovery, code translation, and buffering [DEN75]. Specialized hosts may be installed for purposes such as mail, resource allocation, information retrieval, and mass storage. A control center was developed for the continuous supervision

1

of the network.

Year´72 was devoted to the general design, planning and
staffing of the project. A coordination team, in charge of the
whole project, was set up in the Institut de Recherche
d´Informatique et d´Automatique (IRIA), a government sponsored
research laboratory reporting to the Ministry of Industry.
Participating host centers became active towards the end of´72.

Year´73 saw the implementation of a baby network, which was
publicly demonstrated at the beginning of November´73, with 3
homogeneous hosts, and one packet switch. Facilities available
were Inter-operator communications, File transfer, and Remote
job entry.

From that point on, the network grew rapidly. A presentation in
February´74 featured 4 hosts and 3 packet nodes. The packet
switching network (CIGALE) was made operational for 3 hours a
day, and this aided the testing of host software on the various
sites, as well as giving practical experience in the
operational aspects of a packet switching network.

Software for the terminal concentrator was developed on the
MITRA-15 (the same mini-computer as was used for CIGALE´s
switches). In July´74 there were 4 concentrators installed.

By June´74 CIGALE had 7 nodes, and was made operational for
longer sessions. In addition, CIGALE was available most of the
time over and above regular sessions, for users who wanted to
run tests or experiments.

In February´75, CIGALE shrank to 3 nodes, because of budgetary
constraints. Four concentrators were equipped with host
interfaces. This facility increased the total number of host
interfaces available in the network. This compensated for the
reduction in the number of nodes and allowed us to attach some
hosts to two differents ports. Indeed, a network such as
CIGALE may deliver packets to the same destination through
several ports in order to improve reliability.

To complement the control center a measurement center was also
developed. Both monitor the network in order to gather
statistics and to log abnormalities. The control center is also
used to load programs into nodes dynamically [GRA75b].

Host services had to be provided, if the network were to be of
any use. New developments were rather straightforward, as they
were implemented as user programs interfacing through macros or
sub-routine calls with CYCLADES protocols. Existing
manufacturer software, viz. time-sharing and remote-batch, was
made to interface with the network.

Services available in July´75 were time-sharing, remote-batch,
file transfer, and a facility allowing a terminal attached to a
local host to establish a connection to a remote host. These

services were only available on three hosts. No services were
at that time offered on other machines, save for a few ad hoc
implementations.

Connections were established in August´74 with the National
Physical Laboratory (NPL) in London, in October´75 with the
European Space Agency (ESA) in Rome, and in June´76 with the
newly born European Informatics Network (EIN).

Since early 76, CIGALE has been continuously available,
although the control center is only manned 12 hours a day on
week days. The network´s reliability turned out to be
sufficient without attendance during nights and week-ends.

Out of 20 host computers, 6 are offering services on a regular
basis. Others use the net for their own purposes, such as
experiments, or exchanging files with partners. Typical uses
are remote job entry, conversational time-sharing, and
information retrieval.

1.2. Team organization

The control of the work of a multitude of organizations,
scattered over a wide geographical area would require a very
powerful line of command if tasks were organized on a factory
basis. In a research environment this approach is just
unrealistic. Therefore, there was almost no administrative
control and very few reports or large meetings (no more than
quarterly).

The main idea was to develop friendship among all the
participants, who hardly knew each other before, and to
introduce goals, challenge, enthusiasm, as well as some
redundancy so that no failure would be critical. People were
encouraged to take initiative and see each other whenever
necessary. Mixed teams involving persons from various places
were set up, mostly to break down parochialism and inhibitions.
In order to make sure that no one would be left out, or retire
to an ivory tower, a person from IRIA was assigned specifically
to the job of travelling consultant and gossip carrier. It was
assumed that information around the network would circulate
much better through thousands of informal channels, than it
would through a rigid, formal structure. In particular,
contributions, or lack of contribution, from individuals were
more widely visible. This approach seemed to work [POU75d].

However, there were unavoidably some critical paths, which were
kept under the direct control of IRIA within the headquarters
of the project. These tasks were :

- CIGALE, the packet switching network
- The definition of network-wide protocols
- The implementation of protocols on machines provided by CII
(Compagnie Internationale pour l´Informatique, a French

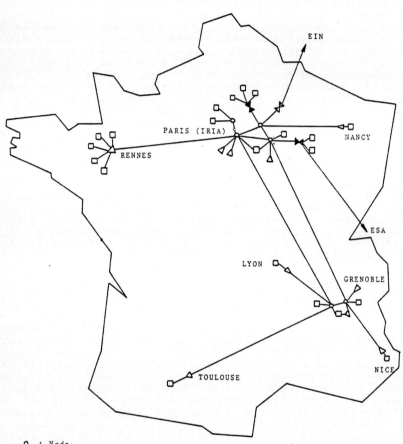

EIN

PARIS (IRIA)

NANCY

RENNES

ESA

LYON

GRENOBLE

TOULOUSE

NICE

O : Node

Δ : Concentrator

M : Gateway

□ : Host

Figure 1.1.(1)—CYCLADES topology (1978)

computer manufacturer now merged with HONEYWELL-BULL), which represented 50 % of the hosts.

With these tasks under control, the team was in a safer position to set at least up half the network on schedule.

Participants saw CIGALE as a black box carrying packets. Thus they did not have to be directly concerned in its construction. The CIGALE effort coincided with the first deliveries of MITRA 15's by CII. This meant teething problems, mainly in technical support, documentation and basic software. In addition to this, our staff were mostly inexperienced programmers.

It took until mid'74 to recover from these early difficulties; well trained professionals from software houses were gradually brought in, and CIGALE got well under control.

The protocol team was initially composed of people from a variety of participants, in order to gain wider acceptance. Some individuals were assigned to IRIA for periods ranging from 3 months to one year. Others worked with the project for short periods, or attended frequent small meetings. As a result, the CYCLADES protocols were already well accepted when their specifications were made available. We experimented with a method of portable definition, intended to facilitate implementation on various operating systems, and prevent ambiguities in interpretation. This approach has been quite satisfactory, as practically no incompatibility problems have been reported from the various sites.

Participants were in charge of developing their own host software, when they could not benefit from the IRIA implementation. In addition, they co-operated in various ways : adaptation of host services to the network environment, demonstrations, simulation of host protocols before implementation, and preliminary studies in view of coming developments. Most of them were given contracts from IRIA to help them set up a local team, and compensate partially for the manpower they provided. On the other hand, they had to make computer time available free of charge for software testing.

A noticeable point was the very strong cooperation obtained from CII in the definition and implementation of host protocols and adaptation of host services. While the basic host to host protocols were designed without the need for operating system modification, this could not apply to existing access methods, designed for directly connected terminals. Furthermore a proportion of participants would not have reacted enthusiastically to the idea of having in their systems modifications unsupported by their manufacturer. In order to anticipate these predictable difficulties, an agreement was reached with CII, whereby this company took the responsibility of maintaining the CYCLADES software on its own computers. A similar problem could have arisen with other manufacturers, but its scale remained much more limited. Modifications were under participant responsibility.

When CYCLADES was initially put into operation, i.e. in the
last quarter of 1974, we relied on each participant to be
present on the network at least 2 hours a day. This did not
work out, as most participants did not consider the network as
really operational, and shunned sessions as a waste of time.

Through a mixture of participant volunteering and political
pressure from the Ministry of Education, it was decided to
expand the duration of sessions to 6 hours, and concentrate all
effort on 2 centers, Lyon and Grenoble, in addition to the IRIA
center. Simultaneously, a campaign was launched to recruit
users and install terminals attached to concentrators. Monthly
meetings were held to review progress, uncover hurdles, and
take appropriate speedy action. All parties involved were
informally invited so as to create a forum-like atmosphere and
to foster the exchange of experiences.

After January´75, the project definitely picked up new
momentum, even though it was only visible to a few
participants. Emphasis shifted from system to user
matters : terminal keyboards, command language, manuals,
session schedules, and training. The real concern was no longer
whether the net worked, but how to make it attractive. Soon
other participants got anxious to climb aboard the bandwagon.

1.3. Personnel and resources

The number of people assigned to the project changed
constantly, and not all persons were assigned full time. As it
was not realistic to keep precise track of the amount of
manpower made available by each participant, we usually relied
on samplings taken at intervals of a few months.

The manpower spent on the project till the end of ´75 was about
150 man-years. Expenses in contracts with participants,
software houses, and CII totaled roughly 20 million French
Francs (MFF) by the end of ´75. Even without reliable figures
on participants´ contributions, it was estimated that they
would equal the amount of subsidies.

The total initial forecasts until the end of´75 were
respectively 140 man-years, and 52 MFF. IRIA´s part was
predicted at 20.8 MFF. It came out at 20.6 MFF [POU74].

Overall, the project was both on schedule and within the
predicted budget. However, tight-rope maneuvering became
necessary to damp out the seesaw funding pattern peculiar to
the French Administration.

It should also be recognized that the extent to which
objectives have been met is not always as we expected. In the
areas of basic software, results are generally beyond our

initial expectations. A second iteration of host protocols was completed by mid´75. CYCLADES and CIGALE have been accepted not only as an interesting experiment, but also as prototypes of commercial products. The transfer of know-how to the computing industry has been faster than could be predicted. On the other hand, the adaptation of existing manufacturer software was more cumbersone than we had hoped.

1.4. The user milieu

Other than the typical software and equipment problems, the main difficulties encountered were organizational and psychological. Users hate changing their habits, and it is always difficult to persuade them to try another computer or system. This may be a reason why we found better response from people who were working on new applications, and who had not yet settled on specific computing services. Computer centers are not organized to deal with very distant customers, particularly in regard to documentation and consulting services. Charging practices are also quite a problem in the typical environment of the French Administration.

It became clear that new methods, policies and tools needed to be devised. A substantial effort has already been devoted to user manuals and on-line help. Consistency has been improved among local command languages and terminal handling. This trend is characteristic of computer network development. Users of several systems find it cumbersome to have to master many variants in software tools, which produce essentially the same functions. Formerly, they were satisfied in learning only one computer system environment.

Finally, applications got off the ground, but slower than we anticipated. It is clearer now that real users do not move until they can verify the practical usefulness of a new tool. With CYCLADES, they discovered that using a computer via a network was about the same as on direct lines. In addition, they could use distant computers, previously too far away, and more attractive systems. Also, they could choose any ASCII terminal. And it all worked at least as well as before.

Except for a few remote batch stations, CYCLADES terminals are used in conversational mode. There are about 100 terminals. 75 % are used by computer people, researchers and students. The rest are used by other kinds of professionals, such as industry engineers or librarians, mainly for technical information retrieval.

1.5. Industrial spinoff

CII and some software houses were continuously involved in the CYCLADES development. This has resulted in acceleration of their learning process in network concepts and know-how.

Numerous industrial   products have been derived from CYCLADES,
for example :

- A computer network architecture and its protocols for a
computer manufacturer.
- A packet switching network, host adaptations, and terminal
concentrators for a military organization.
- A packet switching network for a railway company.
- Gateways and host adapters for public packet networks
- Statistical multiplexers and terminal concentrators
- Virtual terminal   protocols   in   several   administrative
applications   networks   (French   Railways,   French Gas and
Electricity, EURONET-DIANE virtual terminal for the European
Communities).

1.6. Conclusions

As intended, CYCLADES became actively used as an operational
tool.   Apart from its development, it has generated new
research and applications, and it has been a training ground
for a community of experts of international reputation.   The
network technology has been transferred to users and industry
during the development phase. A most striking effect is visible
in professional sociology. No other project before on the
French computer scene had brought together so many individuals.
Interactions have snowballed within traditionally isolated
groups. There is undoubtedly something that we might call
"network power".

1.7. A reader´s map

The presentation of CYCLADES in this book follows an idealized
version of the development of the project.   The overall
architecture of the network along with the underlying basic
concepts are presented first in section 2. The translation of
these general concepts into specific protocols for each layer
of the architecture is then described in section 3. Sections 4
and 5 contain a description of the implementation of CIGALE
(section 4) and of Host and Terminal software (section 5).   The
organization and functioning of network operation is presented
in section 6, along with the services made available to network
users, and figures on network usage resulting from observation
and measurements.   Section 7 gathers results from various
simulations and modelling studies performed about CIGALE and
CYCLADES.   Section 8 is an introduction to the work on
distributed systems initialized in CYCLADES and pursued in an
other project, SIRIUS, on Distributed Data Bases. Finally,
section 9 relates the work done in CYCLADES to the general
development of standards for heterogeneous networks, which was
a major concern in the project.

Of course, the project did not follow this idealized
progression and several iterations were necessary before

reaching the final stage. Each section contains a summarized
history of one specific area in the project. Initial choices
are presented and discussed as well as reasons for subsequent
changes.

Sections 1 and 2 form an introduction to CYCLADES and its major
orientations, which are presently widely accepted. Readers
already familiar with those concepts might want to go directly
to section 3 for presentation of CYCLADES protocols or even to
sections 4 and 5 to get information about implementation
choices. Section 6 on modelling and simulation requires only a
general knowledge of CYCLADES protocols. Readers interested
mainly in packet switching might read section 2, 3.1, and 4,
while those interested in host and terminal protocols may skip
section 4.

Additional information and more detailed or complementary
discussion of various aspects of CYCLADES can be found in the
extended bibliography contained in section 11. This
bibliography contains also references to papers which inspired
CYCLADES or were found to be relevant in the context of
CYCLADES.

CHAPTER 2

CONCEPTS AND SYSTEM ARCHITECTURE

2.1. Concepts

2.1.1. Heterogeneity is a constraint

Heterogeneity of data processing systems

Networks of computers may be homogeneous, but this is the exception rather than the rule. Some organizations, such as IBM, Control Data Corp., and Computer Science Corp., have set up computer networks to provide specific services, using a single brand of machines and operating systems. Sooner or later a new generation comes along and must be installed. Replacing a whole network with new systems in a short span of time is quite unrealistic, thus homogeneous networks are bound to become heterogeneous or die out.

Most computer networks cannot afford to be homogeneous in the first place, since they have to start with existing installations which usually happen to be a mixture of every computer system on the market.

Most large organizations happen to have several types of computers, either as a deliberate choice, or as a result of progressive acquisition of new data processing equipment or successive merging of separate organizations.

This is even more the case for cooperative networks such as CYCLADES which link together computers (and terminals) from a number of independent organizations. Although CII machines are in the majority, CYCLADES started with eight (and there are presently over fifteen) different types of computer systems.

Heterogeneity of data transmission systems

In spite of the standardization efforts pursued in CCITT (see section 9), computer networks are also faced with heterogeneity in data transmission facilities. The same facilities are not available in every country and tariffs differ widely from one country to another. Of course, different data transmission services have different interfaces.

Any large computer network must integrate several
telecommunication facilities (e.g. leased lines, switched
telephone lines and packet switching) for reasons of
availability and/or economy .

Heterogeneity of applications

Most organizations, nowadays, as in CYCLADES, make use of
"informatics" (data processing) for a variety of applications.
When several organizations participate in a network, the
heterogeneity of applications is even more obvious. Such
networks are usually referred to as general computer networks
as opposed to networks dedicated to specific applications. It
should be noted that dedicated networks are usually driven
towards more generality in order to accomodate applications
that were not originally planned (e.g. the SITA network),
[GLO73].

2.1.2. Heterogeneity is an advantage

The capability for a network to be heterogeneous in terms of
data processing equipments, data transmission media and
applications, initially viewed as a constraint, turns out to be
a definite advantage.

It allows one to get the best from each system, since it
removes the constraint of having one single type of system for
all applications. Machines can be dedicated to the work they
are best adapted to (e.g. business oriented, scientific, data
base).

Heterogeneity opens up competition for more cost-effective
service, since various systems can offer the same kind of
service and users can choose freely.

Heterogeneity permits graceful evolution to follow
technological progress, since a new system can be introduced to
gradually replace an old one.

The ability to accomodate various data transmission facilities
allows the network to optimize the cost of its
telecommunications according to tariffs (and their possible
variations).

2.1.3. Sharing implies levels of commonality

The fundamental rationale for building computer networks is
resource sharing.

The sharing of data transmission resources was an initial step.
The use of switching techniques (circuit switching or packet
switching) provided any two users of the network with potential

interconnection.

Switching allows a user to connect to a variety of data
processing systems (servers) from a single terminal equipment,
i.e. the same terminal can be shared between various servers.
Switching allows servers to be called by any terminal on the
network, i.e. a variety of terminals share the same data
processing system. More generally, switching allows any
process (user, program, terminal, etc.) to get connected to any
resource on the network, i.e. all resources can be shared
through networking and switching.

However, sharing implies considerably more than simple
switching :

Access to and use of a resource is governed by a set of rules
and conventions (commands, procedures, messages, etc.) which
the user has to be aware of and follow.

In a heterogeneous network, however, internal conventions
differ from one system to another and thus cannot be used for
external communication.

Letting each system define its own conventions for its users
would be cumbersome for users since they would have to adapt
specifically to each system. Letting each user impose its own
conventions on its servers is not technically acceptable to
servers. Choosing a specific computer system as a model
imposed on the whole network would simply prohibit
heterogeneity, since it would be practically impossible for
other systems to mimic the specific details of behaviour of the
model system.

The only practical solution is to define levels of commonality,
i.e. structured sets of conventions to be used for cooperation
throughout the network. Such conventions must make minimum
assumptions about the internal architecture and conventions of
each system. They only apply to cooperation between components
of the network. Of course, when such conventions are well
established and widely admitted, it may be sensible to use them
also for internal cooperation within a system, but it should
not, in any case, be compulsory. In other words, the idea is
to define a model as an open-ended structure of cooperating
conventions [ZIM78] to which all systems must conform.
Heterogeneous systems can be specifically adapted to this model
since no assumption is made on the internal structure of
components. The model itself can evolve due to its open-ended
structure.

2.1.4. Basic levels of commonality : data transmission and transport

Data transmission

Computer networks make use of existing data transmission facilities which are independent from the computers and terminals to be interconnected. It is therefore essential to recognize a level of commonality corresponding to data transmission. As stated earlier, any large network makes use of a variety of data transmission facilities, i.e. data transmission components are taken for granted and it does not seem realistic in the near future that they should comply with a single model and offer a consistent set of interfaces [POU75a].

Until recently, no data transmission system suitable to computer networks was provided by PTTs or common carriers. This was still the case in 1978 for CYCLADES. Computer network designers were faced with the problem of building their own data transmission systems. At the time CYCLADES was designed, requirements for an appropriate data transmission system could be summarized as follows : [POU73e]

The challenge in designing a data transmission system for a computer network is that only qualitative aspects may be guessed.

No figures are available, since computer networks do not exist. Or at least they have not yet emerged out of the initial building up stage. What we may assume is that there will be computers and terminals, and some barely predictable amount of data traffic between them. Presumably, the amount of traffic will be related to the capability of those devices to generate or accept data. In other words, computer-to-computer traffic, high speed and low speed terminals will likely fall within distinct categories of traffic patterns.

Therefore, the data transmission system will have to simultaneously meet a mixture of requirements pertaining to different classes of data interchange. This comes in addition to carrying dominant flows, depending on the geographical topology of installation clubs.

Since the data transmission system should (1) cater for an unlimited number of computer makes, (2) be suitable for semi-private traffic, and (3) work in an environment of loosely related installations, it cannot depend on any of them. In a context of mutually suspicious parties, the data transmission system will be deemed at fault, unless it has proven itself very reliable.

Furthermore, it should carry, within some limits, a somewhat unpredictable traffic, ranging from low speed conversational messages, up to bursty high speed process-to-process interplay.

New installations may be added, others can be discontinued.
Since the number and type of applications using the network is
a priori evolutionary, there cannot be any favorite
characteristics tailored to some specific traffic.

Although some requirements may turn out to be contradictory,
the data transmission system has to walk a narrow line, and
comply efficiently with a diversity of traffic patterns. This
is called flexibility, in a subjective sense, as opposed to
rigidity.

Carrying data between heterogeneous computers or terminals,
including all sorts of private or semi-public conventions,
would end up in a Penelope´s web type of task, if the data
transmission system had to get involved in data codes, formats,
procedures, etc. Adding constantly new features and fixing old
ones would not make for a reliable system, and installations
would resent being tied to not-quite-satisfactory network
options. A better approach is to make the data transmission
system data transparent, in order to accomodate any type of
code or convention that installations might want to use.

Once a network starts operating, it becomes very frustrating
for users to disrupt its working, particularly if they have
built a substantial investment in software and organizational
structures. A most appreciated virtue of a data transmission
system is to provide for abiding service, so that long term
planning be carried out, counting upon well defined network
characteristics. Data transmission is thus akin to a public
service.

Changes in components of the data transmission system should
not have any visible impact, other than improvement, in the way
installations exchange data. Requiring all users to adapt their
programs overnight would verge on sheer upheaval.

The previous considerations converge towards opting for a data
transmission system as independent as possible from
installations or terminals which it is to serve. On this way,
both users and data transmission system can protect their
investment, and be free to introduce whatever gadget they like,
as long as they keep the same conventions to talk to each
other.

Transport

In most systems, several independent processes run
concurrently. They just happen to share local resources.
Cooperation within the network takes place between individual
processes rather than between systems as a whole. The network
conventions must cater to interprocess communication, i.e.
define how processes get connected to each other and how
information exchanged between processes is passed from one
system to another through the data transmission system. Thus

interprocess communication is the next level of commonality to
be identified above data transmission.

The corresponding set of conventions is usually termed a
transport protocol and the resulting interprocess communication
facility is called the transport service, transport function or
transport box (see section 2.3).

The rationale for identifying this transport component is that
its function is not specific to one application but can be used
by any of them. In other words, all kinds of applications will
share the transport component. They add their own sets of
conventions (or protocols) to define the meaning as well as the
format of data they exchange through the transport box.

As long as the transport component has not been defined and
built, the network cannot exist, since communication is a
prerequisite to sharing.

But the transport component in itself is not sufficient : it
just allows us to get connected to resources, and must be
augmented with conventions about the use of resources. This
latter type of convention is sometimes referred to as
application control.

2.1.5. Application control

It is clear that conventions for the use of all resources
within a network need not and cannot be defined and implemented
in one shot. It is also obvious that some resources are not
widely shared, at least at the beginning of the network's life.
It can be observed, and it is our experience, that the pressure
from users for an application control protocol to be defined
(i.e. for ensuring commonality in the area of applications) is
strictly related to the actual amount of sharing of the
corresponding resource.

It seems to be a general rule that the initial requirement on
any large network is for a set of conventions allowing people
to use the same terminal to access a variety of services. This
commonality in terminal access can be provided by a Virtual
Terminal Protocol [DAY78], which defines a standard behaviour
for terminals on the network as well as a standard way of
handling terminals through the network (see section 3.4).

Then, when users start using the network, they are gradually
led to compare equivalent services provided by different
systems and tempted to use the best of each. The pressure then
builds up for further commonality. For example :

Users want to move their data from one system to another (e.g.
use a text editor on one system to prepare a program and ship
it to another system for execution). This leads one to define a
File Transfer Protocol or more generally a File Management

Protocol.

Secondly, users become infuriated by meaningless differences between control languages of various systems (e.g. different login procedures) and this leads one to standardize the most widely shared procedures between human users and data processing systems.

As long as sharing develops, new requirements for commonality can be identified and new protocols have to be defined. Thus, it is most sensible not to anticipate too much about the actual usage of the network, in order to take advantage of user feedback to adapt optimally to the real world.

2.2. Functional layers

Levels of commonality are implemented by corresponding layers of functions : the data transmission layer forms the basis upon which is built the transport layer, on top of which can be installed a virtual device protocol layer which ensures commonality in terminal access.

These three layers of functions are analysed in the following subsections.

2.2.1. Data transmission

The analysis of the data transmission component must be guided by the following considerations :

A functional analysis of existing and planned data transmission services, pointing out their basic characteristics, commonalities and discrepancies, is required to provide the basis for a unified plan for their integration in the global architecture.

Data transmission systems for computer networks are still in infancy and it is worth paying attention to their design. The fundamental requirements [POU74h] for such systems, taking into account an optimum distribution of functions among all components (data processing and transmission), are best analyzed by computer networks designers. Cooperation between them and telecommunication people would permit both to reach optimum compromises.

Existing data transmission facilities

The existing data transmission facilities were originally designed for telephony. Leased or switched telephone lines were tailored for voice transmission between telephone sets. Noise, failures and delays to serve a call are bearable for human to

human voice communication. For data transmission, modems permit
the transmission of bits over voice grade circuits, with a
reasonable bit error rate (10E-4 to 10E-6). Data link control
procedures allow one to recover from such errors. The
availability and reliability of lines are very dependent on the
environment and are often not acceptable as such (many users
have experienced repair delays ranging from several hours to
several days).

Switching, the prerequisite for sharing, as presently offered
by the switched telephone system, is totally inadequate for
computer communication (low bandwidth and long call
establishment time).

Some PTTs or common carriers began in the early 1970´s to offer
switched circuits specially tailored for data transmission e.g.
[GAB71]. The quality of service was much more acceptable, but
a fixed bandwidth was dedicated to each conversation even if no
data was being transmitted (a circuit between a terminal and a
computer is usually used less than five per cent of the time).
Thus it should be possible to lower cost through a better
sharing of data transmission resources.

Through the use of automatic dialing, modems and data link
procedures, these existing data transmission systems can be
viewed as allowing one to exchange blocks of data between data
processing components with a very low undetected error rate
(10E-10). The remaining drawbacks are : (1) limited switching
capability, (2) low bandwidth, (3) sometimes poor availability,
and (4) the number of physical interfaces to the data
transmission system(s), since there is one physical port per
circuit.

Data transmission facilities for distributed informatics

The initial requirements for such data transmission facilities
have been reviewed in section 2.1.4 : switching, reliability,
flexibility and independence. To the preceding analysis, a more
precise set of requirements or non-requirements can be added.

First, interfaces to a data transmission system are intended to
pass data to the data transmission system, for delivery to the
destination user. Such an interface needs to be duplicated
only for reliability reasons. Traffic to and from various
destinations should be multiplexed on the interfaces with the
data transmission system, since the sharing of interfaces
reduces costs.

Secondly, the size of the blocks accepted by the data
transmission system have to be limited for various reasons,
such as error rate on lines, buffer management and the fair
sharing of resources. In any case, data processing systems will
have to be prepared to fragment data into blocks acceptable for
transmission, and reassemble them upon arrival. Therefore, the

size of the blocks to be transmitted should be simply chosen to optimize the efficiency of interfacing and transmission.

Third, transmission delays must be small. Expensive transmission resources should not be tied up unnecessarily. It appears in particular that sequencing reduces efficiency since reordering means slowing the whole process of transmission and delivery in waiting for laggards (see for instance [CER75a] or [POU76f]).
Reordering outside the data transmission system, if required, is not a serious problem. It already exists in data link control procedures when some blocks are delayed by an error (see for instance "Selective Reject" in HDLC, [ISO77]). When two interfaces to the data transmission system are used, sequencing becomes a disadvantage since additional conventions must be used to tie them together, again raising a reliability problem (see section 3.1.4).

Fourth, packet switching techniques can effectively optimize the sharing of data transmission resources. When used in meshed store-and-forward networks, they provide high availability through adaptive or alternate routing. They can be used on various transmission media such as telephone lines, radio, satellites, and local networks. At present, and for the next few years, packet switching is a suitable answer to the requirements of data transmission for distributed informatics.

In CYCLADES, since no adequate data transmission facility was available for a network of its size, we had to build it ourselves. In such conditions, we had the opportunity to choose an overall design for the network [POU73c] and, in particular, to optimize the distribution of functions and responsibilities between the data transmission system CIGALE [POU73,POU74d] and the transport layer in the data processing systems. For instance, fragmentation of messages into packets and reassembly upon arrival are not provided by CIGALE ; this is done, when required, by hosts that are in a much better position than CIGALE to do it. If a process wants to send or receive messages, it means that it has buffers that can contain them. If fragmentation and reassembly are performed in the hosts, these buffers can be used. CIGALE would have to duplicate all these buffers, if it did reassemble messages.

CIGALE is a simple packet switching subnetwork, providing hosts and terminals with a packet transmission service or "datagram service" as it is called in CCITT terminology. Packets are transmitted within a minimum delay (e.g. less than 200 ms [KAH71,EYR77]) and user equipments can have multiple connections to CIGALE for increased reliability. A functional description of CIGALE is given in section 3.1 and details of its implementation are given in section 4.

Other types of data transmission systems have been designed or planned by PTTs and common carriers. They finally agreed on the definition of a Virtual Circuit service which represents a

compromise between the replacement of existing telephone lines
presently used by data processing systems and providing a
service tailored to the coming distributed informatics. It is
very likely that much progress will still be made by public
data transmission networks to provide cost-effective services
well-adapted to users' requirements.

2.2.2. Transport

The next functional layer in the overall architecture is the
transport layer which caters for interprocess communication. It
implements the set of conventions used by the various data
processing systems to exchange blocks of information through
data transmission facilities. It is essential that variations
in data transmission systems or interfaces not be visible from
the higher layers of the architecture. It is also highly
desirable that the same conventions be used to perform the same
function, regardless of the various data transmission systems.
The first objective leads to a unique definition of a transport
service, provided for the use of the higher layers of the
architecture. The second objective suggests a structured
definition of the transport protocol adaptable to variations in
the data transmission layer of the network. In CYCLADES, this
is done through a structured set of options in the Transport
Protocol [ZIM75] (see section 3.2).

The provision of interprocess communication requires the
definition of a name space (or address space), and the
multiplexing of several conversations between any two systems.
The possibility of error and failure in the data transmission
system requires end to end error control. Since conversations
must be kept independent, individual flow control must be
provided.

The adaptation of the transport protocol to a variety of data
transmission systems includes fragmentation and reassembly of
packets, and support of various data transmission interfaces.

The same principles have been adopted within the IFIP proposal
for an internetwork end-to-end Transport Protocol submitted as
an IFIP contribution to ISO, [CER76].

A detailed description of the Transport Protocol designed for
CYCLADES is given in section 3.2.

2.2.3. Virtual device control

As already explained in section 2.1.5, terminal access is a
basic initial requirement for any network. Users want to be
able to use the network as they previously used telephone
lines, i.e. they want to access their customary data
processing system. The requirement for switched access to
various services follows, soon after the network begins

operation.

Another problem is that existing terminals are not built to be operated through a network. Indeed they interact very intimately with a computer through a physical line. However, it is clear that they cannot be replaced just to accomodate the network.

Less frequent interactions mean that some problems have to be handled on the terminal side :

a) terminals must look more intelligent. In addition, a Virtual Terminal Protocol defines a standard behaviour for all terminals ;

b) all terminals have to look like the model called the Virtual Terminal. It is called "virtual" since it only defines how the terminal has to appear.

The positive aspects of heterogeneity, i.e. the functional differences between terminals, must be taken into account by an appropriate structure of the protocol (e.g. a teleprinter cannot look like a sophisticated data-entry terminal). In CYCLADES, this is obtained by optional features in the protocol, allowing one to define classes of Virtual Terminals.

A detailed description of the Virtual Terminal Protocol designed in CYCLADES is given in section 3.4 and implementation examples can be found in section 5.

2.3. Model

2.3.1. Reference structure

The basic architecture of the network is organized as a hierarchical structure, often referred to as an onion skin or layered architecture. It can be formally represented by the reference structure shown in figure 2.3.(1).

Here, layer(n) of the structure makes use of (n-1)Services provided by the lower layers through the (n-1)Access. Layer(n) is made of (n)Entities that cooperate according to an (n)Protocol.

The specifications of a layer of the architecture must in some way refer to the set of services provided by lower layers. This will be done by making use of access primitives. The set of access primitives to a service should be viewed simply as a means to describe the logical structure of the network. It does not necessarily imply the existence of the corresponding interface in any implementation of a part of the network, since the architecture applies to relations between systems (i.e. to what is seen from outside each system) and not to the internal

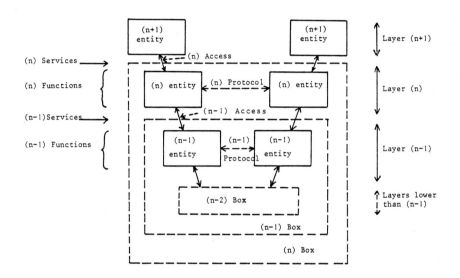

Figure 2.3.(1) - Reference Structure

functioning of these systems. (1)

2.3.2. Independence of layers

Two basic principles are used as a guideline in the definition
of the network architecture and protocols :

a) Define a logical structure that makes minimum assumptions
about the distribution of functions between physical
components.

b) Define a modular structure that minimizes the
interdependency between the various components.

---

(1) We restrict the use of the word "interface" to actual
interfaces in the context of implementations. In the model the
word "access" is used to designate the logical boundaries
between layers of the architecture.

These principles provide the flexibility needed to keep up with
technological progress without having to redesign the whole
network. The reference structure, as previously defined,
provides a model conforming to these principles. Its logical
structure ensures maximum flexibility since it allows us to
replace any box by another one, provided it offers the same
services. The view which one layer has of the underlying boxes
remains unchanged after such a replacement (see section 2.3.3).

The use of such a model with independent layers ultimately
favours a modular architecture. As long as the innermost layers
remain functionally the same, any change in their
implementation or in their internal conventions do not impact
the outermost layers. Thus, it is possible to define a
protocol for (n)Entities independently of the physical
implementation of the (n-1)Box.

This flexibility can be extended to the implementation of each
part of the network, provided that the interfaces between
layers do actually appear. This may be too constraining or too
costly for some implementations. In that case, it might be a
sensible choice to implement several entities of consecutive
layers with a different structure, e.g. as a single piece
without identifiable interfaces. However, if we do this and if
one layer changes, the whole piece has to be changed. The
resulting loss in flexibility is balanced by a lower cost in
implementation and/or operation. The only necessity is that the
external appearance of the set of entities comply with the
model, i.e. protocol visibility remains unchanged.

2.3.3. Functional layout

The reference structure can be used to formally express the
design concepts analyzed in the previous sections 2.1 and 2.2
in the following way. Data transmission facilities constitute
the lower layers of the architecture. Data transmission
services are provided by Data transmission boxes, such as
CIGALE, which provides a Datagram service well suited to
distributed informatics (see section 2.2.1).

Other data transmission boxes/services may be used. It is most
desirable that their variations be invisible from application
programs, which constitute a major investment and must
therefore be kept independent of changes in the data
transmission layer of the network. This is achieved by defining
transport services.

These are provided by a transport box embedding and masking a
possible variety of data transmission boxes (see also
section 3.3.9).

The transport layer is built on top of the data transmission
boxes, and is made of transport entities called Transport
Stations (TS). These transport stations provide transport

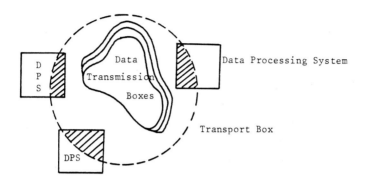

Figure 2.3.(2) - The transport box

services to the higher layers throuh transport accesses.   In
order to provide the transport service, the TS cooperate
according to a transport protocol, a set of rules which define
procedures and message formats for exchanging information
between TS. The TS make use of the data transmission service in
exchanging information (Figure 2.3.(3)).

The Virtual Terminal Protocol and the File Management Protocol,
previously introduced in sections 2.1 and 2.2, are among the
higher-layer protocols making use of the transport services.

2.3.4. Practical flexibility

Building a functional model is not a goal per se ; the interest
of such a model may be derived from its ability to simplify the
implementation of the various layers and its adaptability to
changes in the implementation of a specific layer. This has
been validated by experience in CYCLADES, as the following
example shows :

a) Changes in the packet format

In 1975, it was decided to change the format used for CIGALE
packets, in order to conform to the D-format defined within
IFIP [IFI76]. The transport protocol as well as protocols in
higher layers were kept unchanged.

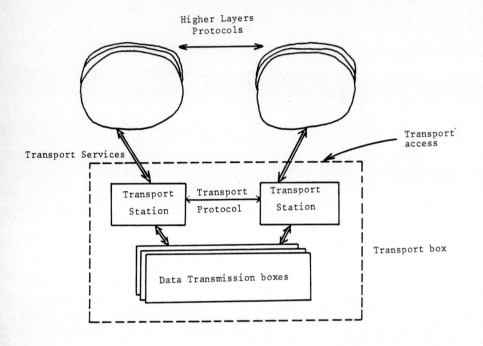

Figure 2.3.(3) - Functional layout

b) Changes in the transport protocol

Simulation and experiments suggested some modifications to the transport protocol [ZIM77]. Again flexibility was most helpful, as transport station software could be changed without requiring modification of data transmission services, or rewriting of existing applications which used the higher level protocols.

2.4. Conclusions

The concept of a layered structure is by no means an innovation. It has always more or less inspired designers of complex systems, whether they be languages, compilers, operating systems, or large application programs. Difficulties in the design of layered systems are not at all in reinventing the principles of embedded layers, but in the identification of appropriate intra- and inter-layer relationships. It is quite easy to draw boxes that look like independent layers on a piece of paper. It is much less easy to maintain independence at the implementation stage.

The design discipline applied all throughout the CYCLADES
project is not just a design exercise. It is intended to
facilitate implementation, and make it reflect thoroughly the
flexibility built in the model. This goal has been achieved,
as the previous examples have shown.

The following section presents a compact description of the
functional contents of the basic layers chosen for CYCLADES.

CHAPTER 3

PROTOCOLS AND COMPONENTS

3.1. CIGALE - The Transmission box

3.1.1. Distributed machine concept

The basic function of CIGALE is to carry packets from sources to destinations. In order to obey the principle of independence between system layers (see sections 2.1.4 and 2.3.2), the internal workings of CIGALE remain invisible from upper layers. Thus, an elementary model is a black box similar to a XEROX copier. It takes an image of a source packet, and after some delay delivers a copy to the specified destination.

On the other hand, additional functions may be necessary for specific purposes such as : help users, take statistics, put out diagnostics, etc. Most computers are delivered with hardware and software tools intended for such purposes. Some of these tools are exercised by a human operator, or a maintenance engineer, through specific devices (e.g. keys, test equipment). Very often, they are not compatible with simultaneous normal system operation [GRA75c].

A packet network is a particular example of a real time system. Availability is a major determinant of the quality of service. Were CIGALE considered as a mere collection of conventional computers exchanging packets, each node would require a duplex system, with constant human supervision. Such an approach was financially unacceptable, and likely unsatisfactory from a technical viewpoint. Indeed, any problem involving more than one node would require the coordination of several persons working at geographically distant sites, with resulting delays and misunderstandings.

Earlier experience acquired within ARPANET showed that simple mechanisms located within nodes could provide for effective remote control and supervision from any node [MCK72]. This approach was adopted by CIGALE, and was turned into a more general design.

In order to provide for completely remote control, CIGALE is viewed as a single abstract machine, with an instruction set, a memory, input-output, and a number of processors. The instruction set and internal communications mechanisms allow

complete control of the whole machine through the equivalent of
a control panel. Building a custom tailored control panel was
undesirable, since any one-off piece of hardware always poses a
reliability problem. Furthermore, lack of experience would
have required several design iterations. A more flexible
approach was to build a set of software tools accessible
through a control language, which could be entered through any
conventional input mechanism. Both the set of tools and the
control language are open-ended so as to allow incremental
implementation and easy changes as more experience is acquired.
Actually, the set of control tools was extended continuously
throughout the development phase, and during the first years of
real operation as well. This approach proved invaluable for
incorporating improvements suggested by practical experience
into CIGALE.

3.1.2. Internal communications

Within a single computer internal wiring provides communication
paths between components. Usually, data and control paths are
physically separate for higher performance. In a distributed
machine such as a packet network, separating communication
paths would require specific mechanisms and transmission
facilities for control and data. The additional amount of
hardware and software required by such a separation would
result in increased cost and complexity. This was certainly
undesirable for CIGALE.

In fact, CIGALE is optimized for its basic function, the
carriage of packets. There is no better way of travelling
within CIGALE than to use regular packets. Thus, there is only
one packet format, for all purposes. This makes the basic
packet handling function a very simple and stable one, since it
does not have to parse packets for a variety of ad-hoc formats.

There remains the question : what is data, and what is
control ? They are in a sense the same. In most computers,
instructions and operands (i.e. control and data) are not
distinguishable in storage. Their interpretation depends on the
nature of the registers to which they are transferred at
execution time. CIGALE uses the same principle. However, a
fixed set of registers with a limited set of instructions would
be a serious hindrance to future evolution. Therefore, the
instruction set is open-ended. Every packet is an instruction,
the semantics of which are defined by the packet destination.

A more refined CIGALE model is given in Figure 3.1.2.(1). It
is organized around a basic service : packet switching. Any
packet directed to the SWITCH service is forwarded to its
specified destination, which may be a Network Service (NS), or
an external destination. At the SWITCH level, there is no
distinction between packets exchanged between external CIGALE
users, and packets exchanged between network services. The set
of NS make up the whole control system of the CIGALE abstract

machine. As will be seen later on in section 4.2.3, they also provide for additional user services, which are made available on request to the benefit of external users.

No assumptions are made in the model about implementation aspects. Typically, some NS are self-contained software modules located within specific nodes. Others are distributed functions scattered over several nodes. Still others are located within specific hosts connected to CIGALE, with appropriate access protection. In other words, the model places no restriction on the implementors.

The IN and OUT services are a bit specific ; they handle acceptance and delivery of packets to and from external users. Typically they are transmission line handlers and procedures. Again, this is but one example of implementation.

The SWITCH service is never specified as a destination, as it is implicitly used as an intermediate relay for any packet exchanged between other services. This approach results in considerable economy and flexibility.

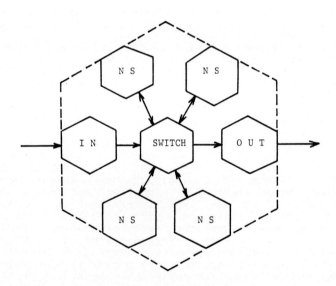

Figure 3.1.2.(1) - CIGALE model

Internally, there is just one type of interface between services : the packet. Modules which implement services can be located anywhere, and even moved around during network operation without affecting other modules.

A closer look at the CIGALE model, without reading the figure
caption, (Figure 3.1.2.(1)) suggests the representation of a
node. Indeed, a CIGALE node is modeled after the whole network
model. This is not just a trick, or an implementation shortcut.
The idea of applying the same model recursively was deliberate,
as it leads to considerable generality, at no cost. Some
implications of this approach are :

a) CIGALE is functionally equivalent to a node ; thus several
interconnected CIGALEs are functionally equivalent to a single
CIGALE.

b) A node is functionally equivalent to a CIGALE network ; thus
any node may be replaced by a network, without affecting
services.

c) Network internal services may be located within specific
nodes, or distributed, whichever is more convenient.

In brief, the CIGALE structure is similar to a crystal. It can
be split or aggregated without losing its functional
properties. On the other hand, it may be observed that earlier
packet networks, and many latecomers, are self-incompatible ;
i.e. they cannot be interconnected with a copy of themselves
without peculiar adaptations. This is the case with ARPANET
and public networks using the X.25 interface.

While the CIGALE design was primarily intended to be built with
mini-computers and transmission lines, it is interesting to
note that the model does not make such an assumption. It would
apply equally well to a ring network, (the ring is the switch),
or to a broadcast satellite network, (the satellite is the
switch). This suggests that the interconnection of networks of
such different technologies should be functionally simple, when
they use the same model. On the other hand, control and
operational aspects raise new problems which point towards
challenging domains for research and experiment.

3.1.3. Logical name space

In computer systems it became customary long ago to address
resources via logical names used as indirect pointers for
accessing physical implementations of these resources (e.g.
mnemonics for peripherals, file names, and user numbers).

Nonetheless, this well proven technique has been overlooked in
most store and forward packet networks, which tend to mimic
antiquated telephone systems in addressing wires rather than
subscribers. In other words, these networks use addresses which
are directly bound to with physical network components,
typically a line number in a specific node [HEA70]. A most
conspicuous case is the X.25 standard for public packet

switched networks. Drawbacks are well known :

Firstly, topological changes affect destination addresses, and
impose service disruptions. Secondly, system failures are
critical when they involve a physical component bound to an
address, because changing this component with another requires
either a change of address or a disruption of service.

In other words, service availability is degraded, unless one
resorts to intricate schemes, such as stand-by duplex systems,
and an alternate set of addresses.

CIGALE does away with these problems by using a logical name
space independent of the physical network structure [POU76h].
Any logical destination is given a name, and CIGALE maintains
tables of all known destinations. These include both network
services and external users. Packets carry logical addresses
all throughout CIGALE.   Conversion between logical addresses
and physical components (node, line, module) is only done by
the SWITCH service.

In the CYCLADES context, external users are transport stations
(see sections 2.3.3 and 3.2). Packets sent and received by
transport stations contain transport station addresses, not
CIGALE node addresses. This capability offers a number of
advantages :

A transport station may be connected with a single address to
several CIGALE nodes, typically two, for reliability purposes.
Indeed, a highly reliable packet net is not a sufficient
guarantee of continuous service, when access to a host computer
relies on a single transmission line. Putting two lines between
a host and a single node is not much better, as both lines are
likely to follow the same geographical route, and the node may
go down. The only way to insure redundancy of access paths is
to run two lines to two geographically distant nodes. This
form of dual homing is easy to do in CIGALE, and it does not
require any additional machinery.

Secondly, a host connection may be moved from one node to
another without service interruption, and without changing the
addresses of the host transport stations.

Third, several transport stations may be located at the end of
a single transmission line. This is particularly convenient
when several transport stations are located within a single
host, or when a host implements virtual machines, or when
several hosts share a front-end computer connected to CIGALE.

A more general case is the connection to CIGALE of a whole
computer network, which appears simply as a collection of external destinations. Examples of such connections are shown in
Figure 3.1.3.(1).

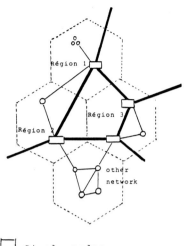

Région 1

Région 3

Région 2

other
network

☐ Cigale nodes

O Host

Figure 3.1.3.(1) - Address space

3.1.3.1. Name space structure

The list of all possible destinations may be bulky, with
resulting storage and look-up overhead. To conserve efficiency,
a well proven technique consists of structuring the name space
in a hierarchy of levels. The CIGALE name space is divided up
into networks, regions, and local destinations. The SWITCH
service handles the successive levels of an address in the
hierarchy, in the obvious top-down manner, just like the
telephone network.

First, packets are switched towards other networks, unless the
network address is CIGALE itself. Second, packets are switched
towards regions, unless they happen to be already in the region
of the final destination. Lastly, switching is performed
towards the local destination.

The complete name space structure is shown in Figure 3.1.3.(2).
Each branch of the tree leads to categories of addressable
entities. However, there may be more than one branch for a
particular category of entities. The rationale for this
structure is the following.

CIGALE was designed for easy interconnection with other
networks. Thus, it had to include the aggregated name space of
all other networks by including a network name in addresses.
The region level was necessary for efficiency in large
networks, since it reduces the size of routing tables and the
switching overhead.
Some hosts may be connected to nodes attached to several

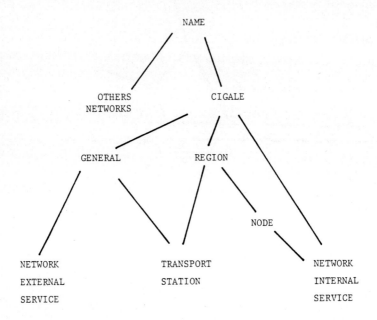

Figure 3.1.3.(2) - Name space structure

regions.   Their   addresses   are made general in order to allow
access from several regions.   Network   internal   services   are
known   in   every   node   when they are distributed, but they may
also be in specific nodes.   Network external services   are   not
attached   to   a   region,   since   they   are presently limited in
number.

3.1.3.2. General address

It may be worth covering further the concept of general
non-hierarchical   address.   Some   examples   help   explain   its
relevance.

In order to avoid disturbances associated with address changes,
it is desirable to work out a stable numbering plan applicable
as   soon   as   the network is operational. According to the plan
users are given regional names, but is is likely that early
network   configurations   will   be   too   sparse. In some regions
there may be only one node, or none at all, which creates a
problem   for   users   located in that region. Dual homing is not
effective with a single node. Thus, it becomes   necessary   that

destinations normally attached to a region become known in
other regions.

Some users may be mobile. They may connect temporarily to a
node, and travel to another place in a different region.
Changing their addresses would be cumbersome.

When a packet has reached the destination region, it is
normally routed to its final address. In some network
topologies, it may happen that the only route goes through a
neighbouring region (see Figure 3.1.3.(3)). This is not
compatible with hierarchical routing, which works top-down
[KAM76].

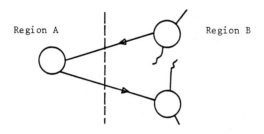

Figure 3.1.3.(3) - General routing

A simple solution to these problems is to place some addresses
into a subset of the name space which is known globally at
network level. If all destinations were in that category, there
would be no hierarchy. These general addresses increase the
number of entries in routing tables, but as long as this is
limited to an acceptable number, the advantages are worth the
cost.

3.1.3.3. Logical networks

In terms of routing, every level of addressing may be
considered as a level in a hierarchy of logical networks.
Regions are actually interconnected logical sub-networks.
General addresses make up a logical network using the same
physical nodes, but distinct from regions.

This technique may be generalized if it appears to bring about
practical advantages. Any set of interconnected nodes may
support one or several distinct logical networks, each one
being assigned a subset of the total name space. Variations in
routing table structure and in look-up algorithms allow
considerable flexibility in the determination of the visible
part of the name space as seen from packet sources. The

keystone for flexibility in the CIGALE addressing scheme is the
aggregation of all possible destination names into a condensed
set comprising both individual destinations and sets of
destinations. As described later in section 4, a node's routing
table entry is either a destination name, or the name of a
destination set. The SWITCH algorithm consists of matching a
packet destination with a routing table entry. A successful
look up means that either the specific packet destination has
been located, or there exists in the table an entry for a set
of destinations which includes the packet destination. Such
explanations might sound superfluous, but they should help the
reader to understand the generalization of this scheme.

In the CIGALE design each node is assumed to know the total
destination name space, either through individual entries or
through set entries in its routing table. Furthermore, all
addresses are supposed to be both sources and destinations.
(Actually, this is not the case with some network services, but
it is not taken into account in the routing scheme.)

Let us assume now that the whole address space is split into
two disjoint sets {A1} and {A2}, in order to share the same
physical CIGALE between two distinct logical networks. Each
logical network allows traffic to be exchanged between sources
and destinations, provided that they belong to the same set
{A1} or {A2}. In telecommunication jargon each set is called a
"closed user group".

A simple way to implement this facility is to provide a 2-step
switch algorithm :

- Look in the routing table for an entry matching the packet
source. This entry belongs to {Ai}. {Ai} is either {A1} or
{A2}.

- Look up only the destinations contained in {Ai} for an entry
matching the packet destination.

It is clear that this scheme may be extended to more than two
logical networks. The additional cost is a look up of a
fraction of the address space restricted to one logical
network. The first look up for the packet origin can also be
eliminated if the packet source can be immediately associated
with a specific logical network, e.g. according to its physical
input line. One might speculate that sophisticated addressing
schemes should increase overhead. It is actually the opposite,
since routing tables located in each node contain only a
limited subset of the total destination name space. This
logical machinery reduces switching overhead.

Further flexibility can be obtained by placing some addresses
in more than one logical network, in order to create partial
overlap between the address spaces of any two logical networks.
In addition, addresses within a specific logical network may be
tagged as source-only, or destination-only. This latter

facility may be useful for dedicated services, such as
statistics gathering, accounting, clock, or supervision, when
they do not require two-way traffic.

As the previous examples illustrate, the CIGALE addressing
scheme is capable of sophisticated extensions, which were not
necessary in the context of CYCLADES, but which may become
relevant for public or private networks in a business
environment. Indeed, communications cannot be developed without
concern for security, privacy, and tariffs. The more networks
expand and interconnect, the greater the need, or the will, to
restrict communications. This may appear paradoxical, but it is
a fact that technological progress in communications is
increasingly facing various kinds of legal restrictions (which
are not necessarily based on valid grounds).

3.1.4. The datagram service

CIGALE does not assume any interdependence between packets.
Each one is accepted, carried, and delivered as a separate
entity. Dynamic modification of routing tables, or repetitions
in case of noisy lines, may change the order within a sequence
of packets travelling from a source to a destination.

In case of node failure, it may happen that packets already
acknowledged for sending nodes are lost before they are
forwarded. Line failure may thwart the transmission of
acknowledgements to a sending node, while received packets are
forwarded correctly. After a delay, the sending node attempts
to route packets onto an alternate path. If it succeeds, some
packets are duplicated.

A transmission service offering these characteristics is called
a Datagram Service [DAV76, POU76f]. CIGALE is the first packet
network designed to take advantage of the characteristics of
datagrams.

Very often, events such as packets out-of-sequence, lost, or
duplicated, are felt as a serious burden, if not a gross
deficiency. The CYCLADES architecture and its transport
protocol are evidence that the datagram service brings
substantial simplicity, cost reduction, and generality as
compared to similar networks such as ARPANET [CAR70] and X.25
virtual circuit networks. This may be attributed to the fact
that the network architecture was optimized as a whole, but
there are specific advantages clearly traceable to the datagram
service itself :

First, multiple host connections to several nodes require no
additional machinery.

Secondly, the datagram interface is a very simple packet
interface to hosts, as opposed to the complexity of such
interfaces as X.25 [CCI77, POU761].

Third, the switching of independent packets is the simplest and fastest way of carrying packets. This is why a number of public and private networks use this form of switching, at least as an internal mechanism. (e.g. BELL Canada, the Dutch PTT, British Steel, the French Navy). However, TRANSPAC [DES72] and a PHILIPS product for private nets use internal virtual circuits.

Finally, as we all know, the simpler the system, the more reliable it is.

Still, the possible loss or duplication of packets make a number of people feel uneasy about the datagram service. To the extent that an appropriate transport protocol takes care of packet losses and duplications, there are no logical consequences, only performance degradation. Actually the matter boils down to the threshold of acceptable performance loss.

Since datagram networks are very few, there are no well known figures about typical performances. Orders of magnitude for CIGALE are :

        duplicates : not observed
        loss due to buffer limit : 0.1 %
        loss due to maximum transit delay : 0.01 %
        loss due to hardware failure : 0.0001 %

Actually, most packets lost are dropped because queue limits are exceeded. This is a crude way of eliminating congestion adopted as a safeguard while more refined mechanisms were under study. Assuming that new traffic control schemes will behave as expected, [POU76d] the loss rate should be determined by the next dominant factor, presently the time-out put on transit delay. Even at this present level of performance, a throughput reduction of 0.1 % is negligible.

It is worth noting that CIGALE deliberately drops packets that could be delivered, but have exceeded a limit put on transit delay. Indeed, end-to-end error control schemes could not be made reliable without some assumption about a maximum transit delay in the transmission layer. Late packets are worse than lost packets, both for efficiency and reliability. This is due to error recovery and synchronization problems in transport protocols [TOM74].

It should be emphasized that the user of a datagram service is not expected to be an application program, but an intermediate layer equipped with end-to-end control functions. This represents an optimal layout from a global viewpoint. However, some network designers feel that a transmission network must offer more refined services than datagrams. Typically, additional refinements include : a) packet sequencing, b) error and flow control.

The result is certainly more complexity and increased costs, both in the transmission network and in the user interface,

since specific procedures are imposed. On the other hand, there
is no evidence that the transmission service offered is any
better in a practical sense.

Indeed, no physical system is perfect, and even with internal
error control, a transmission network experiences some residual
errors. Since end-to-end error control at user level remains
necessary, it is not clear that packet error rates of 0.01 % or
0.0001 % make any difference.

Sequencing might be thought of as improved service, since a
receiver may use fewer buffers when it does not have to store
out-of-sequence packets. But there is the other side of the
coin. Any buffer space saved on the receiver side must actually
be provided by the transmission network. Furthermore,
delivering packets in sequence increases average transit
delays, due to internal network control schemes, and packet
reordering. Thus the sender must provide more buffers to take
into account the longer round trip delay for acknowledgements.

Any error control or sequencing scheme built into a
transmission network has intrinsic limitations :

First, it only applies to a particular transmission network,
within its own boundaries. In other words, it does not provide
any guarantee at the user-to-user level. When packets travel
through several interconnected transmission networks, no one is
in charge of end-to-end control. Some experience of using
transatlantic virtual circuits winding through several public
packet networks is already confirming this point.

Secondly, mechanisms used for internal network control require
that packets be routed through a minimum of two fixed
components, in which packets are labeled on input, and checked
on output. These are called focal points on Figure 3.1.4.(1)
[POU76f]. When one of these components fails, so does control,
without users necessarily being aware. A direct implication is
that dual homing, or multiple host connections to several
nodes, becomes impossible with a single set of addresses. This
is undoubtedly the most damaging impact of sequencing and/or
error control.

The above developments illustrate the complex nature of design
optimization, which is commonplace in computing systems. A
multiplicity of parameters interact with one another, so that
local improvements resulting from a tunnel vision approach turn
generally into global mediocrity.

3.1.5. Network services

While packet switching is the basic CIGALE function, additional
tools are useful for various purposes :

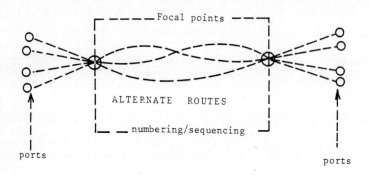

Figure 3.1.4.(1) - Focal points

User aids are necessary to help users in getting information regarding their own traffic, e.g. diagnostics, delays. A particular service is ECHO, which returns packets to their source. This is a very handy tool for host protocol debugging, like a friend in the network.

In order to provide for traffic measurement, a set of tools gathers statistics on real traffic, generating artificial traffic and measuring specific parameters [GRA77].

Troubleshooting requires tools for the observation of CIGALE behaviour and for taking corrective actions on network components. Operator aids designed for human interaction allow an operator to control CIGALE, load nodes, take dumps, open and close transmission lines, etc. All network services are described in detail in section 4.2.

It can be inferred from the above list that some services may serve multiple purposes, e.g. ECHO is also used for measurement and troubleshooting. Thus, it would have been wasteful to design specific tools for limited purposes by a piecemeal approach. As mentioned earlier in section 3.1.1, CIGALE is viewed as a distributed machine. Network services are an instruction set, rather than specific subsystems. Each service is self-contained, and as simple as possible.

Any meaningful action usually requires a combination of several services, very much like a sequence of instructions. A difference from a conventional computer is that instructions may run in parallel, but this is also the case with high speed or multi-processor computers. This suggests some structural similarity between multi-processors and packet networks.

CIGALE services execute packets, which they receive from the SWITCH service. As seen earlier, network services belong to the CIGALE destination name space. The execution of a packet may change the state of some CIGALE components. Some packets may be generated and handed on to the SWITCH service, and so on. This is typical of a machine executing a program. Packet-instructions may be generated by an operator using a teleprinter connected to a node. (Formatting packets, and handling operator input-output are again network services). Packet-instructions may also be generated by hosts, at least for the services they are allowed to access. Elaborate programs may be fed into CIGALE and monitored from a host. This is typical of the capabilities of a measurement center, which is another network service.

Morever, network services have been used mostly for the purposes indicated previously. But this basic mechanism could lend itself to applications in other areas, e.g. a) automated execution of diagnostics of network components, for preventive maintenance, b) information center for CIGALE users, c) broadcasting multi-address packets, d) various adaptation chores, such as code conversion, terminal polling, and equipment monitoring. With its open-ended kit of network services, CIGALE is the kernel of a hybrid system integrating data processing and communications.

The concept of a hybrid system may appear in contradiction with the layering principles stated in section 2. This is indeed a point worth clarification.

The CYCLADES architecture makes every effort to separate functional layers with well defined interfaces and protocols. As long as the same discipline is applied to implementation, changing a component has no adverse effect on the rest of the system. This is particularly helpful when a computer network is made up of evolving heterogeneous components. CIGALE is a different case. The same rationale is applicable to the architecture, as this is a well proven approach in system design. This is why CIGALE follows a rigorous model, (presented earlier in section 3.1.2). In the context of CYCLADES, CIGALE is dedicated to packet switching. Thus, it would have been undesirable to introduce more functions than were required for the purpose of being a simple transmission box. But this is not the only environment in which CIGALE could be used.

Indeed, CIGALE is built as a homogeneous distributed machine. Although its present functions are limited to packet transport, its structure allows the insertion of any additional function which might be desirable. This results from its open-ended instruction code. One might, for example, add a distributed file system, a task monitor, input-output peripherals, and CIGALE would become a homogeneous distributed data processing machine. Packet transport would no longer be a service to the outside world but an internal component of a distributed operating system.

3.1.6. External interface

The external interface is the set of conventions allowing packets to be passed to or received from CIGALE. It comprises three levels : a) packet format, b) data link control, c) physical and electrical interface.

3.1.6.1. Packet format

A packet contains a header (12 octets), and a text field of 0 to 255 octets, (Figure 3.1.6.(1)). The figure for the maximum length appeared convenient. A number of other nets have taken the same length, or a smaller one. This could bring some simplification in the case of interconnecting with other networks. Indeed, since a CIGALE packet carries at least the same text length as other networks, it is usually possible to map a single packet received from another network into a single CIGALE packet. Thus there is no need for fragmentation and reassembly of oversize foreign packets.

The choice of a packet size must also take into account transmission overhead due to the header. With a 12 octets header and 255 octets field, the transmission overhead resulting from the packet format is 12 octets over a total of 267, less than 5 %. This is a very acceptable figure indeed.

The packet size is also related to the overhead incurred when erroneous packets are retransmitted. Indeed, the longer the packet, the higher the probability that it could be damaged. On the other hand, if packets are very short, the header overhead becomes dominant. Clearly, there must be an optimum size between very long and very short packets. Studies have shown that line efficiency is near the optimum for a large range of packet sizes between about 2000 bits and 10,000 bits [MET73]. These figures depend on line error characteristics, but most leased circuits present similar performances. Such conclusions should not be extended to other transmission technologies (radio, satellite, fiber optics).

The header structure is shown in Figure 3.1.6.(2). It is biased towards octet machines, since they represent a dominant part of the market. However, the header length (96 bits) is such that it does not create boundary problems on computers of different word sizes. (The figure 96 is a multiple of 6, 8, 12, 16, 24 and 32). Fields do not straddle 16-bit boundaries in order to avoid processing overhead. Most mini-computers used for communications have 16-bit words and registers.

The header starts with format control fields intended for easy parsing and future evolution. CIGALE uses a single packet format, but packets may travel through various networks, and new packet formats may be introduced in the future. For these reasons the header format was laid out in order to accomodate inter-network traffic [POU74g]. This conforms to a proposal

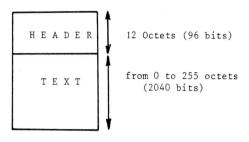

Figure 3.1.6.(1) - Packet structure

Header Format	Header Length	Text Length
Packet Identification		
Facilities		
Destination Network		Source Network
Destination		Station Transport
Source		Station Transport

Figure 3.1.6.(2) - Packet header

worked out within IFIP-TC.6, and known as the D-format [IFI74].

The packet identification field is not processed by CIGALE. It is just carried as is, end-to-end. Its purpose is to provide CIGALE with some way of referring to a packet when diagnostics are produced. Indeed, many packets carry the same source-destination addresses when they are exchanged between a pair of users. Differences, if any, are in the text. It was undesirable to use the text field for packet identification, because it is too long, and no general convention could be defined. A better solution is to provide for a specific field, which transport stations label in their own way, so that they can relate diagnostics to their data streams.

The facility field is used for requesting some network services. Address fields reflect the name space structure covered earlier (see section 3.1.3). Destination fields appear prior to source fields, because they are looked up more often. Thus, the parsing of a packet header remains straightforward even in the case of variable length addresses.

More details are given in section 4.2.

3.1.6.2. Data link procedure

Packets are exchanged between CIGALE and physical host equipments through a synchronous transmission procedure operating in data transparent mode. The question was which of CIGALE and the hosts had to adapt to the other. Host transmission procedures are buried into sensitive parts of manufacturer's software. Changing it would create persistent adaptation problems, and increase costs. Thus, it was decided to implement manufacturer transmission procedures within CIGALE. Fortunately, only two different procedures were necessary, CII's and IBM's. In the future, it is expected that HDLC will become generally available from computer manufacturers.

3.1.6.3. Physical and electrical interface

The use of special hardware was strongly resisted as it would have created endless maintenance problems. Standard modem interfaces are used (CCITT V24 and V35). Line speeds go from 4.8 kbits/s up to 48 kbits/s.

Thus, all that is necessary to link a host to CIGALE is to order a PTT leased circuit, a pair of modems, and use one port of a telecommunication interface, which is a standard product from every computer manufacturer. This approach requires only off-the-shelf equipment, and does not put any constraint on the geographical distance between a host and a CIGALE node. In summary, the CIGALE interface is as simple as possible, with the objective of minimizing host adaptation problems.

3.1.6.4. Network services interface

It is often contended that networks should turn back diagnostics or signaling packets in some circumstances. (E.g. the X.25 interface defines various network diagnostics packets). Contrary to common prejudices these packets are basically a burden for user systems. Interpreting them takes additional logic, and does not help users very much. The CYCLADES transport protocol is self sufficient : it does not need any CIGALE diagnostics to detect and recover transmission errors.

On the other hand, CIGALE diagnostics may be extremely helpful
for specialized users carrying out tests, measurements, and
other network hobbies. Therefore, the CIGALE SWITCH service is
totally   silent   and   unobtrusive.   Any feedback has to be
explicitly requested by users in the form of packets sent to
network services, or invocation of facilities. (It may become
necessary to make one exception to the above rule for traffic
flow control, (see section 7.5.4).

3.1.7. Network supervision

In a distributed system using long distance transmission lines,
failures must be expected as normal events. Provided that
enough investment is put into reliability, communications
between users should always find at least two distinct paths
through separate physical components.   In   such   a   context,
failures   should   not   disrupt   communications. Component
malfunctioning should only cause a reduction of available
resources. To that end, CIGALE components are constantly
monitored, either by themselves, or by other components. In
case of abnormal behaviour, components try immediately to
ensure their own survival through proper adjustments, and
subsequently report their observations to a control center.
Repair depends on human initiative.

Tools are necessary for network supervision. Instead of being
thought of as local node functions, they are organized into a
network-wide   distributed   control   system,   because   network
control implies mutual cooperation between nodes. Furthermore,
the concept of distributed control is in line with the design
of CIGALE as a distributed machine.

Network services are usually exercised from external sources of
commands (operar or hosts). Rather than design a specific
network   control   machinery,   it   was   much simpler to think of
network control as a variety of network services,   except   that
instructions triggering actions are generated by CIGALE itself,
based on scheduled or random events. This is an extremely
flexible approach for an incremental implementation of control
tools built upon practical experience. Here are some network
services.

3.1.7.1. TIME service

This service maintains a synchronized network clock in every
node, as well as scheduling of dependent events.

3.1.7.2. Node self-monitoring

Each node observes significant events, such as : transmission line status, buffer availability, power failure, or use of control panel keys. Status reports are sent to a control center. Statistics are gathered and made available to a measurement center.

3.1.7.3. Adaptive routing

This service maintains, in every node, tables of best routes for the benefit of the SWITCH service. It uses a propagation scheme inspired by ARPANET [FRA72, FUL72]. Its objective is not to spread traffic depending on load, but only to adapt routes in case of component failure. Indeed, traffic transients are too sharp to be handled effectively by a mechanism which necessarily responds more slowly. Spreading stochastic traffic in a meaningful way is still a research area. Thus, the CIGALE adaptive routing scheme does not take into account packet queue lengths. It was changed from periodic to event driven updating, because simulation results pointed out significant improvements (see section 7.4).

3.1.7.4. Traffic control

This refers to the set of mechanisms which maintain input traffic within limits compatible with the amount of resources available to the network [POU76].

At the time CIGALE was designed, there was very little known about traffic control, except that packet networks were subject to traffic jams, as in busy cities [DAV71, KAH72]. Recipes advocated by network designers were without scientific or experimental justification. Thus, the policy adopted for CIGALE was twofold : a) make no commitment, make no investment in mechanisms which were not proven, b) put in safeguards preventing network congestion.

It was obvious from other networks' experience that traffic did not build up quickly. Even after several years of operation, real traffic in ARPANET remained much below its potential capacity. Thus, it was realistic to delay the implementation of traffic control within CIGALE. On the other hand, it was felt necessary to prevent pathological situations, not necessarily in an efficient manner.

The mechanism adopted initially to prevent congestion is crude but effective : dropping packets. Each output queue is assigned a maximum number of packet buffers. When the maximum is reached, or when the free buffer pool is depleted, nodes drop incoming packets, which are nonetheless acknowledged. Thus, excess packets vanish instead of clogging the network. Simulation shows that throughput is reduced when CIGALE is

saturated, due to packet drops [IRL75c]. But traffic does not
get blocked as is usually the case when a network is congested
(see section 7).

However, it was clear that a more efficient scheme was
desirable in order to keep packets out of the network, rather
than discarding them on the way to their destination.

Some network designers contend that traffic control requires an
internal identification of data streams, so that the network is
capable of separately regulating each data stream, depending on
available network resources and acceptance rate at the receiver
end [DES75]. Various related schemes based on this principle
have been implemented. They fall in the category of Virtual
Circuits (VC). The CCITT recommendation X.25 (see
section 9.3.1.2) is now a well known example of the VC approach
to packet transmission.

Basically, a VC is a logical association established through a
packet network between network logical ports. Packets sent over
a VC are delivered in sequence to the other end, and the
network enforces flow control per VC in slowing up the sender
when the receiver or the network become congested. Since
sequenced delivery of packets is always associated with a VC,
packets must pass through a minimum of two fixed places: one
where they are numbered on entering the network, the other
where they are checked before delivery. These places have been
called focal points, (see section 3.1.4). This approach has a
number of drawbacks :

First, focal points within the transmission network reduce
reliability, because the failure of a focal point causes
service disruption. The establishment of a new VC without
packet loss appears to be practically unfeasible, especially
when the user access circuit is disabled.

Secondly, the external interface is complex and raises
adaptation problems, as is now well known with X.25.

Third, the VC machinery is unadaptable to traffic patterns
consisting of short messages exchanged with a large number of
sources or destinations, e.g. point-of-sale, meter reading,
transactions in general.

Fourth, the number of carriers involved in international VC's
and their differences in implementing the interfaces, require
several conversions at network boundaries. This results in
transit delays of several seconds and various persisting
conflicts in service functionalities.

Thus, the VC approach was not taken in CIGALE, due to its
sizable overhead and lack of generality.

After a thorough examination of various research works, it
became clear that the critical resource is bandwidth, not

buffers. A traffic control scheme called the Channel Load
Limiter (CLL) was designed, simulated, and implemented [MAJ79,
POU76d]. This aspect is covered further, in section 7.5.
Practical evaluation of its value is not yet fully completed.

In summary, the CIGALE approach to traffic control aims at
simple and robust mechanisms, as transparent as possible to
users. Packet drop is considered an acceptable counter measure,
as a second line of defense, while one tries to minimize its
occurrence. Finally, traffic control is to be treated in the
context of a service policy. In order to achieve a good
utilization of network resources and satisfy user needs,
classes of services should be defined, with associated
guaranteed characteristics and tariffs [POU76]. This is an area
for future investigation.

3.1.7.5. Control center

As seen from CIGALE the control center is a network service to
which some packets are sent by other network services. This
does not make assumptions about its physical nature, which can
be varied in time, e.g. a software module within a node, or a
specialized host.

Functionally, the control center is the control panel of a
distributed machine. It receives reports from all over the
network whenever a significant event is observed by monitoring
services, e.g. a line going down. All network reports are
recorded for further analysis, and critical events are
presented to a human operator for appropriate action.

The control center takes no active part in CIGALE operation.
It just listens. For convenience, its functions may be housed
in a specialized host, but they may also be distributed among
several machines (nodes or hosts). Practically, it is
convenient to use the same kind of mini-computer used for
nodes. This provides for easy back up and allows one to reuse a
major part of the node software.

Debates occur sometimes about the possibility of having two
control centers, for extreme reliability. This is more an
organizational problem than a technical one. CIGALE might be
cut by an arbitrary line, each node reporting to one of the
control centers, or both. This is straightforward. The
responsibility of each control center operator must be clearly
defined with regard to physical components of the network.
Procedures are required for passing responsibilities from one
center to the other in case of trouble (see section 6).

3.2. Transport station

3.2.1. Transport service requirements and protocol structure

The transport service [ELI75,GAR75,ZIM75] provides support for point-to-point conversations, i.e. it relieves higher layers of the problems associated with the sharing of data transmission resources.

It therefore defines Ports (PT) as a common name space for addressable entities (e.g. resources, user processes, terminals) and provides means to exchange messages and to establish Liaisons (LI) for private conversations between ports. Thus, the transport service relieves higher layers of the problem of multiplexing several conversations on communication links. High reliability of the transport service implies end-to-end error control. Alternate transmission routes may lead to misordering and thus require possible reordering by the transport layer. Independence of conversations requires individual flow control for each conversation.

As data processing systems evolve toward a distributed structure, it is important that transport stations handling the transport protocol for each data processing system also be implemented in a distributed manner. This leads one to structure the transport protocol in two sub-layers as in Figure 3.2.1.(1) :

- A multiplexing sub-layer provides access to individual ports within each system. It also permits us, within the context of a given port, to identify several liaisons with distinct distant ports (see figure 3.2.2(2)).

- The second sub-layer performs end-to-end error control, flow control, etc. according to a port-to-port procedure.

If one attempts to model the transport protocol after the detailed list of desirable features of a local interprocess communication facility, one is faced with endless diversity which may be traced to different assumptions made by designers about the process environment (e.g. shared buffers, message queue, access protection). If network conventions had to encompass every possible approach, the whole implementation would become too massive and more likely impossible. In a heterogeneous computer network, only strict minimal assumptions can be made. There are definitely valid arguments in favour of a process-to-process interface based on bit, or byte, or message streams, with fixed or variable length items, and a number of additional functions for contact, synchronization, etc. Unfortunately, it does not appear possible to devise a scheme ideally suited to all environments.

A few minimal assumptions appear to be generally valid in a heterogeneous computer network environment :

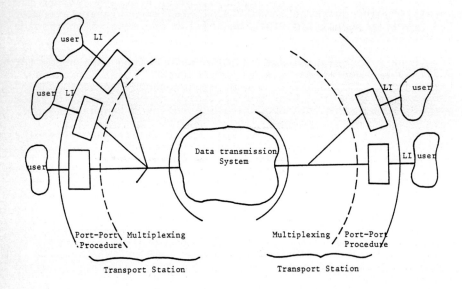

Figure 3.2.1.(1) - Structure of the transport protocol

a) Data exchanged between processes usually travel through I-O channels and undefined transmission media.

b) Many systems are not able to transmit or receive data streams of unbounded length.

c) Some transmission media are not very reliable.

Practically, these observations point out explicit constraints. Both computer I-O machinery and transmission error recovery require data to be transmitted in blocks of limited length. This may not be the most appropriate form of data exchange, as seen from some level of system or application program. However, it is possible to build an I-O package presenting a different data structure interface as seen from within the computer.

Therefore, the basic service provided by the transport layer
consists of the copying a buffer of the sender's memory into
the receiver's memory. This is similar to a "move" operation
in existing data processing systems. In CYCLADES, blocks of
information moved from one port to the other are called Letters
(LT). In addition to moving buffers, the transport service also
transmits Telegrams (TG) which are similar to the notion of
events commonly used by processes located in a single system.
In order to keep application programs independent of the
variations of transmission facilities, the size of letters is
kept independent of the size of packets. The corresponding
adaptations, if required, are provided by the transport layer.

Lastly, transport stations must be prepared to adapt to a
variety of data transmission services and interfaces (see
section 2.2.1). This is obtained with a modular structure : the
interface to data transmission as well as functions specific to
particular data transmission services are grouped in an adapter
module (bridge) and clearly isolated from common functions (see
section 3.3).

The following description of the transport protocol in CYCLADES
takes into account the data transmission service and interface
provided by CIGALE.

3.2.2. Ports and Liaisons

Each individual process or resource belongs to a data
processing system. Data processing systems are themselves
assembled into the network. It is therefore sensible to reflect
this hierarchical structure in the transport name space :

At a first level, data processing systems are identified with
transport station addresses (TS-NB) used by the data
transmission system to route information to the proper
destination.

At a second level within each data processing system,
communicating entities are identified with port numbers (PT-NB)
which are sub-adresses of transport stations interpreted by the
multiplexing function of the transport station as in
Figure 3.2.2.(1).

It would not be possible to integrate already existing names in
a common name space [POU76i] since each system has its own way
of naming its processes, resources, I/O streams, etc. Rather,
port names constitute a convenient network-wide naming
convention for all communications. Each system is then
responsible for mapping its local names into ports. Outside
each individual system, ports are used to identify resources
and their users. As already discussed in section 2.2.4, the
sharing of resources between several users as well as the
concurrent use of several resources by a single user imply that
several conversations be anchored on the same port, i.e. ports

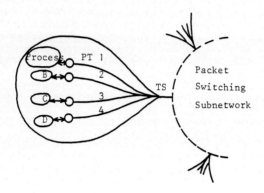

Figure 3.2.2. (1) - A transport station is a collection of ports

must be capable of accepting several liaisons at the same time.
It has also been shown that pairs of resources usually carry
only one conversation at a time. Therefore, it is sufficient
that only one liaison be permitted between a pair of ports. A
liaison is then simply identified with the pair of port
addresses as in Figure 3.3.2.(2) :

Liaison identification = (TS-NB/PT-NB) (TS-NB/PT-NB)

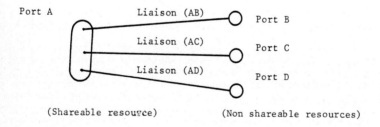

Figure 3.2.2.(2) - Ports to shareable/non shareable resources

This scheme is somehow similar to the one used in the telephone
system where a company or an individual is identified with a
phone number. As seen from the outside, the phone number of a
company is shareable, since several conversations can proceed
at the same time, and the caller does not have to worry about

already existing conversations. On the other hand, the phone
number of an individual is non-sharable since he can process
only one conversation at a time. A sharable resource (e.g. a
time sharing system) will permit several liaisons on its port
while a non sharable resource (e.g. a terminal) will only
accept one liaison at a time.

All commands exchanged between a particular pair of transport
stations are related to a liaison, i.e. transport commands, can
be viewed as transmitted from a sending port to a receiving
port by the multiplexing function. Each command contains the
identifications of both sending port and destination port as
indicated in Figure 3.2.9.(1).

In the present implementation of transport stations on
CYCLADES, it has been decided, for the sake of simplicity, that
information from different liaisons would not be multiplexed
within the same packet, i.e. each packet is dedicated to a
single liaison. This type of multiplexing can be done (e.g. for
efficiency or economy reasons) with minor modifications of the
multiplexing part of the transport station.

3.2.3. Letters and Telegrams

On a liaison, the port-to-port protocol provides transportation
of letters and telegrams :

A letter is a container of information with a variable length
presently limited to 4 K octets. Practically most physical
records would fit into a single letter, thus avoiding further
fragmentation. As explained in section 2.2.1,
fragmentation / reassembly is performed in the transport layer
and not in CIGALE. A letter is given as a whole by the sending
process, fragmented if necessary by the TS into several
commands to fit into packets, reassembled upon arrival and then
delivered as a whole to the receiving process. Thus in the
transport station, buffer management is handled at letter
level. Since error control and flow control are tied to buffer
management, they are also introduced at letter level (see
sections 3.2.5 and 3.2.6).

A telegram is a fixed length piece of information (16 bits)
intended for interrupt-like use. It could appear at the user
interface as an event, as an interrupt, as a contingency, etc.
Telegrams are not subject to error or flow control : they are
transmitted and delivered independently of letters. Each TG is
sent in a (LI-TG) command. Its format is given in
Figure 3.2.9.(1).

3.2.4. Fragmentation and reassembly

When necessary, a letter is divided into fixed length Fragments
(FR) except for the last. Each fragment is sent as a one packet
command with proper control information (see Figure 3.2.4.(1)).
The size of the fragment is directly derived from the size of
the packet text. Each letter carries an 8-bit reference
(MY-REF) unique within the liaison, so as to avoid mixing
fragments of different letters on the same liaison.

Fragments are numbered (FR-NB) within the letter and an
End-Of-Letter (EOL) flag indicates the last fragment of the
letter. Both FR-NB (7 bits) and EOL (1 bit) fit within one
octet. The format of the corresponding (LI-LT) command is given
in Figure 3.2.9.(1). Upon arrival, fragments are reassembled
into a copy of the letter. Since packets may get lost,
reassembly is protected by a time-out associated with each
letter under reassembly. This time-out is set upon receipt of
the first delivered fragment, it is reset on receipt of each
fragment, and finally turned off when all fragments of the
letter have been received. If the time-out occurs, reassembly
is aborted and the letter considered erroneous. With error
control in effect, the error will normally be recovered.

3.2.5. Error control

To be able to recover from packet loss, the sender must keep a
copy of the data being sent until an acknowledgement is
received. Since buffer management is done at letter level and
the loss rate on packets is assumed to be low, error control is
performed on letters and not on fragments. This reduces the
amount of reverse control information (ACK), since
acknowledgements are sent for letters and not for fragments.

When in use on a liaison, error control is performed in both
directions and works as illustrated in Figure 3.2.5.(1) :

a) The sending TS sends letters with cyclically re-used
sequential references "MY-REF" and expects acknowledgement
within a maximum delay after the last fragment of the letter
has been sent.

b) The receiving TS acknowledges letters promptly, i.e. within
a maximum delay after the last fragment of the letter has been
received. It sends back "YR-REF" (your reference), meaning that
the letter with this reference and all preceding ones have been
received without error and passed to the receiving process. The
aknowledgment means that the LT has been made available to the
receiving process. It does not mean that the process has read
it. It does not mean that the process agrees with its
contents. It just means that the process agreed to receive a LT
on that LI, and that the LT was correctly received by the TS
and made available to the receiving process.

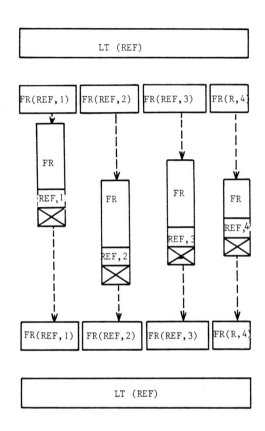

Figure 3.2.4.(1) - Fragmentation reassembly

The acknowledgment can be sent in a special command (LI-ACK) or with a fragment of the reverse flow (LI-LT) if there is one to send (see Figure 3.2.9.(1)).

c) If an acknowledgment is not received by the sending TS within the prescribed delay, all unacknowledged letters will be assumed lost and sent again, starting with the first unacknowledged letter. Acknowledgment will again be expected within the given delay. If acknowlegment is not received, this process will be repeated.

d) If a letter has been sent "N" times without success, the sending TS will declare an unrecoverable error, inform its user and quit (for that liaison).

e) Duplicate letters must be discarded, but an acknowledgment must be sent back by the receiving TS. To ensure uniqueness of letter references, possible anticipation is restricted to half a reference cycle.

f) The source TS should not send letters with references higher than half a reference cycle - 1 (i.e. 127) ahead of the last acknowledged letter.

g) The destination TS should not accept letters with references higher than half a reference cycle ahead of the last acknowledged letter, i.e. the receiver´s window is restricted to 128 letters. Moreover, the reference cycle is long enough to make sure that late letters do not arrive in the next reference cycle.

At initialization of error control, all references on the liaison are initialized to zero. The first letter is sent with MY-REF equal to one.

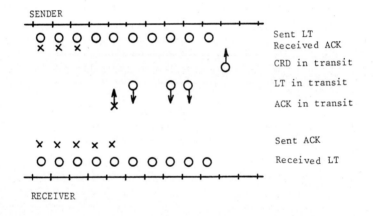

Figure 3.2.5.(1) - Error and flow control on letters

3.2.6. Flow control

For buffer management reasons flow control is performed at letter level. When in use on a liaison, it is associated with error control and performed in both directions as follows (see Figure 3.2.5.(1)) :

a) The receiving end allocates Credits (CRD) to the sending end. One credit represents the permission to send one letter. Each allocation is associated with an acknowledgement (YR-REF) within a LI-LT or LI-ACK command (see Figure 3.2.9.(1)). The

4-bit Credit Number (CRD-NB) parameter means : "you may send letters with references going from (YR-REF) + 1 up to (YR-REF) + (CRD-NB)", unless CRD-NB = 0, which means "do not send any letter".

b) The sending TS restricts itself to this upper limit that progresses under receiver control. This limit is updated as LI-ACK or LI-LT packets are received.

c) CRD-NB has a maximum value of 15, i.e. when flow control is used, the maximum number of letters in transit is 15. Such an anticipation seems to be sufficient with the delay and bandwidth properties of present technology.

3.2.7. Optional services

Error and flow control are optional services. Liaisons can be operated in the following modes :

a) Basic service : the transport station performs only fragmentation-reassembly, if needed, without error or flow control. No initial exchange of information is required prior to sending a letter. This has sometimes been referred to as a Lettergram service [EIN76].

b) Additional services :
. Error control on letters
. Error and flow control on letters

For optional services, the required initialization is done on user request (OPEN) by exchanging LI-INIT commands (see Figure 3.2.9.(1)), which contain the requested options. When optional services are no longer needed or when an unrecoverable error has been detected, termination is done by exchanging LI-TERM commands. The corresponding state diagram is given in Figure 3.2.7.(1).

3.2.8. Transport access

A variety of user interfaces can be provided [DEC77, GAR75, RAS75, ZIM75c]. We just indicate one partial set of primitives that could be offered as a Transport Access Method :

```
    OPEN-PT  : Activate a port
    RECV-PT  : Receive a letter addressed to that port from any
    port
    RINT-PT  : Receive interrupt (TG or initialization)
    addressed to that port from any port
    CLOSE-PT : Deactivate a port
    OPEN-LI  : Activate the local end of the liaison and
    initialize optional services if required
    RECV-LI  : Receive a letter on the liaison
```

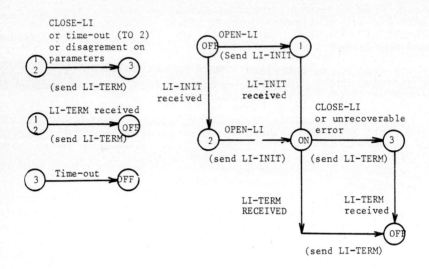

Figure 3.2.7.(1) - Session negotiation state diagram

SEND-LI : Send a letter on the liaison
RINT-LI : Receive interrupt (TG) on the liaison
SINT-LI : Send interrupt (TG) on the liaison
CLOSE-LI : Deactivate the local end of the liaison and
terminate any optional services in effect

An example in Figure 3.2.8.(1) in which a terminal wants to access a server illustrates
the possible use of the transport functions.

3.2.9. Command format

Transport commands should contain the identification of the liaison they pertain to. To avoid unnecessary overhead in practice, the TS-NB part of the addresses already placed in the packet header is not repeated in the command itself.

The format of transport commands is given in Figure 3.2.9.(1).

3.2.10. Transport station supervision

The same principle used in CIGALE with addressable network services is also applied at transport level. Specific ports can be dedicated to supervisory functions such as echoing,

Server(PT A)	TS_A	TS_B	Terminal (PT B)
OPEN-PT(A)	Create PT context		
RINT-PT(A)	Expect something...		
	Distant request (A-B)	LI-INIT (A-B)	OPEN-LI (A-B)
OPEN-LI (B-A)	LI-INIT (B-A)	Liaison successfully opened	
	Liaison successfully opened		RECV-LI (A-B)
SEND-LI(B-A)			

Figure 3.2.8.(1) - Use of the transport function

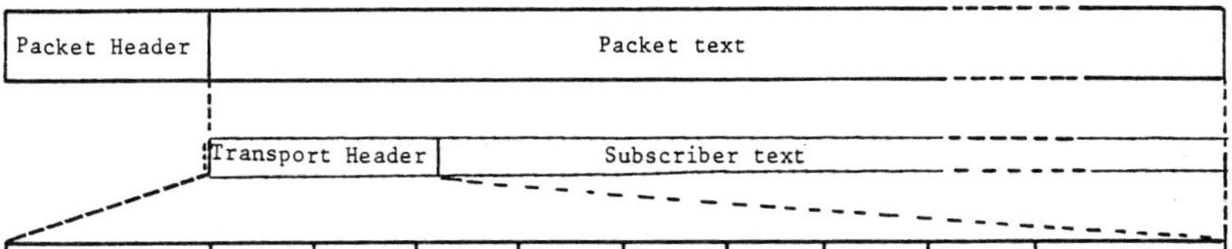

Octet 0		1	2	3	4	5	6	7	8	....
LT-LI	CRD-NB	DEST PR-NB		SRCE PT-NB		YR-REF	MY-REF	EOI/FR-NB	FR-TEXT	....
LI-ACK	CRD-NB	DEST PR-NB		SRCE PT-NB		YR-REF				
LI-TG		DEST PT-NB		SRCE PT-NB		TG-TEXT				
LI-INIT		DEST PT-NB		SRCE PT-NB		SERVICES AND PARAMETERS				
LI-TERM		DEST PT-NB		SRCE PT-NB		TERM-REASON				

Figure 3.2.9.(1) - Transport command format

statistics gathering, accounting, debugging, etc. Processes responsible for these functions communicate by means of letters according to their own protocols.

3.3. Transmission interface

The transport station handles letters on liaisons, with end-to-end error and flow control. An ideal transmission service should be able to accept letters and deliver them to their destinations within a predefined time delay. There is no transmission service possessing such a capability.

3.3.1. Typical public transmission services

Specialized transmission systems could be built, but they remain exceptions, since transmission is typically a service controlled by state monopolies (PTT), or regulated common carriers. In the following, only publicly offered services are considered.

3.3.1.1. Circuit oriented services

These services use dedicated or switched circuits conditioned for certain classes of bandwidth and signaling speeds. Bit rates vary from 50 bits/s up to 48 Kbits/s. Many carriers in industrialized countries offer higher bit rates. However, speeds higher than 48 Kbits/s are not available internationally, and they can only be installed in some specific geographical areas, where good quality circuits exist. There are several standards for the physical and electrical interface, but this is a minor problem, as appropriate line adapters are usually available from computer manufacturers.

There are two major categories of interfaces :

Asynchronous interface :

The transmission service carries individual characters of 5 to 8 bits framed with a START signal and a STOP signal. Within each character the bit rate is a characteristic of the circuit. More precisely the bit rate is defined by the type of Data Circuit terminating Equipment (DCE) connected at each end of the circuit. However there is no time relationship between successive characters, (hence the qualifier asynchronous). There is no error control, but the character code may provide for a parity bit. Flow control does not exist on circuits. Characters sent must be picked up by the receiver, or else they are lost. Transit delay is almost negligible (5 to 15 ms).

Synchronous interface :

The transmission service carries bit strings (blocks) of any length at a bit speed determined by DCE´s. There is no imposed character structure, but a few synchronization patterns are necessary at the beginning of each block for DCE´s to get synchronized. Public networks do not provide for any error control facility on synchronous interfaces, as it is assumed to

be implemented in user´s equipments. Flow control does not
exist since bits must be transmitted at a predefined rate.
However, line adapters for synchronous transmission services
are commonly equipped with augmented capabilities intended for
error detection. They include :

On transmission :

    a) generation of synchronization patterns,
    b) generation of special patterns for block framing and
    data transparency,
    c) generation of a Cyclic Redundancy Check (CRC) appended
    to each transmitted block.

On reception :

    a) character alignment on 8-bit groups,
    b) detection and removal of framing characters,
    c) verification of the CRC validity.

With these services added by user equipments (or equivalent
software) a synchronous transmission service appears to carry
blocks of 8-bit characters with automatic error detection. With
blocks of a few thousand bits and 16-bit CRC the undetected bit
error rate is lower than 10E-10. However nothing can reveal the
loss of entire blocks. Since bit error rates on lines vary from
10E-3 to 10E-6, blocks must be limited in length in order to
bring the ratio of block error rate down to an acceptable
figure, e.g. 10E-2. If this is not possible, a fallback
expedient is to use a lower bit rate.

3.3.1.2. Message oriented services

There is no well defined service ; it varies with systems. As a
general trend, it is a computerization of telegram-like
services. Input is in the form of character strings of variable
length with imposed formats and alphabets. Messages carry
multiple addresses and transit delays vary between a few
minutes and several hours. Message labeling and acknowledgement
offer some error detection capabilities.

These services are only available in some countries. They are
also made available by private networks for certain groups of
users, such as airlines [GLO73], banks, and meteorology.

3.3.1.3. Packet oriented services

The datagram service (see section 3.1.4) is only available with
private packet networks. The 1980 vintage of X.25 introduced a
datagram service as an extension to X.25, but it may take some
time before existing public networks make it available.

A virtual circuit service has been defined for public networks,
and is offered in some countries. The interface is X.25.
Broadly speaking, its characteristics are : a) the same
physical and electrical interface as for synchronous
transmission, b) a data link control procedure of the HDLC
family, c) a packet level interface [CCI77].

The packet level itself comprises again a transmission
procedure different from HDLC, and about 15 packet formats. It
provides for Virtual Circuits (VC) between user equipments, not
between ports. The packet level procedure performs error and
flow control per VC, but control during data transfer applies
only to the segment of a VC between user equipment and network,
(see Figure 3.3.1.(1)). Thus there is no guarantee of error
free transmission. Error detection and recovery must anyhow
rely upon the transport protocol.

This matter of end-to-end control has been a continuous
controversy from the beginning of packet switching. As will be
explained in more details later (see section 9.3.1.2), some
public packet networks offer a restricted form of end-to-end
error control within their own boundaries. However, this may
not be considered as a generally available service.

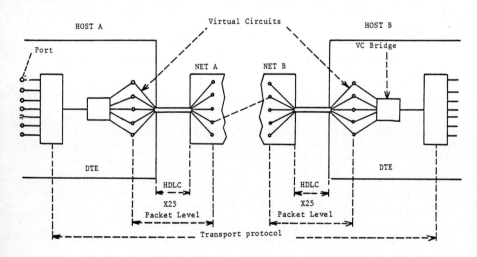

Figure 3.3.1.(1) - Virtual circuit interface

3.3.1.4. Mixed services

PTT´s are studying interworking between classes of services. It is conceivable that some future service might appear as an X.25 virtual circuit interface at one end, while the other end was a real circuit with a synchronous interface. The transmission network could assume interface conversions.

3.3.2. The transmission bridge

The descriptions given above show that there is no "letter" oriented transmission service. Some adaptations are necessary to bridge the gap between transport station functions and transmission interface.

The asynchronous interface is the most manageable. Letters could be transmitted as a sequence of 8-bit characters. Checksumming would be necessary to insure bit integrity, and speed is limited to 1200 bits/s. These constraints may be acceptable for some classes of terminal traffic.

The synchronous interface could allow the transmission of complete letters, as long as they are short enough to cope with transmission errors. Letters received with checksum errors must be dropped. The transport station error control can recover lost letters. A data link control procedure (e.g. HDLC) may be introduced at circuit level, because error recovery is quicker and more efficient at this level. Such an additional facility is only useful when performance is substantially affected by a high error rate. When letters exceed the maximum block length, they must be fragmented for transmission and reassembled on arrival. Beside that, all of the above discussions on the synchronous interface apply again (see section 3.3.1.1).

The X.25 interface imposes two levels of procedure, and a large number of packet formats. It is a complex interface. Furthermore, X.25 does not accept packets longer than a certain maximum size, which depends on the carrier, (a typical limit is 128 octets). Thus, fragmentation of letters may be necessary.

In summary, the transmission bridge contains one or several of the following functions : a) letter ckecksumming, b) letter fragmentation and reassembly, d) the packet level of the X.25 procedure, c) a data link control procedure.

The case of message oriented services has not been examined, because it is not typical in a computer network environment. The datagram interface is covered in the following.

3.3.3. The CIGALE bridge

In the design of the CYCLADES transport station it was assumed
that a typical environment would be : a) synchronous
transmission interface, circuit or packet oriented, b) letters
possibly longer than the maximum acceptable transmission block
or packet.

A consequence is that letter fragmentation and reassembly had
to be provided in any case. Instead of designing a separate
layer of limited functional significance, it appeared simpler
and more efficient to include fragmentation in the transport
station capabilities.

Every computer system with synchronous transmission adapters
provides some data link control procedure. CIGALE is adapted to
host transmission procedures, and requires only one packet
format. Therefore, the only difference between the CIGALE
interface and a synchronous transmission interface is that
letter fragments must be sent with a CIGALE header. This is the
only price to pay for the switching capability of CIGALE.   On
the other hand several manufacturers have implemented an X.25
bridge. They all came up with 3 to 4000 machine instructions,
just for the packet level.

3.4. Virtual Terminal Protocol

3.4.1. Introduction

Prior to the development of computer networks, terminals were
attached to computers either locally, as any other peripheral
device, or remotely, by means of a telephone line. The move
towards networking brings up two constraints on the
organization of the relationship between terminals and
computers : autonomy and compatibility.

Autonomy

On a physical line, the transmission delay for control
information may be considered as negligible (e.g. 10 ms to
transfer 3 octets at 2400 bit/s). Moreover, the transmission
cost is not related to the amount of information transferred on
the line.   This made possible very intimate and frequent
interactions between terminals and computers (e.g. character at
a time interaction, including echoing and padding, or the
polling of terminals on a multidrop line).

Packet networks introduce a delay (often about 200 ms) and make
transmission costs depend on the number of messages being
exchanged, i.e. on the amount of interaction between the two
parties. It is therefore sensible to design terminals with
increased autonomy, i.e. more intelligence, to be able to drive

themselves and thus, minimize the amount of control information
transferred through the network. This is made practical   for
new terminals with microprocessors, while other terminals must
be provided with additional intelligence, often by   a   terminal
concentrator.

Compatibility

The   terminal   market is developing very rapidly. The number of
terminals installed is growing much faster than the   number   of
mainframes, and at the same time terminals are getting more and
more intelligence to perform new functions.

Computer   manufacturers   provide   the   software required in
mainframes to control their own terminals, i.e.   they provide
compatibility between the various products they sell. This has
been sufficient for the last generation of star-like networks,
in which one terminal was connected only to one mainframe.

The new generation of informatics networks makes use of packet
switching to provide communication between any two entities
within the network. In particular each terminal can now access
all of the mainframes participating in the network. This raises
the need for network compatibility between terminals and
mainframes, through standard conventions for controlling
terminals on the network.

The transport protocol (see section 3.3) provides a basis for
compatibility, since it provides communication between any
application-like process in a computer and any   terminal
handling process elsewhere on the network. An additional layer
of conventions is required for terminals   and   applications   to
understand each other (e.g. message formats, character code).
Such a set of conventions, generally called a Virtual   Terminal
Protocol (VTP), defines :

a) a logical model for each class of terminals, called a
Virtual Terminal (VT),

b) a specification about how to drive this virtual terminal
(message formats, etc.).

A   virtual   terminal   is   a   logical model in the sense that it
defines an abstract model of a terminal in terms of logical
functions that can be interpreted differently on different real
terminals.

Another way to provide standardization would have been to
choose a specific (existing) terminal "X" in each class, and
require all terminals of that class in the network to be
compatible with "X". The virtual terminal approach offers the
advantage of not being biased by specific implementation
decisions. It is also best adapted to programmable terminals
that will gradually replace existing hard-wired terminals. In

addition, it provides some compatibility between classes of terminals, since the same logical functions can be found in different classes.

The pratical use of a Virtual Terminal Protocol has been demonstrated in CYCLADES as well as in several other networks.

Existing applications only need to be adapted to drive a new type of terminal, the Virtual Terminal, while new applications can take it into account from the very beginning (see section 5.2).

Programmable terminals can be modified to emulate a virtual terminal (see section 5.5), while hard-wired terminals have to be adapted through some conversion package (see section 5.3).

The early design of CYCLADES included the definition of a VTP [ZIM75c,ZIM75d]. This protocol was adopted for all initial implementations and experimented with for about two years. Network-wide usage of the protocol on a daily basis forced us to learn a lot about the requirements and non-requirements for a virtual terminal protocol, with much better evidence than was provided by hours of discussion.

We then had to decide whether or not to replace the VTP currently in use in CYCLADES by a new one, in accordance with our experience. We came to the conclusion that the change would be worth the cost provided ; (1) the move would be decided as soon as possible, avoiding new implementations to be started with the old protocol, and (2) the consensus on this protocol could be extended beyond CYCLADES. It turned out that we could rapidly come to an agreement with CII on a revised version of the virtual terminal protocol, to become a common standard and be put into operation within a minimum delay. As a result of this, CYCLADES has been equipped since 1977 with this second version of VTP [ZIM76b], used for conversational as well as batch terminals. In our view, the next move is to be made only when an international agreement is reached on a standard VTP, since we are technically satisfied with the CYCLADES/VTP. This opinion is now being shared within the international networking community and much effort is being made to force the advent of such a standard.

Out of discussions, conducted in particular within EIN [EIN77] and EURONET [EUR79], and enlarged within IFIP, a proposal is emerging as a possible candidate for official standardization [IFI78]. As compared with the present CYCLADES/VTP, the concepts are identical, but the overall structure is more general and the formats are simpler. We have thus decided to describe here this latest version of VTP rather than the former.

3.4.2. The virtual terminal layer

The virtual terminal layer (see Figure 3.4.2.(1)) is built on
top of the transport box. It provides additional functions
required for terminal oriented communications, for example
between a human user at a terminal and an application program
in a host computer.

Each communication provided by the virtual terminal service is
handled by a pair of virtual terminals, located in the virtual
terminal layer, one at each end of the liaison provided by the
transport service (see section 3.3). Cooperation between a pair
of virtual terminals is governed by the virtual terminal
protocol. The use of a pair of virtual terminals to describe
the virtual terminal service (as opposed to a single one with
no specific location) makes it easier to implement the
different views the two users may have of the data structure
presented on the terminal(s) (see section 3.4.4.1), due to
concurrency and network delays. For instance, there is a delay
between the write operation performed by an application program
and appearance of the corresponding modification on the remote
display ; in between, the two ends have different views of the
data being displayed. In addition, the location of the data
structure is important for some applications, in particular for
implementation of error recovery.

A virtual terminal may, for instance, be implemented as :

        - An intelligent terminal which directly handles the
        virtual terminal protocol (see section 5.5).

        - A terminal with the additional logic (e.g. in a
        concentrator [WEB77]) required to handle the virtual
        terminal protocol (see section 5.3)

        - An access method providing application programs in a
        host with some kind of virtual terminal access method.

However, the structure of a virtual terminal implementation is
not visible through the protocol : each end may simply assume
that there is a virtual terminal at the other end, without
worrying about its implementation. In other words, the only
constraint is to look like a virtual terminal. This is the
reason why it is called "Virtual".

3.4.3. Virtual terminal classes

The virtual terminal protocol is intended to cover several
classes of terminals with different functional capabilities,
corresponding to different classes of applications.

First, a scroll-mode virtual terminal class covers simple
sequential terminals such as teleprinters, displays in scroll

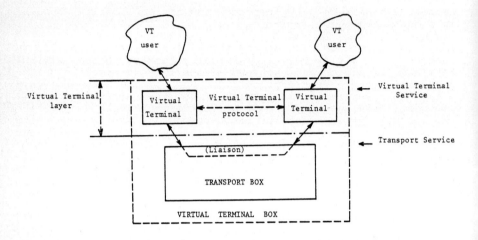

Figure 3.4.2.(1) - Virtual Terminal Layer

mode, card readers and punches, line printers, etc.

Secondly, a page-mode virtual terminal class covers simple terminals which offer direct addressing within the page.

Third, a data entry virtual terminal class should cover terminals with field and attribute capability.

Fourth, of course, a number of functions are common to different classes, thus providing some elementary compatibility between classes.

The virtual terminal service/protocol will be defined starting with scroll mode. The definition of page mode will then refer to the definition of scroll mode. The definition of data entry, which is not included here, should in turn refer to the preceding ones.

3.4.4. Scroll-mode virtual terminal class

3.4.4.1. Definition of the service

Text data structures

The virtual terminal service allows pairs of users to have a common view of a text data structure. Each user is provided with a local "copy" of the data structure located in his (local) virtual terminal. Both "copies" of the data structure are coupled by the virtual terminal service, i.e. a modification at one end causes the corresponding modification to occur at the other end. The use of two "copies" of the data structure (rather than a single shared one) makes it easier to render the different views that both users may have, due for instance to network delays. In addition, the location of a "copy" of the data structure is important for some applications since the "copies" may be in different states. We will simply consider that there are two data structures, one in each virtual terminal, which are coupled by the virtual terminal service.

A virtual terminal contains a primary data structure and possibly one or several secondary data structures. At one point in time, only one pair of data structures (both primaries or both secondaries) can be coupled by the virtual terminal service. They are referred to as the "current" data structures.

A text data structure is made of a sequence of NL lines, each line being made of a sequence of NC character positions. Each character position may either be empty or contain a graphic character pertaining to a character set (the "overprint" option allows us to superimpose several characters in the same character position).

A pointer to the current character position is associated with each data structure.

Modifications of the current data structures

A VT user can modify the contents of the current data structures by performing transactions of elementary modifications on its (local) data structure. The virtual terminal service updates the other end data structure according to the result of the transaction, i.e. the new contents of the data structure and the new value of the pointer. The sequence of elementary modifications within the transaction is purely a local matter (see Figure 3.4.4.(1)).

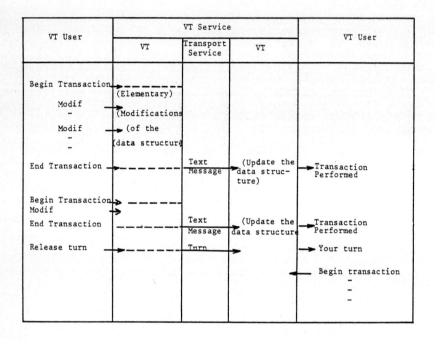

| | VT Service | | | |
VT User	VT	Transport Service	VT	VT User
Begin Transaction	(Elementary)			
Modif	(Modifications			
-	(of the			
Modif	(data structure			
-				
-				
End Transaction		Text Message	(Update the data struc- ture)	Transaction Performed
Begin Transaction Modif				
End Transaction		Text Message	(Update the data structure	Transaction Performed
Release turn		Turn		Your turn
				Begin transaction
				-
				-

Figure 3.4.4.(1) - Transaction of modifications of the data-structure

Scroll-mode updating rules

The result of a transaction of modifications on a data structure in a scroll-mode virtual terminal must obey the following rules :

- lines preceding the line which was the "current line" before the transaction started cannot be modified,

- lines following the line which is the "current line" at the end of the transaction cannot be modified.

The consequences of these rules are that the pointer cannot be moved to a preceding line, and that the current line is the last one (according to sequential order of lines in the data structure) which has been modified.

With regard to modifications, a data structure may either be :

- a source, i.e. it can be modified only by the local VT   user
(an example of a source could be a card reader)

- a sink, i.e. it can be modified only by the virtual terminal
service, as a consequence of a transaction of modifications
performed on the distant data-structure (an example of a sink
could be a printer)

- a source/sink, i.e. it can be modified by either end (an
example of a source/sink could be a   conversational   terminal).

Of course a source can only be paired with a sink or a
source/sink (see Figure 3.4.4.(2)).

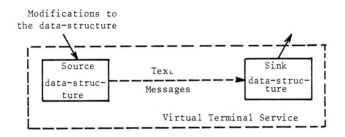

a) A text source VT must be paired with a text sink VT

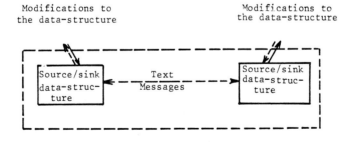

b) Text source/sink VTs must be paired together

Figure 3.4.4.(2) - Text source, sink and source/sink VTs

In case of source/sink pairing the virtual terminal service
offers two modes of coupling data structures. Alternating mode
and free-running mode.

In alternating mode, the ´turn´, i.e. the right to perform a
transaction of modifications, is allocated to only one VT user
at a time. At the end of the transaction, the VT user may
either keep the turn and perform another transaction or give it
back to the virtual terminal service which will then pass it to
the other VT user when the update of his data structure has
been performed.

In free-running mode, the virtual terminal service performs
updates of data structures at each end on a first come first
served basis. In this mode, if both VT users happen to start a
transaction of modifications at the same time, updates will be
performed at both ends in a different order (see
Figure 3.4.4.(3)). It is the VT users´ responsibility to
perform transactions of modifications in an orderly fashion, if
they want both data structures to remain identical. This mode
might be used by some applications for which messages being
sent and received are not directly related (e.g. some remote
batch systems), but it is intended mainly to cater for those
cases where adapting an existing host to the virtual terminal
from the outside does not permit one to identify which end is
supposed to perform the next transaction of modifications. A
misinterpretation could cause a deadlock in alternating mode.
For example, after having sent a question, the host expects a
reply from the terminal, but if the host adaptation does not
recognize the end of the question (in many cases, only the user
is able to recognize it), it will not pass the turn to the
terminal, which will not be able to send the reply.

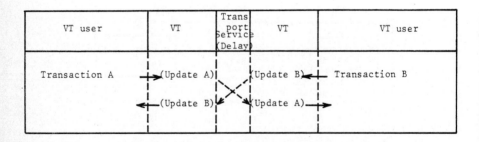

Figure 3.4.4.(3) - Concurrency of updates

Purge

At any time, any VT user may request the virtual terminal
service to perform a purge operation : the current transaction
(if any) is aborted and both data structures are reinitialized,
i.e. all character positions are emptied and pointers are reset
to the first position of the first line of the first page. The
"turn" is not affected by a purge operation.

Attentions

In addition to communication by means of data structures, the
virtual terminal service provides VT users with means of
exchanging qualified attention signals. The meaning of the
qualifier associated with an attention signal is out of the
scope of the virtual terminal service, which only passes the
signal without interpreting it. The attention signal is passed
on a channel independent of the one used to update data
structures and thus cannot be delayed by an update. This
independence also implies that both ends may have a different
view of the order in which updates and attentions occur.

Configuration

A virtual terminal may have a default configuration or be
equipped with "options". Each VT user may request a specific
configuration for his virtual terminal, or let the virtual
terminal service decide the configuration. If requests from
both VT users are compatible, the configuration of both virtual
terminals will be determined by the virtual terminal service.
The parameters which describe options of a scroll-mode virtual
terminal are shown in Figure 3.4.4.(4).

3.4.4.2. Definition of the protocol

The protocol will be described as an exchange of primitives
(assembled into messages, themselves passed in letters) and
telegrams on the liaison provided by the transport service, for
communication between two virtual terminals. The mapping of
primitives onto letters will be described in section 3.4.6.

a) Configuration procedure

The configuration procedure is the subset of the virtual
terminal protocol which is used to determine (if possible) the
configuration of both virtual terminals according to VT users'
requirements. As long as a specific configuration has not been
determined, both virtual terminals have default configurations.
Each end can enquire about the range of configurations
acceptable to the other end by sending a

PARAMETERS	POSSIBLE VALUES
<Terminal Class>	Scroll-Mode (default)
<Primary data structure>	Yes (default)
<Secondary 1>	Yes/No (default)
<Secondary 2>	Yes/No (default)
--------	-------
For each existing data structure :	
<Source/Sink>	Source/Sink free-running (default) Source/Sink alternating Source Sink
<Line length>	Undefined (default) $N \leqslant 255$
<Replace/overprint>	Undefined (default) Overprint Replace
<Current data-structure>	Primary (default) Secondary $\neq$ i
<Location of the turn>	My turn Your turn

Figure 3.4.4.(4) - Scroll-Mode Virtual Terminal Parameters

REQUEST-PARAMETERS-RANGE primitive (see Figure 3.4.4.(5)).

Either end can select a configuration by sending a SET-PARAMETERS-VALUE primitive, which is answered either by an

Virtual Terminal	Transport Service	Virtual Terminal
	REQUEST-PARAMETERS-RANGE	
	INDICATE-PARAMETERS-RANGE	

Figure 3.4.4.(5) - Information on configuration capabilities

AGREE primitive or a DISAGREE primitive. In the latter case the configuration is kept unchanged (see Figure 3.4.4.(6)).

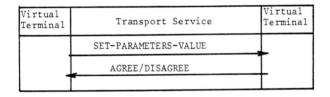

Virtual Terminal	Transport Service	Virtual Terminal
	SET-PARAMETERS-VALUE	
	AGREE/DISAGREE	

Figure 3.4.4.(6) - Configuration setting

Each SET-PARAMETERS-VALUE primitive contains a ´random number´ which is used to solve potential contention when both virtual terminals issue a SET-PARAMETERS-VALUE primitive at the same time. The primitive with the lower random number is ignored. Primitives used by the configuration procedure are summarized below. Parameters of scroll-mode virtual terminals are given in Figure 3.4.4.(4).

> - REQUEST-PARAMETERS-RANGE   <List   of   parameters identifiers>
> - INDICATE-PARAMETERS-RANGE   <List   of   parameters range>
> - SET-PARAMETERS-VALUE   <Random   number>   <List   of parameters value>
> - AGREE
> - DISAGREE

b) Updating procedure

The updating procedure is the subset of the virtual terminal protocol which is used to update the current data structure at

one end according to the result of a transaction of
modifications performed at the other end by the VT user on its
current data structure. Primitives corresponding to a
transaction of modifications are grouped into a text-message. A
TEXT-SEGMENT primitive is used to write a sequence of
characters in the sequence of character positions starting with
the current character position. After the primitive has been
executed, the pointer is set to the position following the last
character position of the sequence.

START-OF-LINE and NEW-LINE primitives are used to set the
pointer to the first character position in the current line and
in the following one respectively, while the NEW-PAGE primitive
sets the pointer to the first character position of the first
line of the page following the current page.

The updating procedure for scroll-mode virtual terminals
conforms to restrictions indicated in section 3.4.4.1.

Alternation of the "turn" makes use of a "your turn"
indication, possibly associated with text messages.

Primitives used by the updating procedure are summarized below.

          - TEXT-SEGMENT <Sequence of characters>
          - START-OF-LINE
          - NEW-LINE
          - NEW-PAGE

c) Purge procedure

The purge procedure is used to purge the current data
structures. It consists of a double handshake (see
Figure 3.4.4.(7))

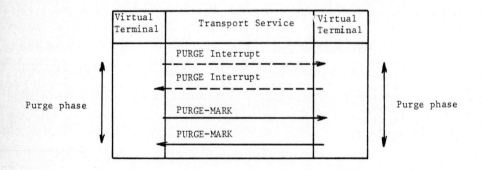

Figure 3.4.4.(7) - Purge scenario

The first handshake consisting of the exchange of PURGE telegrams permits us to initiate the purge operation, regardless of flow control on the flow of letters (in which primitives are normally passed). The second handshake, consisting of the exchange of PURGE-MARK primitives is used to relate the purge operation to the flow of updating primitives. The symmetry of the purge avoids any collision problem. As seen by one end, the "purge phase" starts when a PURGE telegram is initially sent or received, and ends when a PURGE-MARK primitive is last sent or received (see Figure 3.4.4.(8)). In addition to exchanging PURGE telegrams and PURGE-MARK primitives, the following actions are taken by both virtual terminals :

- At the beginning of a purge phase, local transactions of modifications, current sending of modifications, and current sending of updating primitives, if any, are aborted.

- During the purge phase, any updating primitive received is dropped.

- At the end of the purge phase, the local data structure is reinitialised, i.e. all character positions are emptied and the pointer is reset to the first character position of the first line of the first page.

Primitives and telegrams used by the purge procedure are summarized below :

      - PURGE   (sent as a telegram)

      - PURGE-MARK

d) Attention procedure

The attention procedure consists of the passing of attention signals within ATTENTION telegrams, upon the VT user's request. ATTENTION telegrams contain the qualifier which is not interpreted within the virtual terminal service :

      - ATTENTION   <Qualifier>   (sent as a telegram)

3.4.5. Page-mode virtual terminal class

3.4.5.1. Definition of the service

The definition of the page-mode virtual terminal service differs from scroll-mode in the following points :

The number of characters per line and the number of lines per page in the primary data structure may not be undefined.

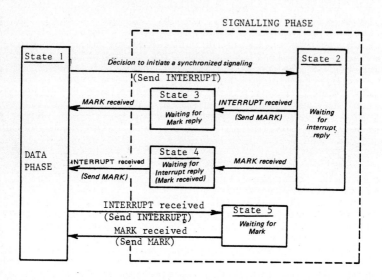

Figure 3.4.4.(8) - Purge automaton

Secondly, updating rules for the primary data structure are the following :

   - Pages preceding the page which was the "current page" before the transaction started cannot be modified.
   - Pages following the page which is the "current page" at the end of the transaction cannot be modified.

3.4.5.2. Definition of the protocol

The definition of the page-mode virtual terminal protocol differs from scroll-mode in the following points :

a) In the configuration procedure, <terminal-class> must be "page mode" while <line length> and <page length> for the primary data structure may not be "undefined".

b) In the updating procedure for the primary data structure, a POSITION primitive is used to set the pointer within the current page (NEW-LINE and START-OF-LINE are not available) :

      - POSITION   <line number> <character number>

3.4.6. Message format considerations

Interaction between virtual terminals is based on the exchange
of telegrams and primitives forming messages passed in letters.
Each message may contain several primitives in the same
procedures, i.e. primitives from different procedures may not
be mixed in a message :

        <message> ::= <primitive><primitive>...<primitive>

Restrictions imposed by the transport service might require the
use of several consecutive letters to transfer one message.
Each letter should then contain an integer number of
primitives.

The coding of primitives within letters in CYCLADES, also
adopted in many other networks, uses an item structure. A
letter starts with a <letter header> followed by a sequence of
<items>. The letter header contains namely the identification
of the procedure and possibly the end of message and the "turn"
indications. Each item starts with the indication of its
length, followed by the description of the primitive :

        <letter>   ::= <letter header><item><item>...<item>
        <letter header> ::= <procedure id.><EOM   indication><your
        turn indication>
        <item>   ::= <item length><primitive description>

3.5. File transfer

3.5.1. General problems

The use of the CYCLADES computer network started with access to
different systems from a single remote terminal. This was made
possible by standard conventions to handle terminals over the
network, provided by the Virtual Terminal Protocol (VTP) just
discussed.

The need for some standard ways of handling files appeared
rapidly as network usage developed, for example distribution of
new software, tape transfer and distributed applications,
(e.g., a source program edited on one computer and compiled on
another).

The VTP allows users to switch from one system to another, from
the same terminal. To take full advantage of the network, the
user also needs to be able to easily transfer his files between
systems. This raised the need for a network file management
service.

Files

A File is a container of information, considered as a whole
(i.e., it can be identified as such), without any reference to
the meaning of the data that it contains. This is in
contradistinction to a data base, which deals with the meaning
and structure of the data itself, without reference to its
"physical" representations within files.

Within a file, data is represented according to local operating
system conventions, (e.g., text characters can be coded in the
ISO code on eight bits, or in EBCDIC code). A file is often
structured in blocks of information called logical records (or
logical units). If a file is structured in logical records,
then they represent the basic unit in which information can be
accessed within the file.

File management

A File Management Service (FMS) usually provides two kinds of
services :

a) a file access method, which consists of a set of standard
primitives to store data into files and retrieve it (often in
terms of logical records),

b) a set of file maintenance programs or services, whose usual
functions are : (1) to make a copy of a file (i.e., move data
from one container to another, possibly with changes in its
physical structure), (2) to delete a file (i.e., suppress all
access to the file and its contents), (3) to rename a file
(i.e., change its identification), and (4) to reorganize a file
(i.e., get back unused space).

As opposed to data base management, which provides access to
the actual information, file management permits manipulation of
the "physical" representation of this information.

Network file management

A general network file management service could consist of the
extension of local file management services over a network.
These services would be accessed through a standard File
Management Access Method (FM-AM) which would include :

a) A remote or network file access method, for accessing data
contained in a remote network file,

b) Network file maintenance services, which would provide
remote access to local file maintenance services,

c) A network file transfer service, to extend the "copy"
facility, usually available locally over the network.

The cooperation between the network File Management Access
Method (FM-AM) and the File Management Systems (FMS), as well
as between the file management systems themselves, would be
governed by means of a File Management Protocol (FMP), (see
Figure 3.5.1.(1)).

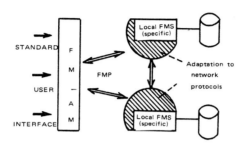

Figure 3.5.1.(1) - Network file management

Problems raised when one tries to provide network file
management services belong to two classes, as is typical in
distributed computing : a) Questions related to the
distribution of control between various participating
activities over the network, b) Problems resulting from the
heterogeneity of the different elements involved.

In the first class one finds problems like :

a) Synchronisation between activities needing to cooperate at
some point in time, e.g., for resource allocation,

b) Coherence of information accessed when stored in different
places, e.g. when dealing whith multiple file copies or network
file catalogs,

c) Security and privacy of information under distributed
control.

In the second class, the heterogeneity of the systems involved
leads to considerable problems, at the level of interworking
between network file management systems, namely physical
representation of data. Three main features usually differing
from one system to another can be considered :

a) File identification, which generally includes a device name,
a volume name, a file name, an account number, a password, etc.

b) File structure, which can be record-oriented or not and
accessed sequentially, by indexes, or randomly.

c) Data representation, which depends also on the nature of data, e.g. characters (EBCDIC, ASCII, BCD), integers, floating point or formatted data of any kind.

Most of these problems are not specific to file management services. They also belong to wider fields of investigation, such as distributed data bases and operating systems or network control languages. The approach chosen in CYCLADES [GIE77, GIE77b] was to limit file management services offered over the network to a minimum, which would satisfy most of the users' requirements, and to leave most of the problems mentioned above to longer term studies (see section 6).

The main simplifications made were to reduce network file management services to a simple file transfer service and to define only the control environment of file transfer operations.

3.5.2. File transfer service

Except for the file transfer service, all other file management operations (i.e. file access and file maintenance) involve only one FMS at a time : the one handling the file. Remote access to local file management services of a system is provided to network users by means of a VTP (interactive or batch access), thus allowing the user to perform these file management functions. The burden, put on the user, is that he has to know the control language of every file system he wants to access. This would not be acceptable in the long run but it provides a first step towards an adequate solution.

On the other hand, file transfer operations, which involve cooperation between at least two systems (i.e. two file access methods), impose the definition of some common network-wide conventions, namely a File Transfer Protocol (FTP) to provide a file transfer service through a File Transfer Access Method (FT-AM), (see Figure 3.5.2.(1)).

Some of the file management problems mentioned earlier need still be considered. They concern file identification, data representation within files and mechanisms for transferring data.

a) File identification problems have not been solved in full generality within CYCLADES. No network-wide convention exists for the naming of network files. The usual way of identifying a file over the network is to identify the system handling the file, using its address as known by the transport service, and then use local conventions within that system.

b) Data representation within files depends on local FMS conventions. Files can be structured into logical records or not, and codes, byte sizes, etc. are usually different. One requirement for a file transfer service is that it must provide

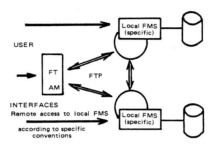

Figure 3.5.2.(1) - Network file transfer

some code conversions and file organization mappings between
the systems involved, in order to provide a useful service
[SCH75]. To make this possible, it is necessary to define some
standard file organization and data representations that can be
mapped onto every system and that will be used as the standard
conventions to represent data travelling over the network.

The conventions defined for a minimum file transfer service
cover only sequential files, containing text information
grouped into records which constitute logical units (i.e. "text
messages") accessible individually and sequentially.

Except for homogeneous or compatible systems, other types of
file organization and data representation are not considered.
Nevertheless, a "transparent" mode of operation is provided,
which allows the transfer of any kind of file between
homogeneous or compatible file systems.

However, transfer of binary data between heterogeneous file
systems is not very significant. Most user needs are satisfied
with transparent file transfer in a homogeneous environment and
a transfer of text files between heterogeneous computers.

c) Mechanisms for transferring data constitute the area where
most of the effort has been applied. They have been designed in
a general context so that simplification to particular cases
will not prevent future extensions. These mechanisms, which
constitute most of the file transfer protocol, are described in
the following sections.

3.5.3. File transfer architecture

Architecture of a network File Management System (FMS)

A network file management can be considered [NEI73, GIE78] as
being composed of two kinds of components. First, service
points provide access to local file handling facilities.
Secondly, control points monitor and synchronize the operation
of service points in order to perform actions on files, as
requested by users (or application programs).

A sequence of file management operations, which involves one
control point and one (or two) service point(s) is called a
transaction.

In order to complete a transaction, a dialog takes place
between a control process (the controller) at a control point
and a server process (the server) at a service point.

In the case of a file transfer one controller and two servers
are involved : one controller at the control point, e.g. where
the user is located, one server at the service point where the
source file resides (the producer), and one server at the
service point where the file has to be transferred (the
consumer).

In this case, a dialog will also take place between the two
servers (see Figure 3.5.3.(1)).

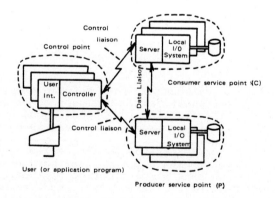

Figure 3.5.3.(1) - General architecture

One server operates only on one file at a time, and one
controller and one server cooperate only for one transaction at
a time. Several transactions could be handled in parallel
involving the same control and service points ; they will be
considered here (i.e. in the model), as being performed by
different instances of controller and server processes.

Communication means

To conduct their dialog, controller and server(s) communicate
through the transport service provided locally by a Transport
Station (TS) residing on each site. This transport service can
be considered as an inter-process communication facility which
establishes liaisons between process ports.

A liaison established between a controller and a server is
called a control liaison ; between two servers (for a file
transfer), where it will be used to transfer actual data, it is
called a data liaison (see Figure 3.5.3.(2)).

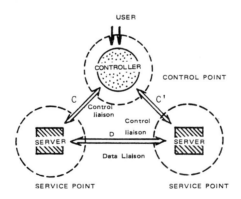

Figure 3.5.3.(2) - File transfer general architecture

Simplified architecture for a file transfer

A simplified model [NEI73, DAY77, HLP77] can be derived from
the one described above, where controller and server functions
happen to lie within the same systems (see Figure 3.5.3.(3)).
In this case, user requests must be directed to the site where
one of the files resides.

This approach does not affect the basic mechanisms involved in the protocol ; it simplifies synchronization and restart problems between distant sites (in case one liaison is broken), since only two systems have to be controlled during a transaction (instead of three).

Formats for exchanging commands and replies on the control liaison are different from formats used for transferring data on the data liaison. It is easy to distinguish them, so that they can be multiplexed on the same liaison to further simplify synchronization and restart problems between both ends (see Figure 3.5.3.(3)).

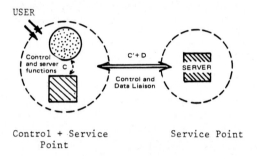

Control + Service   Service Point
      Point

Figure 3.5.3.(3) - Minimum architecture for file transfer

This simple architecture allows easy experimentation with the basic file transfer protocol mechanisms.

As can be seen in the figures above, the move to the general model where control and data transfer functions are well isolated, will have a greater impact on implementation and structure of the different modules involved in controller and server processes, than on the actual protocol primitives.

3.5.4. File transfer primitives

File transfer primitives are grouped into two classes :

a) Commands/replies (exchanged on the control liaison) to control file transfer operations,

b) Data transfer primitives (exchanged on the data liaison) which allow safe transfer of the actual data.

File transfer commands/replies

These primitives are exchanged in an alternate mode
(demand/response). They are used to initiate and terminate a
transaction (i.e. a file transfer). They are :

D-SENDFILE   <Transparent/Standard Mode> <File Identification>
               <Rewind/Resume> <Mark>

and the corresponding reply :

R-SENDFILE   <Reply code> <File Structure>

or :

D-RECVFILE   <Transparent/Standard Mode> <File Identification>
               <File Structure> <Rewind/Append/Resume>

and the corresponding reply :

R-RECVFILE   <Reply Code> <Mark>

These pairs of commands/replies are used to initialize a file
transfer, in either direction.

CLOSEFILE   <Code>

is used to terminate a transaction (i.e. a file transfer).

As parameters of these commands, file identification and file
structure are given either in transparent mode when systems are
homogeneous or compatible, or in standard mode when systems are
incompatible. In the latter, only a limited number of file
structure types can be handled.

A position parameter indicates whether the transfer must be
executed from the beginning of the file (Rewind) or if the file
must be appended to an existing one (Append). A <Resume>
indication allows one to restart a transfer previously
interrupted. In this case, the <Mark> parameter indicates a
restart checkpoint from which to recover.

Data transfer primitives

a) DATA primitives are used to transfer the actual data (on the
data liaison). The data blocks exchanged can be structured into
records, a concept which is similar to the VTP message concept
(see section 3.4). An End Of Record/Message (EOR/EOM)
indication is available to specify the end of a logical record.
The last record indicates the End Of the File (EOF).

In transparent mode, if specified by the initiation commands,
(i.e. through the <mode> parameter of the D-SENDFILE/D-RECVFILE
commands), the structure and representation of the data

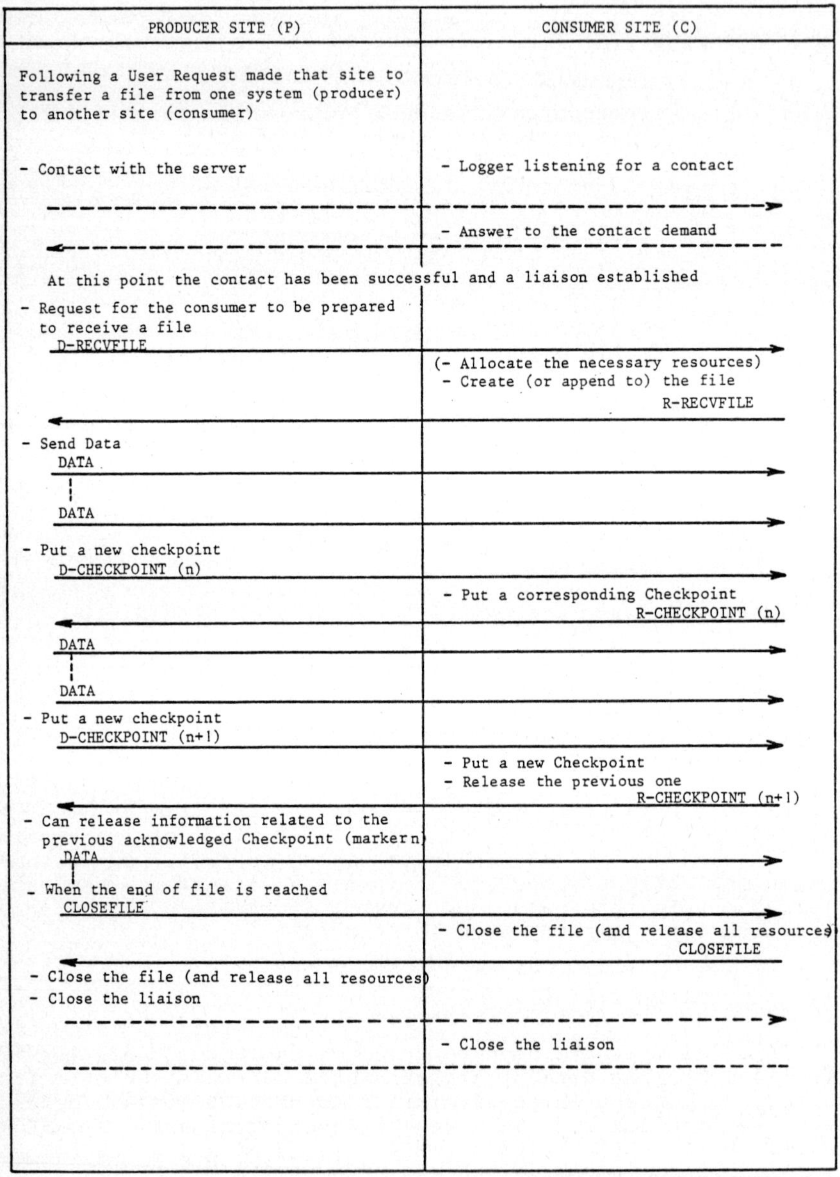

PRODUCER SITE (P)	CONSUMER SITE (C)
Following a User Request made that site to transfer a file from one system (producer) to another site (consumer)	
- Contact with the server	- Logger listening for a contact
	- Answer to the contact demand
At this point the contact has been successful and a liaison established	
- Request for the consumer to be prepared to receive a file D-RECVFILE	
	(- Allocate the necessary resources) - Create (or append to) the file R-RECVFILE

- Send Data
  DATA
  ┊
  DATA	

- Put a new checkpoint D-CHECKPOINT (n)	
	- Put a corresponding Checkpoint R-CHECKPOINT (n)
DATA ┊ DATA	
- Put a new checkpoint D-CHECKPOINT (n+1)	
	- Put a new Checkpoint - Release the previous one R-CHECKPOINT (n+1)

- Can release information related to the previous acknowledged Checkpoint (marker n)
  DATA
  ┊	

- When the end of file is reached CLOSEFILE	
	- Close the file (and release all resources) CLOSEFILE
- Close the file (and release all resources) - Close the liaison	
	- Close the liaison

Figure 3.5.4. (1) - Functional scenario

contained in the blocks exchanged (structured or not into records), is in a form known by the receiving end.

In standard mode, records contain data, structured and represented according to standard conventions as specified in the <file structure> parameter of the R-SENDFILE/D-RECVFILE primitives.

b) Control primitives (CTRL) are used to control the orderly progress of a transaction (i.e. a file transfer), e.g. to be able to recover later on, should a failure occur [SCH75].

They are exchanged in alternate mode (on the data liaison). This exchange cannot occur in the middle of the transmission of a record, and can be activated only after an EOR indication has been transmitted. These primitives are :

D-CHECKPOINT   <Mark>

Sent by the producer after the setting up of a checkpoint, and

R-CHECKPOINT   <Mark>

Sent by the consumer to acknowledge the setting up of a corresponding checkpoint.

Figure 3.5.4.(1) gives an example of a functional scenario.

3.6. Conclusions

This section 3 has presented the various layers of the CYCLADES network. The objectives and the functional capabilities of their protocols have been described and discussed. At this point, it should be apparent that the functional independence maintained between layers allows a great deal of flexibility for future changes, if needed.

On the other hand, this layer independence should not be interpreted as the freedom to design each layer blindly, as if functions performed by other layers were totally irrelevant. Actually, the distribution of functions among the various layers is a fundamental choice bearing on the whole architecture. In the CYCLADES project there were only limited historical constraints imposed on the design. Thus, choices made for each layer attempt to optimize the architecture as a whole, by making each layer simple and general, while useless redundancies are eliminated.

The following sections 4 and 5 present a description of the implementation of the CYCLADES layers.

CHAPTER 4

THE IMPLEMENTATION OF CIGALE

4.1. Introduction

Although the hosts and terminals to be integrated in CYCLADES already existed and were used by local users on each participant centre, the packet switching subnetwok CIGALE was a brand new component to be introduced between centres.

The two major alternatives were to implement this packet switching function either within hosts, or within dedicated machines. The latter choice was made for the following reasons.

Most hosts were large or medium size machines well suited for processing of applications, but not adapted to data transmission (the same consideration leads one to equip these hosts with front-end processors in charge of data transmission).

Heterogeneity of hosts (more than ten different types of systems) would have led us to replicate the software development effort, while usage of a single type of machine for all switching nodes allowed us to develop the switching software only once. The reliability and availability of hosts are clearly insufficient, compared to the requirements of an operational packet switching network. Finally, coordination between the team developing the packet switching and those adapting hosts to network protocols is much eased by the existence of a physical interface between their respective systems. The choice of the mini-computer for CIGALE was straightforward : the major French mini-computer MITRA 15, not being inadequate, was adopted...

4.2. The design and components of the distributed machine

4.2.1. Hardware

CIGALE nodes are CII-MITRA 15 mini-computers with the following configuration : a micro-programmed CPU with a 800 ns cycle time, 16-bit words, 32 interrupt levels, 24 K words of primary memory, a teleprinter, and up to 14 line adapters.

CIGALE nodes are interconnected through dedicated telephone lines provided by PTTs. Line speeds range from 4.8 Kb/s to 48 Kb/s. Hosts are also connected to nodes through telephone lines. For short distance connections, typically in the host-to-node case, 19.2 Kb/s base band modems are used.

4.2.2. CIGALE services

As previously discussed, CIGALE was conceived as a "machine" offering a set of specific services [POU73, POU74d, GRA75c, GRA76a]. These services are grouped into classes, as shown in figure 4.2.2.(1).

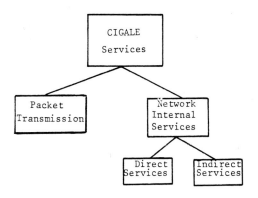

Figure 4.2.2.(1) - CIGALE services classes

a) Packet Transmission

This service is implicit for each packet entering .CIGALE. It consists of carrying packets from source to destination by forwarding them from node to node. This involves the two following functions in each node :

Switching : essentially it computes the function : $L = f(D)$, where D is the destination of the packet and L is the outgoing line over which the packet is to be transmitted in order to reach its destination. This function is computed by lookup in a routing table as shown in figure 4.2.2.(2).

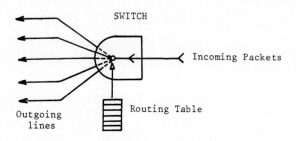

Figure 4.2.2.(2) - Switching function

Data transmission : packets are transmitted between node and
host by using standard manufacturers' procedures. Some of these
procedures were not well suited for packet transmission since
they were designed long ago for multipoint configurations
operated   in half-duplex mode with considerable overhead.
Therefore, a specific procedure called MV8 has been designed
for node-to-node transmission (see section 4.4.1).

b) Network Internal Services

Some   additional   services are also needed to help with
debugging, maintenance and monitoring of the network [GRA76,
GRA76b,   GRA77a].   Network   Internal   Services (NIS) are
implemented within CIGALE and most of them are available in
each node. As opposed to the Packet Transmission, NIS are
provided only on explicit request. Depending on the way of
requesting them, NIS have been broken down into two classes :
Direct Services and Indirect Services.

A request for a DIRECT SERVICE simply consists of sending a
packet to it.   In fact, part of the CIGALE name space is
reserved for addressing direct services.   Direct   service
addresses consist of a "node number" and a "NIS number".

In addressing a direct service, the node number may be set to
zero, standing for "any node". This facility enables the user
to invoke a service without having to know its location. For
instance, as a debugging aid, a host user may want his traffic
to be "echoed" or "dropped" by CIGALE. He can do it without
knowing anything about the network node numbers.

CIGALE's direct services are :

ECHO
Returns the received packet to its SOURCE. An obvious use is

for checking all the components between the SOURCE and the echoing node : if the packet does not come back, then something failed somewhere in the network.

TIME
Returns to the SOURCE a packet containing the synchronized clock of CIGALE (see section 4.4.4).

TTY
As mentioned earlier (see section 4.2.1), each node is equipped with a teleprinter. The TTY service prints out received packets on the teleprinter. On the other hand, it sends packets entered from the teleprinter keyboard. The TTY service may be used for exchanging messages between people located at various nodes. However, its main use is to provide easy access to all network services from any node.

DEBUG
Extracts debugging commands (e.g. DISPLAY, PATCH, SEARCH, DUMP) from received packets, executes them and returns packets containing answers to the source. When coupled with TTY, the DEBUG service is quite powerful since it allows debugging of any node from any node.

TRAFFIC
Sends packets according to certain preset parameters (e.g. length, frequency, destinations) in order to create artificial traffic for measurements, study of pathological cases, and so forth.

STATISTICS
Sends packets containing statistical information about the functioning and use of the network.

DROP
Discards received packets. This service is provided to destroy packets that cannot be forwarded through the network for any reason (e.g. ill formatted packet, unknown or unreachable destination, congestion, too old packet). The DROP service is also used to absorb artificial traffic sent by the TRAFFIC service.

AID
Receives commands from the network control center and transmits them to a neighbour node, which is being reloaded remotely (see section 4.5).

An INDIRECT SERVICE may be requested by turning on the corresponding bit in the "facility" field of the packet header.

CIGALE´s indirect services are :

TRACE
If the TRACE bit is set in a packet header, each node traversed sends back a TRACE packet to the source of the incoming packet.

The TRACE packet contains a copy of the traced packet header (source, destination, identification, length, etc.) and some additional information such as input time, identity of this node and input line number.

PROBE
Each node traversed adds a set of information to the packet text such as time, input line number and node number. The user may also indicate whether he wants to keep the oldest or the latest data in case of packet text overflow.

ROUTE
The packet text contains a list of outgoing line numbers. Each intermediate node extracts a next line number from the list and forwards the packet over this line. The packet is therefore routed according to the predefined itinerary contained in the text. When the end of the list is reached, normal switching mechanisms take over to carry the packet up to its destination.

DIAGNOSTIC
If a packet is discarded by CIGALE, the DIAGNOSTIC bit is checked in the header. If it is set, a DIAGNOSTIC packet is returned to the SOURCE. In addition to the reason for discarding the packet, the DIAGNOSTIC packet text contains the same kind of information as the TRACE packet.

Finally, there is the question of compatibility among NIS requests. For efficiency, it is desirable to be able to request several services with one packet.

Direct services are incompatible with each other since a packet is delivered to a single destination.

Indirect services are all compatible with one another. Furthermore, any combination of indirect services (i.e. of bits in the "facility" field) is allowed in the same packet.

Compatibility between direct and indirect services depends on the packet text utilization. For instance, DEBUG is not compatible with PROBE since both of them use the packet text in different ways. On the other hand, DIAGNOSTIC does not use the packet text and is therefore compatible with any direct service. For the same reason, DIAGNOSTIC and TRACE can be invoked in regular host-host packets.

4.2.3. The CIGALE packet

As seen previously (see section 3.1.1), a CIGALE packet is not only a container of data to be transmitted through the network. It also carries all the control information necessary for CIGALE to route these data towards their destination and provide requested services [POU74c, IFI76]. Furthermore, inside a node, it is also a vehicle for control information passed between the various software modules. These design

principles are reflected in a unique packet format.
 It contains the context necessary for processing the packet at
a given component level. The part of the packet format which is
not used for the next component is just removed when leaving
the previous one (see figure 4.2.3.(1)).

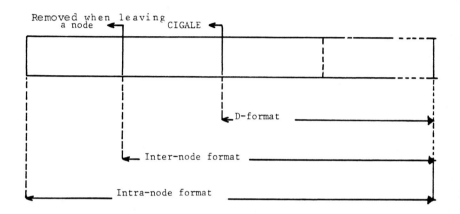

        Figure 4.2.3.(1)- General packet format

Three parts can be distinguished.

Figure 4.2.3.(2) shows the fields within the various packet
header parts. The coding of the facilities and address fields
is given in figure 4.2.3.(3) and figure 4.2.3.(4).

4.3. Node software organization

4.3.1. Software components

The MITRA 15 software comprises the following components : the
supervisor, various tasks attached to specific interrupt
levels, and buffers [GRA75, GRA75a].

The SUPERVISOR contains system and process tables and system
service routines (SSR). The SSR's consist of reentrant sections
of code, called by means of SVC's (supervisor calls) and
executed at the same interrupt level as the calling processes.
They mainly take care of queue management and event handling.

TASKS attached to interrupt levels are   decomposed   into
immediate tasks and permanent tasks.

Start of Intra-node header

bits   cumulative octets

Node arrival time   16   [   ]   2

Input line number   8   [   ]   3

Output line number   8   [   ]   4

Error code   16   [   ]   6

Facility flags   8   [   ]   7

Not used   8   [   ]   8

Start of Inter-node header

CIGALE flags   8   [   ]   1   9

CIGALE exit time limit   8   [   ]   2   10

Start of Datagram header

CIGALE format type   2   [0 0]
D-format type   2   [1 0]
D-header length   4   [0 1 00]   1   3   11
(- 8 octets)
Text length (0 to 255   8   [   ]   2   4   12
octets)
Packet identification   16   [   ]   4   6   14

Facility   16   [   ]   6   8   16

Destination PSN address   4   [0 0 0 1]
length
Destination PSN address   4   7   9   17
Source PSN address length 4   [0 0 0 1]
Source PSN address   4   8   10   18

Local destination address 16 [   ]   10   12   20

Local source address   16   [   ]   12   14   22

End of datagram header

End of Inter-node header

End of Intra-node header

Start of Datagram text

Datagram text   0-2040   [   ]
(0 to 255 octets)

Figure 4.2.3.(2) - Header format

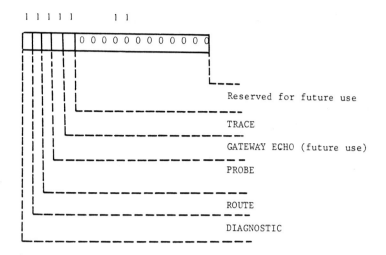

Figure 4.2.3.(3) - Facility field

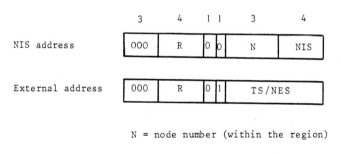

N = node number (within the region)

R = Region number

NIS = Network Internal Service number

TS = Transport Station number

NES = Network External Service number

Figure 4.2.3.(4)- Local address field

IMMEDIATE TASKS (IT) are attached to interrupt levels triggered
by an external device (line adapter, clock), which they handle.
The interrupt level is deactivated by the IT itself at the end
of the task execution. For the line handling, there is one IT
per transmission line. The same reentrant section of code is

executed when the same transmission procedure is executed on behalf of several lines. Other IT´s are attached to different interrupt levels such as clocks, operator keyboard, teleprinter and power on/off.

PERMANENT TASKS (PT) are attached to software triggered interrupt levels. A PT consists of a number of processes. All PT processes are synchronized with software events. The event handling primitives (Post, Wait) take care of the activation and deactivation of the interrupt levels to which the PT´s are attached. There are two PT´s in a CIGALE node, SWITCH and BACKGROUND. SWITCH processes packets coming from lines or NIS and switches them toward their destination, i.e. a line or an NIS. The SWITCH is executed by only one process. BACKGROUND groups all the functions of the NIS. There is generally one process per function. They are : ECHO, TIME, TTY, DEBUG, TRAFFIC, STATISTICS, DROP, AID, ROUTING and Indirect NIS (TRACE, ROUTE and PROBE).

BUFFERS contain packets in transit and the process contexts.

4.3.2. Software functional structure

The functional structure of the node software can be represented by a network of processes as shown in figure 4.3.2.(1).

Processes communicate by means of queues. An event is associated with each queue on which a process can wait. The event status changes when the queue becomes empty or when a packet arrives.

The IT associated with each transmission line is divided into two parts : SEND, for transmitting packets on the line, and RECEIVE for receiving them. SEND extracts packets from its associated queue, transmits them according to the line procedure and releases the packet buffers. RECEIVE gets free buffers, receives packets coming from the line according to the line procedure and attaches them to the SWITCH input queue.

SWITCH extracts one packet from its input queue, extracts from the routing table an output line number for the destination, and attaches the packet to the corresponding output queue. Packets overflowing the output queue are directed to DROP. Packets overflowing the DROP queue are simply returned to the free buffer pool.

The communication interface between SWITCH and the background functions is the same as between SWITCH and the line handling functions : there is one input queue per function and all output packets go to the unique SWITCH queue.

IT´s and PT´s are attached to different interrupt levels, thus introducing different priorities in executing the associated

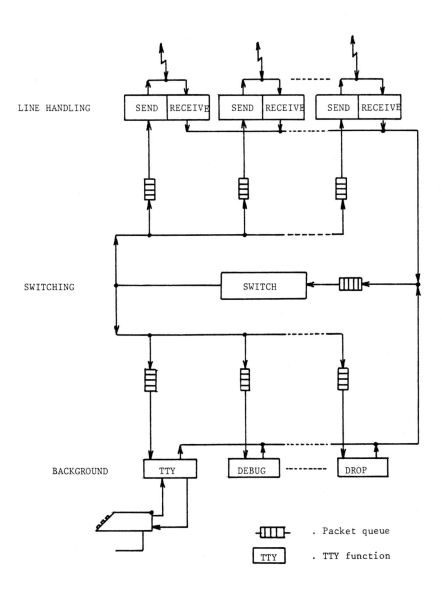

Figure 4.3.2.(1) - Functional node software structure

processes. Task priorities are (in decreasing order) :

    Power off
    Power on
    Clocks
    Line handling
    Operator keyboard
    Teleprinter
    Switching
    Background

4.4. Implementation of CIGALE services

4.4.1. Line handling

To transport packets towards their destination, CIGALE forwards them from node to node over synchronous lines. Since lines introduce delays and errors, some line handling procedures are needed to provide for efficient and reliable transmission [POU74i].

For error detection, a 16-bit cyclic redundancy check (CRC) is a common feature of synchronous procedures. The polynomial used is the ISO standard : $X**16 + X**12 + X**5 + 1$, which is recommended to maintain the error rate below 10E-10.

4.4.1.1. Computer manufacturers' procedures

In order to avoid any special hardware or software for host connections, two standard manufacturers' procedures were made available in CIGALE, TMM-UC and BSC.

TMM-UC is a CII standard procedure [POU73g]. It allows full duplex symmetrical transmission, i.e. physical transmission in both directions at the same time. However, a stop-and-wait scheme is used to control message transmission : a new message can be transmitted over the line only when the previous one has been acknowledged. A time-out is set before transmitting each message. If it expires before receiving the acknowledgment, the message is retransmitted. A sequential message numbering scheme allows us to detect and discard duplicated messages. Since the transmission of a message must wait for the acknowledgement of the previous one, any delay in acknowledgment transmission leads to the waste of a portion of the bandwidth. In particular, short message traffic may be considerably slowed down by long messages transmitted in the reverse direction, because their acknowledgments are delayed by the transmission time of the long messages [GEL77].

BSC (Binary Synchronous Communication) is an IBM line control procedure [DEN73]. The one implemented in CIGALE nodes derives from the BSC of "multileaving" HASP. This procedure is typically half-duplex, and asymmetrical. Blocks of characters are transmitted in data transparent mode. A new block can be transmitted only when the previous one has been acknowledged. When an error occurs, the receiver sends a negative acknowledgment to the transmitter which repeats the last block transmitted. A flow control mechanism allows the receiver to regulate the flow of blocks transmitted by the other end. This line control procedure is much less efficient than full-duplex procedures [POU73g].

4.4.1.2. The node-to-node procedure : MV8

CIGALE´s performance (transit delay and throughput) depends critically on the performance of the node to node line procedure [DAN75a]. From that point of view, full-duplex transmission and anticipation in receiving acknowledgments were considered as minimum requirements. At the time CIGALE was designed, the definition of the HDLC standard procedure was not stabilized and no hardware was available for handling the HDLC frame.

It was therefore decided to design and implement a new line procedure called MV8 (Multi-Voie 8) [PAY75]. MV8 was basically derived from the IMP-IMP procedure used in the ARPANET [BBN72, HEA70]. MV8 is a full-duplex procedure in which each direction of the line is divided into eight "virtual" channels. A channel used for transmitting a packet is blocked until an acknowledgment is returned indicating that the next node has successfully received the packet. Acknowledgments are carried "piggy-back" by traffic sent in the opposite direction (see figure 4.4.1.(1)). A copy of each transmitted packet is held at the sending node until an acknowledgement has been received. After a predefined time-out period, unacknowledged packets are retransmitted.

The acknowledgment mechanism works as follows. When a packet is sent on a channel it is assigned an "alternate" bit. This bit is the opposite of the alternate bit assigned to the previous packet that used the same channel. A retransmitted packet takes the same channel and alternate bit as the original one. When the packet is received by the other node this alternate bit is recorded in the n-th bit of an acknowledgment octet where n is the number of the channel used by the packet. This acknowledgment octet is piggy-backed to the sending node with the next packet transmitted in the opposite direction.

When the sending node receives the acknowledgment octet, it "exclusive-or"s this octet with an octet holding the alternate bits most recently assigned on each channel of the line. The result is an octet in which every zero entry corresponds to an acknowledgment (possibly redundant). Channels are scanned, copies of newly acknowledged packets are discarded and corresponding channels unblocked. If the alternate bit of a received packet is the same as in the previous packet received

on the same channel, then the received packet is a duplicate :
it is discarded and acknowledged.

Acknowledgment Frames (AF) are sent when no regular packets are
available for immediate transmission, or when all channels are
temporarily blocked.

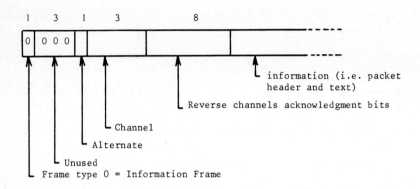

Figure 4.4.1.(1) - MV8 Information Frame format

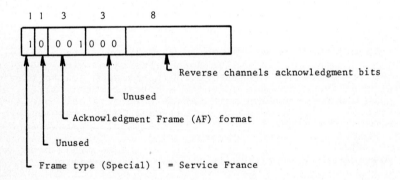

Figure 4.4.1.(2) - MV8 Acknowledgment Frame format

An AF contains only acknowledgments (see figure 4.4.1.(2)) and
does not use a channel number. The intent of these service
frames is to improve the responsiveness of the acknowledgment
mechanism in cases of unbalanced traffic (substantially more
packets in one direction than in the other) or when, for some
reason, all channels are busy for an extended period of time.

In order to give priority to very short packets, three classes
of traffic were defined according to packet text length :

    Short   0 - 10 octets
    Medium   11 - 127 octets
    Long   128 - 255 octets

Packets of each class form separate output queues.

Each class is allocated a certain number of channels (see
figure 4.4.1.(3)). Short packets may be sent on every channel
(0-7). Medium packets may be sent only on channels 1, 3, 5, 7,
and long packets only on channels 2, 4 and 6. Short packets are
always transmitted first.

Various MV8 simulation studies [IRL76a, DAN75, FAB76] validated
its basic principles and some results suggested the inclusion
of a few additional features to improve performance.

4.4.1.3. Line monitoring

In order to detect transmission troubles as fast as possible,
each CIGALE node monitors telephone lines. It maintains a "line
status" (UP or DOWN) reported periodically to the Network
Control Center (see section 4.5). The UP status corresponds to
normal line behaviour. The DOWN status means that the line is
unusable for traffic because of some permanent failure : other
end's equipment, hardware adapter, modem, telephone line and so
forth. A line is declared DOWN after several consecutive
unsucessful transmissions of the same message.

A line comes UP again when several consecutive messages are
transmitted successfully. In the absence of data traffic,
service messages are transmitted over an UP line in order to
detect and report promptly any failure.

With MV8, line monitoring and status handling are performed at
procedure level. A "CALL frame" (CF) and a "RESPONSE frame"
(RF) are used for that purpose. Each end of the line
periodically sends a CF to be answered with an RF. Each end
handles the line status by monitoring the ratio of answered CF
over a predefined period of time. In addition, both CF and RF
contain the sending node's address (see figure 4.4.1.(4)), in
order to easily detect accidental conditions of looped back
lines.

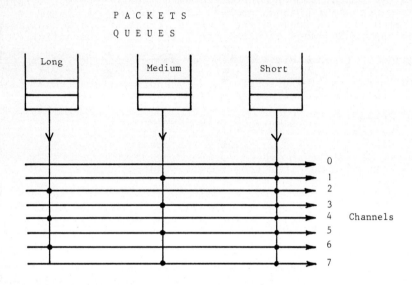

Figure 4.4.1.(3) - MV8   channel assignement

The looping of lines is a convenient method for testing link
components :   line, modem, adapter, procedure. On the other
hand, the loop detection mechanism automatically excludes the
lines that are accidentally looped back from use in the
network.

Computer manufacturer´s procedures do not usually provide such
facilities. Additional traffic must be generated at the packet
level, independently of the line procedure, in order to
maintain a minimum level of line monitoring. Consequently, for
TMM-UC and BSC, both ends transmit periodically a "Bubble". A
Bubble is defined as a packet in which the destination network
address (PSN) is zero (see figure 4.2.3.(2)).

4.4.2. The SWITCH Module

4.4.2.1. Main function

As previously shown in section 4.3, the SWITCH Module (SM)
occupies a central position in the node functional
organisation : all packets entering the node or generated

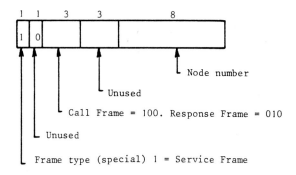

Figure 4.4.1.(4) - MV8 Call/Response Frame format

locally by NIS are processed by SM.

The basic function of SM is to forward packets to the appropriate output queue, according to their destination. A packet may be switched to either a line queue or an NIS queue.

4.4.2.2. Packet validity check

SM is a CIGALE process which is automatically activated when its queue contains some packets (see section 4.3). After extracting a packet from its queue, SM checks the packet format for validity. In case of error, SM sets an appropriate error code in the intra-node header (see figure 4.2.3.(2)) and switches it to the DROP queue (see section 4.4.7).

4.4.2.3. Processing of indirect services

When a packet contains requests for indirect services in its facility field, it is necessary to check that they are completed. To that effect, the intra-node header contains facility flags set by the Indirect NIS after processing the requests. Before any other processing, requests for indirect services are checked by looking at the facility field of the packet header. If any request still remains unprocessed, as indicated by facility flags, the packet is switched to the Indirect NIS queue (see section 4.4.7).

4.4.2.4. Forced switching

Once all requested indirect services are processed, the output line number field of the intra-node header is checked. If a

line number is specified the packet is switched to the
indicated line queue regardless of its destination. In the
regular switching case no line number is specified. This is
indicated by a specific value for the line number. The forced
switching facility is used by the ROUTE indirect service (see
section 4.4.7) and by the node to node propagation mechanism
(see section 4.4.3).

4.4.2.5. Regular switching

If no output line number is specified, the regular switching
mechanism takes place and the output line number is determined
by the routing tables.

Due to the hierarchical organization of the CIGALE name space,
each node holds five routing tables allowing us to forward
packets towards the following types of entities :

- networks
- general addresses
- regions
- external addresses (i.e. Transport Station (TS) or Network
  External Service (NES))
- nodes

In addition, each node is initialized with the CIGALE network
number, its own region number, its own node number and the list
of general addresses.

The switching process consists of analyzing the destination
addresses in the packet header, in order to extract the output
line number from the appropriate routing table entry. The
packet is then attached to the corresponding output queue. The
following paragraphs describe how the destination address is
analyzed according to its hierarchical structure (see figure
4.4.2.(1)).

a) First, if the destination network number (PSN field in
figure 4.2.3.(2)) is different from the CIGALE network number,
it is used as an index to the NETWORK routing table to get the
output line number.

b) If the destination network number is CIGALE, the local
destination is matched against the general address list. The
matching entry index, if any, is used as an index to the
GENERAL ADDRESS routing table to get the output line number.

c) If it is not a general address, the region number is then
isolated from the local address. If it is different from the
node region number, it is used as an index to the REGION
routing table to get the output line number.

d) If the packet is already in the destination region and if it
is an external address (see figure 4.2.3.(4)) the TS or NES is

used as an index to the EXTERNAL address routing table to get
the output line number.

e) If it is an NIS address and if the switching node is not the
destination node, the destination node number is used as an
index to the NODE routing table to get the output line number.

f) Finally, if the packet has reached its destination node,
then the destination NIS number is used to select   the
corresponding NIS queue.

4.4.2.6. Implicit switching

An exception is made in the above scheme when both the region
number and the node number are zero in an NIS destination. This
is a particular convention to specify that the required NIS may
be provided in any node of the network : practically, in the
first node traversed. In this case, after checking that it is
not a general address, the first node traversed directly uses
the destination NIS number to select the corresponding NIS
queue.

4.4.2.7. Queue overflow

When a packet is switched to any output queue, it may happen
that the queue is full. After setting an appropriate error code
in the intra-node header, the packet is attached to the DROP
queue. If the DROP queue is also full, the packet is
eventually discarded.

4.4.3. Adaptive routing

4.4.3.1. Introduction

Meshed networks are intended to provide path redundancy. The
routing function consists in defining the best path between
each source-destination pair in the network. Paths are recorded
by the nodes in "routing tables" which contain the "best"
output line number for each destination.

In the first CIGALE version, routing was fixed and routing
tables were built up manually by an operator. It was quite
difficult to prevent mistakes in entering tables, thus causing
incorrect or inefficient routing.

It turned out very quickly that routing tables needed to be
computed automatically in order to provide for fast and
reliable routing adaptation to topology changes (e.g. line
and/or node failures, new host connections, etc.).

A possible approach is to compute routing tables at a single
place in the network called : the Network Routing Center (NRC),

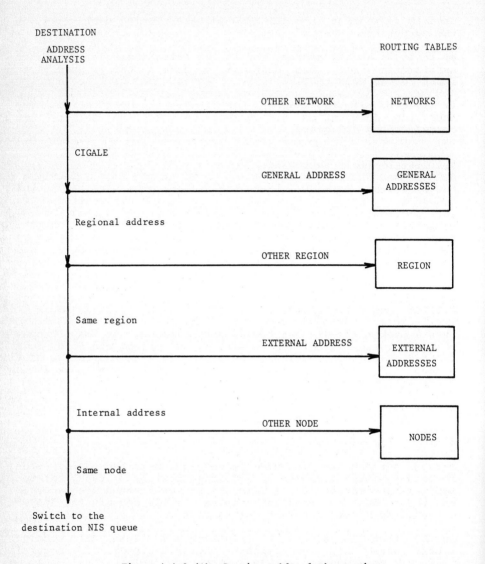

Figure 4.4.2.(1) - Routing table. look-up scheme

possibly located at the Network Control Center. In this type of centralized scheme each node reports information about its own state and observed traffic conditions to the NRC. Knowing the topology of the network, the NRC is able to integrate received information and compute new routing tables, which are sent back

to the nodes. An obvious drawback of such a centralized
solution is its vulnerability : unfortunate combinations of
failures may isolate a part of the network from the NRC.
Moreover, a failure of the NRC itself may have catastrophic
consequences.

Another problem with centralized routing is accuracy of routing
adaptation. Theoretically, sophisticated algorithms may compute
nearly optimum paths, provided that the NRC knows the
instantaneous state of the whole network. In practice, they do
not make much sense since reports received from the nodes are
more or less obsolete and inconsistent due to possibly
inaccurate node clock synchronization and variable transit
delays. Accuracy is also affected by transit delays experienced
by new routing tables travelling from the NRC to the nodes.

The inconvenience of centralized techniques suggested the
design of a distributed routing algorithm for CIGALE [GRA74].
There is no NRC in CIGALE and nodes cooperate with their
neighbours to compute their routing tables. However, nodes are
also given enough autonomy to keep performing the routing
function in spite of neighbour or line failures. The
feasibility of such distributed algorithms was demonstrated by
the ARPANET experience [MCQ74]. The distributed scheme for
CIGALE has been simulated [IRL76, COC75] and implemented.
Further details are given in the following sections.

4.4.3.2. Design principles

The purpose of a routing algorithm is to compute and
dynamically set up the "best" path between each
source-destination pair. Indeed, some path evaluation
mechanism is needed to make it possible to compare paths and
select the "best" one.

In fact, paths may be evaluated according to various criteria
corresponding to different service requirements, e.g. minimum
delay, maximum throughput, lowest cost, highest security, etc.
Since these requirements are sometimes incompatible or even
contradictory, a sensible approach would be to establish
several (perhaps distinct) paths, one path being specifically
optimized for each requirement. Traffic entering the network
should then specify a Traffic Class corresponding to the
required service characteristics, thus allowing one to forward
it through the appropriate "best" path.

Actually, these routing techniques are still a research area.
Problems related to path stability, path interferences, traffic
load splitting, relationships with congestion control, and so
forth, are not yet fully understood.

For safety reasons, it was therefore decided to implement in
CIGALE a simplified and practical scheme : only one best path
is established for each source-destination pair. Paths are not

bifurcated and are optimized for minimum delay in an empty
network.   In CIGALE, this turned out so far to be satisfactory
in practice.

In order to further describe the "best" path computation
technique, the following terms need to be introduced :

A HOP is defined as being a node and a line connected to that
node. A hop is directed, i.e. traffic goes from the node to the
line. In particular, two adjacent nodes constitute two hops
(see figure 4.4.3.(1)).

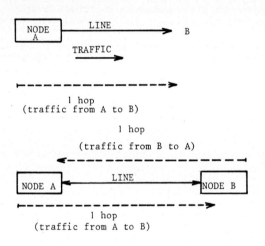

Figure 4.4.3.(1) - Hop definition

A PATH is defined as a chain of connected hops, the last hop
being connected to a destination (see figure 4.4.3.(2)).

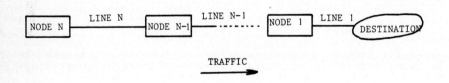

Figure 4.4.3.(2) - N-hop path.

A HOP GRADE is defined as a numeric evaluation of a hop. If there are several Traffic Classes, several hop grades may be computed for the same hop according to different evaluation criteria.

A PATH GRADE is defined as a numeric evaluation of a path. A path grade is computed by combining the hop grades of each hop of the path. Depending on Traffic Classes, several path grades may be obtained for the same path by combining appropriate hop grades.

A BEST PATH is defined as the path which has the minimum path grade among the existing paths for a given source-destination pair. Again, several best paths may be obtained for the same source-destination pair, depending on Traffic Classes.

A BEST GRADE is defined as the path grade of a best path.

A BEST OUTPUT LINE is defined as a line of a hop which belongs to a best path.

For clarity, a single Traffic Class is considered in the following. Interested readers can easily generalize the mechanisms presented to several Traffic Classes.

The basic principle of distributed routing computation is propagation of path grade information from node to node. Figure 4.4.3.(3) illustrates this mechanism.

In practice, path grades are computed as follows : according to predefined rules (see below) each node of the network sends to its neighbours the best grade from itself to each destination.

In the following, $G(x)$ will refer to the grade value of x, x being a hop or a path. Let us consider a destination (D) and a node (N). Let us assume that each neighbour (Mi) of N knows the grade $(G(Pi))$ of the best path (Pi) from itself (Mi) to D (see figure 4.4.3.(3)).

Each Mi sends $G(Pi)$ to (N). (N) is therefore able to combine each received $G(Pi)$ with the corresponding $G(Hi)$. Then (N) obtains the grade of each path (Qi), formed by connecting (Hi) to (Pi) and going from itself to (D) :

$$G(Qi) = G(Hi)*G(Pi)$$

where * represents the operation which combines grades.

Clearly the best path from (N) to (D) is (Qj) with j such that :

$$G(Qj) = MIN (G(Q1), G(Q2), ..., G(Qn))$$

Therefore (N) computes and keeps track of $G(Qj)$ and j :

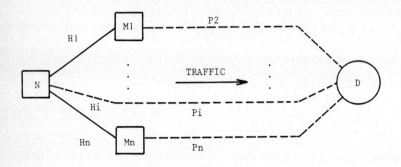

```
N  =  a node
D  =  a destination
Mi=  a neighbour of N
Hi=  hop from N to Mi
Pi=  best path from Mi to D
```

The best path from N to D is (Hi, Pi) with i such that

$$G(Hi) * G(Pi) = MIN\left[(G(H1) * G(P1)), (G(H2)*G(P2)),\ldots, (G(Hn)*G(Pn))\right]$$

- G(E) refers to grade value of the entity E.
- Symbol * represents the operation which allows us to combine
  grades related to the Traffic considered.

Figure 4.4.3.(3) - Path grade propagation

- G(Qj) is its best grade to (D) and is sent to its neighbours.

- j determines its best output line to (D), i.e. the line of
hop (Hj) over which packets destined to (D) are to be
forwarded.

Practically neighbours of (N) are not synchronized for sending
their G(Pi). To compute G(Qj) at once, (N) would need to keep
in memory each received G(Pi). Because this propagation scheme
applies indeed to all destinations, the required memory space
could turn out to be prohibitive for large networks : the
number of grades to be kept in a node would be the total number
of destinations times the total number of lines connected to
that node. If there are several Traffic Classes, this number

must be multiplied be the number of classes.

Since only G(Qj) and j are actually used by a node to propagate
grade information and forward traffic, it is sensible to keep
only these values and update them when a G(Pi) is received.
This is described by the following algorithm :

                         SYMBOLS USED
GQJ = current best grade to (D)
  J = corresponding hop, best output line and neighbour number
GPI = received path grade
  I = corresponding hop, line and neighbour number
  G = function allowing to compute a hop grade
  * = operation allowing to combine hop grade and received path
      grade
CHALLENGER = path grade to (D), candidate to become the best
grade.

                         Algorithm
begin
CHALLENGER := G(I)*GPI ;
if I = J
then comment
     update of the grade for the same best path ;
     GQJ := CHALLENGER
else comment
     check if CHALLENGER is better ;
     if CHALLENGER < GQJ
     then comment
          update the best path ;
          begin
          GQJ := CHALLENGER ;
          J := I
          end
end

By using the above algorithm, it is only necessary to maintain
within each node : a) the best path grade for each destination,
b) the best output line number for each destination.

4.4.3.3. Initialization

Since the best grade computation in a node is based upon the
best grade received from its neighbours, this propagation
scheme must be initialized. When a node starts operating, best
grades and best output line numbers are initialized with an
infinite value, i.e. a special value meaning that no path is
known. As part of its initialization the node knows the
destinations that are directly connected to it. For each of
them, it computes the hop grade related to the connecting line.
This hop grade and the connecting line number are then used as
best grade and best output line to the corresponding
destination, thus initializing the path grade propagation

mechanism.

4.4.3.4. Implementation principles

Node modules that perform the routing algorithm need to
exchange path grades. A convenient way is to assign a network
address to these modules and to send path grades in regular
packets. This allows one to implement the routing scheme at a
very low additional cost since the addressing and transmission
mechanisms needed to forward routing packets already exist.

Adaptive routing in CIGALE is therefore simply implemented in a
node as a regular addressable NIS called ROUTING. ROUTING NISs
of neighbour nodes exchange "Routing Packets", which contain
their best grade to each destination.

However, in order to facilitate topology changes, CIGALE nodes
are kept in ignorance of the addresses of their neighbours.
Therefore, a node cannot use the regular switching mechanism to
send routing packets. Again two facilities already existing in
CIGALE (see section 4.4.2) are used to solve this problem :

a) Forced switching. The number of the line over which a
routing packet is to be sent is put by the ROUTING NIS into the
output line number field of the routing packet header. This
forces the routing packet to be switched to the specified line,
regardless of its final destination.

b) Implicit switching. Since the neighbour address, i.e.
region and node numbers, cannot be specified in the routing
packet, both numbers are set to zero by the sending ROUTING
NIS. This allows it to reach the neighbour ROUTING NIS without
having to know its address.

4.4.3.5. Path grade evaluation

As already mentioned it was decided to implement in CIGALE a
simplified but safe routing scheme. Thus, best paths are
selected according to a simple criterion : lowest delay in an
empty network. Therefore :

a) A hop grade value is in reverse proportion to the bandwidth
of the related line if it is UP, (see section 4.4.1.4). If the
line is DOWN, the hop grade is set to infinite, a special value
meaning that no path can go through this hop.

b) The operation used to combine hop grades and best grades
received from neighbours is addition.

4.4.3.6. Routing loop control

In case of line or node failure and particularly if it causes a
destination to become unreachable, routing loops may appear in
the network. A simple example of loop formation is described in
figure 4.4.3.(4). Smart readers might be able to construct
smarter examples.

A mechanism has been proposed to prevent loop formation in the
particular case of length-two loop (i.e. between two adjacent
nodes). However, simulation [IRL76] showed surprisingly that
there are cases where it caused a significant improvement and
cases in which there was a significant deterioration.

A more general mechanism is implemented in CIGALE in order to
detect and destroy routing loops of any length : in addition
to the path grade, each node computes and propagates a path
length for each destination. Since nodes involved in a loop
keep exchanging routing packets, the looped path length
increases continuously. In fact, the length of the longest
possible path without loop may be calculated from the network
topology, the number of nodes being an upper limit.

Thus routing loops may be detected and destroyed by setting the
grade to infinite when the path length reaches this maximum
value.

4.4.3.7. Processing of received routing packets

Routing packets contain the grade and length of the best path
to each destination : i.e. networks, general addresses,
regions, nodes and external addresses (see figure 4.4.3.(5)).

When a node receives a routing packet from a neighbouring node
belonging to a different region, only path grades and lengths
to networks, general addresses and regions are processed.
Indeed, information about nodes and TS´s of one region is not
relevant for a node of another region.

4.4.3.8. Strategies for sending routing packets

In the first adaptive routing implementation, routing packets
were sent periodically. A dilemma is that the sending frequency
should be low in order to save line bandwidth and high to allow
the network to adapt rapidly to changes.

The chosen compromise was to make the sending frequency
proportional to the line speed so that routing packets take no
more than 5% of the line bandwidth. Taking into account line
control procedure efficiency [POU73g], this led us to send a
routing packet every 0.6 second over a 48 Kb/s line.

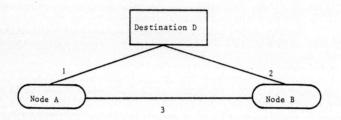

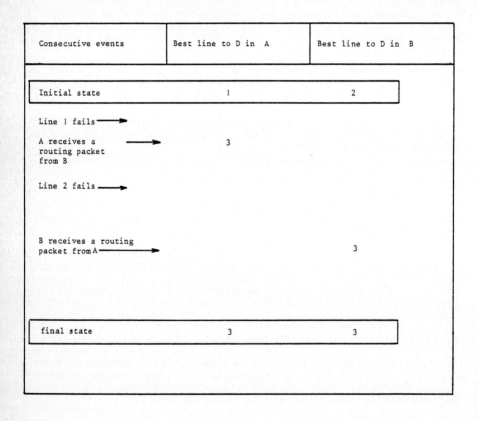

Consecutive events	Best line to D in A	Best line to D in B
Initial state	1	2
Line 1 fails →		
A receives a routing packet from B →	3	
Line 2 fails →		
B receives a routing packet from A →		3
final state	3	3

Figure 4.4.3.(4) - Routing loop formation

Another scheme was proposed and simulated.   Instead   of   being
sent   at   regular   time   intervals, routing packets are sent as
soon as a change occurs in routing tables. In addition, routing
packets are sent   at   a   very   low   frequency   (e.g.   every   20
seconds)   as   a protection against a possible loss of a routing
packet.

However, it was observed from simulation [IRL76]   that   a   node
occasionally accumulates several routing packets in its queues.
An   avalanche   can even occur when arriving routing packets all
cause changes in routing tables (e.g. an initialization).   When
this happens,   the   propagation   of   regular   traffic   and   new
routing   packets   is   slowed down by the old ones. The old ones
carry obsolete information since   more   timely   information   is
contained   in   the   newer   routing   packets. This can therefore
cause temporary wrong update of routing   tables,   when   routing
packets   are   sent   over a transmission line operated with MV8,
which   does   not   necessarily   preserve   order   in   packet
transmission.   In   order   to   avoid these problems, a "Slotting
Period" (SP) was introduced to guarantee   a   minimum   time   lag
between   two consecutive routing packet generations.   The whole
scheme is designed   so   that   the   network   adapts   quickly   to
topology   changes   while   avoiding   a useless loss of bandwidth
when there is no change.   Simulation pointed out a   significant
performance   improvement   [IRL76].   Therefore,   this scheme has
been implemented in CIGALE.

4.4.3.9. Protection

It is clear that routing is a vital   function   in   CIGALE.   The
propagation   of   wrong   routing   information   could   have
catastrophic consequences. The adaptive   routing   mechanism   is
therefore protected against various possible threats :

a) Routing packets received from lines connected to hosts or to
other networks are just destroyed.

b) A   checksun   is   sent along with routing packets.   Corrupted
packets are destroyed.

c) A checksum is also associated with vital data   used   by   the
node   for initializing the routing propagation algorithm :   its
own node number, its   own   region   number,   external   addresses
direcly   connected to it, etc. It is checked before each access
to any of these data. If an error is detected the only sensible
choice for the node is suicide.

4.4.4. Synchronized network time management

4.4.4.1. The purpose of Network Time

In order to   correlate   time   measurements   made   at   different
network   sites,   e.g.   for   statistics   or   accurate   host

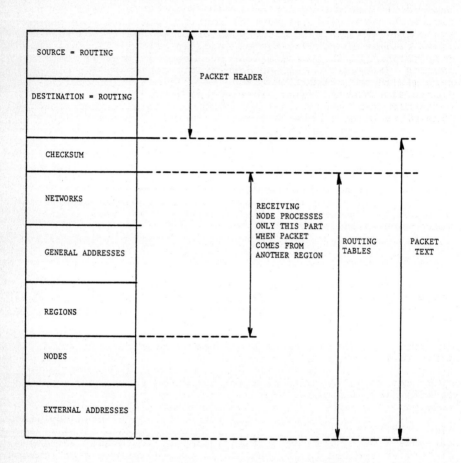

Figure 4.4.3.(5) - Routing packet structure

synchronization, a synchronized network time (SNT) must be
provided. SNT is also used by the maximum transit delay control
mechanism (see section 4.4.5).

4.4.4.2. Principle

Each node manages its own time using its internal hardware
clock. However, this local time has to be synchronized
periodically (e.g. every minute) to compensate for hardware
clock drift. In order to maintain an SNT, CIGALE uses a
propagation scheme based on the same principles as the adaptive
routing (see section 4.4.3) : each node sends is own SNT to
each of its neighbours. Each neighbour updates its own SNT only
if the received SNT is greater than its own in order to
guarantee uniqueness of SNT values. This results in network
time being driven by the fastest clock of all nodes.

4.4.4.3. Implementation

SNT management is a CIGALE supervision service and is
implemented in a NIS called TIMAN (Time Management). As in the
case of adaptive routing, neighbouring nodes exchange their SNT
by means of regular packets addressed to TIMAN. They are called
"time packets". In practice, time packets may experience a
variable (and generally non negligible) delay to travel between
TIMAN´s of two neighbour nodes : software processing time and
queueing transmission delay.

If the time packet were stamped with SNT by the sending TIMAN,
any correlation with the receiving TIMAN SNT would be erratic
due to variable transit delays. In order to solve this problem
the following scheme was implemented in CIGALE :

In order to eliminate both queue and processing delays, the
time packet is explicitly recognized by the line handling
software. Then the sender SNT is placed into the time packet
just before transmitting it over the line. On the other end,
the receiver SNT is recorded in the time packet just after
receiving the last bit (see figure 4.4.4.(1)).

The difference between the two SNT´s recorded in the time
packet reflects the line service time for the time packet and
the difference of the SNT´s of the two nodes. Since the
receiving TIMAN NIS knows the time packet length, it can derive
the transmission delay from the line speed. This yields the
actual time lag between SNT´s in the two nodes. If this
indicates that the neighbouring node´s SNT is in advance, then
the local SNT is advanced.

Problems related to TIMAN addressing in the neighbour node are
the same as in adaptive routing. Identical solutions apply for
SNT management (see section 4.4.3)

4.4.4.4. Initialization

When a node is loaded, its SNT has obviously an unpredictable and meaningless value, which should therefore not be propagated to its neighbours.

The intialization scheme is as follows : the newly loaded node does not send any time packets to its neighbours until it has received a time packet from one of them. The first received time packet is used to initialize the SNT.

Finally, when the whole network must be restarted, setting the SNT in any one node is sufficient to boot-strap the propagation mechanism. Typically this is done manually from the control center.

4.4.4.5. Security and protection

Since SNT is driven by the fastest clock, it could go malfunction in the case of clock failure. As a protection, if the SNT lag is too large (more than a few seconds) the receiving node does not update its own SNT.

In addition, time packets received from hosts or from other networks are destroyed.

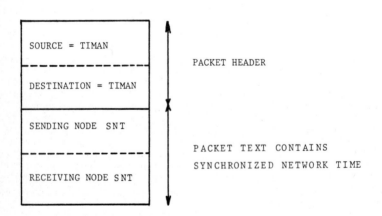

Figure 4.4.4.(1)   - Time packet structure

4.4.5. Maximum transit delay

In order to simplify the design of reliable end-to-end control at the transport protocol level, the packet transit delay should have an upper limit, too old packets being worse than lost packets. The rationale for this is detailed in [TOM74]. The CIGALE network provides for transit delay control and does not deliver too old packets, the maximum transit delay being kept to less than a few seconds (e.g. 5 seconds).

Each packet entering the network is time-stamped (see exit time limit field in the packet header in figure 4.2.3.(2)). This time stamp indicates the latest time by which the packet must leave CIGALE. It is obtained by adding the maximum transit delay to the current value of the Synchronized Network Time (SNT). Before transmitting a packet, each node traversed matches packet exit time limit against the SNT. If the time is exceeded, the packet is dropped.

A few precautions are taken in the design of such a mechanism.

First, transit delay control is by-passed for packets requesting FORCED ROUTING service (see section 4.4.7) : a forced route may be arbitrarily long (e.g. for testing purpose).

Secondly, Remote Load, Remote Dump and Debug packets are normally submitted to the same rule of maximum transit delay. However there may be some unusual conditions in which an exception is necessary. Such a condition is shown in figure 4.4.4.(2) : remote load and dump traffic need to travel through the network area A where the SNT has not been initialized. It is to be noted that in this case the SNT must not be initialized in area A since, by reloading the dead node, the SNT will be automatically initialized and propagated from area B to area A.

4.4.6. Traffic control

CIGALE is a resource sharing system : node CPU, node packet buffer capacity and line bandwidth are shared among users of the network. In order to reach its destination, each packet needs to be stored in intermediate nodes (buffers), switched from node to node (CPU) according to its destination and routing table contents, and transmitted (CPU and bandwidth) over intermediate lines.

In resource sharing systems, performance generally tends to collapse when the offered load reaches a critical threshold : the throughput of the system tends to fall down drastically while waiting time tends to increase accordingly. This phenomenon is known in data processing systems such as time sharing systems, as well as in other types of networks such as road, electricity, or telephone networks. In packet switching

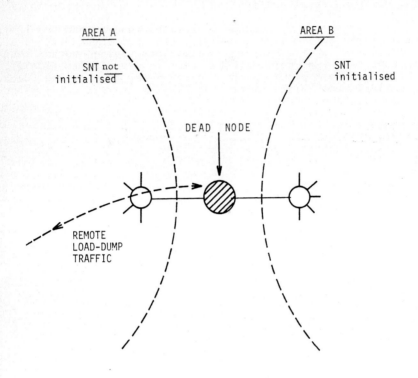

Figure 4.4.4.(2) –

The remote load/dump traffic exception

networks it is called "congestion" (see figure 4.4.6.(1)).

Simulation studies [IRL75a, IRL75b, IRL75c] clearly showed that CIGALE was potentially subject to such congestion and that preventive control mechanisms were needed.

Traffic control in CIGALE was designed as a set of mechanisms intended mainly to control incoming traffic, in order to prevent congestion, thus keeping network performance at an acceptable level. A discussion about the CIGALE approach to traffic control appears in section 3.1.7.4. The mechanisms implemented are described in the following sections.

4.4.6.1. Maximum transit delay

This mechanism has already been described in section 3.1.4, while section 4.4.5 gives more details about its

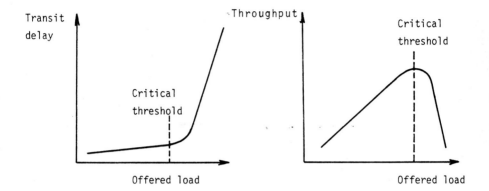

Figure 4.4.6.(1) -

Congestion phenomenom in packet switching networks

implementation. Although it is primarily intended to provide end-to-end protocols with a guarantee against the delivery of aging packets, dropping these packets also helps in preventing congestion since deadlocks or excessive use of network resources by any one packet are automatically eliminated.

4.4.6.2. Maximum queue length

This consists in limiting the length of each output queue in a node to a maximum value. Whenever a packet is destined to a full queue, it is dropped. The purpose of this mechanism is to prevent a single queue from monopolizing all available buffers. It is clear from figure 4.4.6.(2) that, if queue lengths are uncontrolled :

a) the total throughput of the node may be reduced to the throughput of a single line,

b) the transit delay through that node may become excessive due to increased waiting time in the queue, and

c) traffic destined to other output queues may not be forwarded since all buffers are allocated to the same queue.

Considerable work (using both simulation and analytical models) [IRL75, IRL75d, KAM80] has been conducted in order to investigate various questions related to maximum queue length policy. Irland showed by analysis and simulation [IRL77] that the collapse of throughput under excessive offered load in a

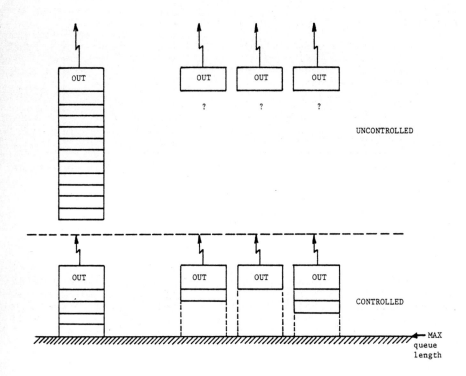

Figure 4.4.6.(2)   - Queue length control

node (see figure 4.4.6.(1)) is indeed due to unrestricted buffer sharing, and he found both optimal and approximate rules for restricted buffer sharing to prevent this. Detailed results are given in section 7.3.

The options taken in CIGALE implementation are in line with these results : the maximum length is set to the same value for all queues in a node. This value is a function of both the total number of buffers available in the node and the number of output lines. A typical figure for the maximum queue length in a CIGALE node is 6 buffers.

4.4.6.3. Buffer sharing policy

If the optimum value for maximum queue length is chosen to minimize packet drops, it usually happens that the sum of the maximum values of all queues in a node exceeds the total number of available buffers in that node. This means that the node may run out of buffers while queues are not necessarily full. In this case, the node drops incoming packets until new buffers are released. However, these packets are acknowledged as if they had been accepted normally.

This mechanism is primarily intended to prevent deadlock occurrence and widespread congestion. Indeed, if a congested node A does not acknowledge packets sent by a neighbour B, the latter may become also congested, and will in turn reject packets sent from A. Neither A nor B could relieve this situation.

4.4.6.4. Discussion

These mechanisms illustrate design choices meant to satisfy the service policy defined for CIGALE, viz. maximize throughput while meeting constraints of limited transit delay, and limited packet loss rate.

Packet loss is considered as an acceptable implication of traffic control, to the extent that the loss rate remains below a certain threshold, say 10E-4 to 10E-6, under any load condition. Indeed, dropped packets are retransmitted, as a normal function of an end-to-end transport protocol. It is only necessary that the overhead incurred in packet retransmission remain negligible.

On the other hand, pathological conditions leading to substantial service degradation, such as deadlocks or persistent congestion, are not considered as acceptable, even if their probability of occurrence is negligible. Therefore, mechanisms preventing deadlocks and persistent congestion had to be installed.

Since all additional machinery has a price, in throughput, overhead and/or potential failure, every possible effort was made to design simple, robust and easily understandable mechanisms, so that they could be developed, tested, and operated independently at minimum cost.

4.4.6.5. Channel load limiter

The mechanisms described in the previous sections are basically intended to protect the network itself against troubles caused by congestion. These mechanisms are quite effective for this purpose but they are not satisfactory in terms of quality of service, since the rate of dropped packets grows beyond an acceptable figure when the offered load exceeds maximum throughput, (see figure 4.4.6.(3)).

Additional mechanisms are needed to keep the offered load under the threshold where packets start to be dropped. A major difficulty in designing such a mechanism is to find a parameter or a set of parameters through which potential congestion can be predicted and control mechanisms be triggered, before congestion actually occurs.

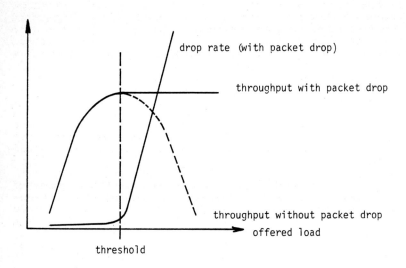

Figure 4.4.6.(3)   - Congestion traded for packet drop

Simulation studies of CIGALE were carried out in order to discover such sensitive factors upon which effective and simple traffic control mechanisms could be based. Results from these simulations [IRL75b, IRL75c, IRL75d] suggested that individual line loads could be adequate to predict network congestion. On this basis, a traffic control mechanism, called the "Channel Load Limiter" (CLL) [POU75b, POU76, POU76d], was designed (see section 3.1.7.4) and implemented in CIGALE, as described in the following.

The Channel Load Limiter mechanism comprises the following four functions : (1) the Network load state estimation by which potential congestion is predicted, (2) the Host information by which hosts are requested to reduce the load they offer to the network, (3) the Host reaction, which indicates how hosts

should react to host information received from the network, and
(4) protection against improper host reaction by which the
network takes proper actions to prevent congestion, even if
hosts do not react as they should. These functions are
described further in the following sections.

a) Network Load State Estimation

For each individual node, the network load is viewed as the set
of loads of each path from itself to each destination. The
corresponding path load states are evaluated by a distributed
computation in which all nodes participate just as they do for
distributed route computation (see section 4.4.3).

The basis for this distributed evaluation is the estimate by
each node of the load state of each outgoing channel (one
direction of transmission over a line), which will then be
integrated along each path. The channel load state is computed
as a discrete variable derived from the smoothing of the
instantaneous channel load.

CHANNEL LOAD MEASUREMENT by sampling and smoothing is described
in the next following section. Then follows the CHANNEL LOAD
STATE COMPUTATION and the distributed PATH LOAD STATE
EVALUATION. A specific problem due to hierarchical addressing
is then discussed and the last section deals with the question
of initialization of the whole mechanism.

CHANNEL LOAD MEASUREMENT

A transmission line is considered as being made of two
channels, each corresponding to one of the two possible
directions of transmission on the line. Each end of the line
sends data over one channel and receives data over the other.
Each node handles a Busy Channel Flag (BCF) associated with the
sending channel of each of its transmission lines as
illustrated in figure 4.4.6.(4). BCF is set to 1 when the
sending channel of the line is busy, and to 0 when the sending
channel of the line is not busy.

The sending channel is defined as busy whenever not immediately
available for transmission of a packet ready to be sent. In
particular, for the TMM procedure, the channel is busy from the
start of transmission of a packet until reception of the
corresponding positive acknowledgement. For the MV8 procedure,
the channel is busy either when transmitting a packet or when
no virtual channel is available (see section 4.4.1.2).

The BCF of each channel is periodically observed and used to
update the value of the channel load CL (between 0 and 1)
according to the following exponential smoothing formula :

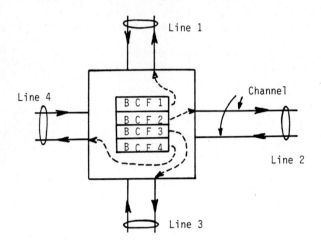

Figure 4.4.6.(4)   - Busy Channel Flag for outgoing channels

$$CL := BCF * (1-ALPHA) + CL * ALPHA$$

where ALPHA is the smoothing constant, which can be set to any
value between 0 and 1 as a system tuning parameter. The use of
a smoothing function is intended to prevent over-reaction to
transient load changes. In order for the channel load
measurement mechanism to automatically adapt to changes of line
speeds in the network, it was initially decided to have the BCF
observation period in inverse proportion to the line speed.

CHANNEL LOAD STATE COMPUTATION

The traffic control mechanism will not react until the path
load reaches a certain threshold. Therefore, it is not
necessary to propagate the exact value of the channel load, and
the channel load CL is locally transformed into a Channel Load
State (CLS) which represents the state of the channel load with
regard to critical thresholds. The CLS is a ternary variable
which can assume the values Normal (N), Warning (W) or Alarm
(A) depending on the current value of CL. In order to reduce
oscillation, double thresholds are used. The conversion is
performed periodically by the CLS-update algorithm shown below.
The time interval between two consecutive updates is called the
"Update Period" (UP) and is independent of line speed. The

CLS-Update algorithm illustrated in figure 4.4.6.(5) is :

CL = current value of the channel load
CLS = current value of the channel load state (i.e. N, W, or A)
TL(x) = lower threshold of the state x
TU(x) = upper threshold of the state x

Note : Threshold values are set to values such that

0 = TL(N) < TL(W) < TU(N) < TL(A) < TU(W) < TU(A) = 1

begin
if CL < TL(CLS) then decrease CLS ;
if CL > TU(CLS) then increase CLS ;
end

Note : the initial value of CLS is supposed to be N and
"increase" and "decrease" are defined in the natural way (i.e.
N < W < A).

PATH LOAD STATE EVALUATION

Path load state is defined as the maximum channel load state,
over all channels belonging to the hops of the path. The
notions of path and hop have already been introduced in section
4.4.3 "Maximum" is defined here in the natural way, i.e.
assuming that N < W < A. Thus, the Path Load State is a
ternary variable which can assume the same values as the
Channel Load State, i.e. "normal", "Warning" and "Alarm". Since
all data traffic is forwarded only along best paths, the Path
Load State needs to be computed for best paths only.

The Path Load State of a best path can be computed on a hop
basis by propagation along the path. This organization of
distributed computation is very similar to the one used for
computing path grade in order to determine best paths within
CIGALE (see section 4.4.3). It is therefore natural to forward
path load information along with routing information in routing
packets. In practice, each node puts the Path Load State into
routing packets sent to its neighbours (in addition to the path
grade and length used for adaptive routing) of the best path
from itself to each destination. Let us consider the best path
between a node N and a destination D. Let M be the neighbour of
N on the best path to D as illustrated in figure 4.4.6.(6)
where :

N = a node
D = a destination
M = the neighbour of N on the best path from N to D
RLS = received path load state between M and D (received
by N from M in routing packets).
CLS = channel load state between N and M (computed by N).

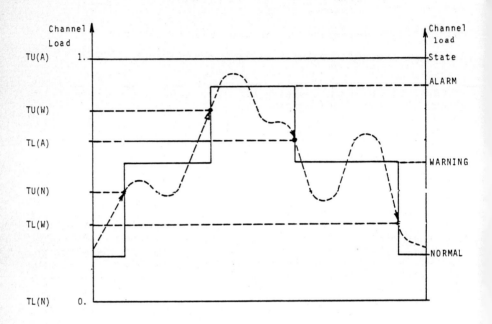

Figure 4.4.6.(5) -   Channel Load and Channel Load State

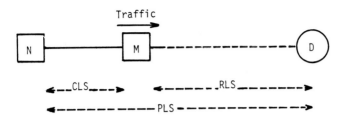

Figure 4.4.6.(6)   - Path Load State propagation

The path load state between N and D is computed as :

PLS := MAX (CLS, RLS)

In practice, when N receives a routing packet from M, the
following algorithm is executed to compute the Path Load State
(PLS) for each destination D, possibly triggering transmission
of routing packets :

```
begin
X := MAX (CLS, RLS) ;
if X <Not equal> PLS
            then begin comment
            if the path load state to D changed, then
            update it and send a routing packet to
            neighbours (containing new PLS) ;
            PLS := X ;
            Send routing packet to neighbours
            end
end
```

This update algorithm must be executed each time the Path Load
State is liable to change, i.e. not only when a routing packet
is received (as indicated above) but also each time the Channel
Load State is computed for update (periodic update, see CHANNEL
LOAD STATE COMPUTATION above).

Note: As we will see later in this section, normal operation
of the congestion control could simply be based on observation
of local channel load state by each node, without propagation
of path load state. However knowledge of path load states at
entry points in the network allows the traffic of ill-behaving
hosts to be discarded or blocked immediately, without
unnecessarily loading the rest of the network.

PATH LOAD STATES TO REGIONS

Best paths from one node to the various destinations in the network(s) have a tree structure corresponding to hierarchical addressing. For instance, best paths from one node to all destinations Di within another region follow the same best path to that region R (see figure 4.4.6.(7)).

Path load state computation must follow the same hierarchical organization :

Path load states to individual destinations Di (external addresses and nodes within the same region, as well as general addresses) are computed on an individual basis.

Path load states to destinations within another region or another network are computed as the path load state to that region or network as a whole. As a starting point a conservative rule has been chosen for evaluation of the path load state to the whole region. The last node (N") in the destination region (R) indicates to its neighbour (N´) a path load state PLS(R) as the highest value of path loads to individual destinations PLS(Di) within the region, (i.e. PLS(R) = MAX (PLS(Di)).

This is illustrated by the following algorithm executed by each node before sending a routing packet :

used symbols

Rr = a region
N1, N2....., Nn = nodes of the region Rr
E1, E2....., Em = external addresses of the region Rr
PLS(x) = Path Load State to x (contained in routing tables and sent in routing packets).

algorithm

```
begin
PLS(Rr):= MAX (PLS(N1), PLS(N2),..., PLS(Nn), PLS(E1),
               PLS(E2),..., PLS(Em)))
end
```

PATH LOAD STATE INITIALIZATION

As is the case for path grade, the path load state computation in a node is based upon path load states received from its neighbours. This propagation scheme has therefore to be initialized. When a node starts operating, path load states to all destinations are conservatively set to "warning".

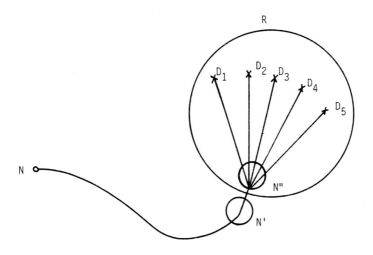

R = a region
N"= a node in R
Di= a destinataire in R
N'= a node outside of R
N = a node outside of R

Figure 4.4.6.(7) - Path Load State to regions

b) Host Information

Path load state evaluation allows each node to be aware of
potential congestion to a destination whenever path load state
to that destination reaches the Warning state. Unless the
corresponding load offered by hosts is reduced, congestion
might occur and packets could be dropped. Therefore, warning
information needs to be passed to, and only to, hosts sending
packets to that destination (selectivity). This is simply done
by sending them Choke Packets as explained below.

Each time a node switches a packet, it checks the load state of
the path over which the packet is to be forwarded. If it is in
the Warning State, a choke packet is generated and sent back to
the source host, while the packet is forwarded to its
destination. In addition, the packet is tagged by setting a
flag in its inter-node header in order to prevent it from
triggering additional Choke Packets on its way.

More precisely, for each packet to be switched by a node, a
Choke Packet is to be generated if the three following
conditions are satisfied simultaneously : 1) the Path Load
State is Warning (The Path Load State is extracted from the
routing table, by using the destination of the packet, see
section 4.4.2); 2) the packet is not tagged (flag in the
"CIGALE flags" field of the inter-node header); 3) the packet
has not been already processed by the CHOKE NIS as explained
below (flag in the "Facilities Flags" field of the intra-node
header).

If the above conditions are verified for a packet being
switched, the Switch Module attaches it to the queue of the
CHOKE NIS. The CHOKE NIS will be responsible for generating the
corresponding Choke Packet and will return both packets (normal
and choke) to the Switch Module (see figure 4.4.6.(8)).

If any of the above conditions are not satisfied or if the
CHOKE NIS queue is full, the Switch Module directly attaches
the packet to the output line queue towards its destination as
already explained in section 4.4.2. However, if the path load
to the destination of the packet is in the Alarm State, the
packet is dropped (see section d) below).

The CHOKE NIS is activated when packets are stored in its queue
(as any NIS) and it performs the following actions on each
packet in its queue :

1) if the source of the packet is an NIS address, no Choke
Packets will be generated. The packet is simply tagged
(inter-node header), marked as already processed (intra-node
header), and sent back to the Switch Module queue. In other
words, traffic from hosts only is to be reduced in case of
potential congestion, without affecting network control
traffic.

2) if the source is not an NIS, the CHOKE NIS tries to get a
free buffer in order to build up a Choke Packet. If a buffer is
available its source field is set to the CHOKE NIS address
(i.e. node number and NIS number) and its destination is copied
from the source field of the packet which caused the choke to
be generated. Its intra-node header is also copied into the
text field of the Choke Packet (see figure 4.4.6.(9)). Flags
in its intra-node header and inter-node header are turned on in
order to signify the Switch Module that the packet has been
processed by the CHOKE NIS and that it triggered a Choke Packet
effectively. Then both packets are attached to the Switch
Module queue and the CHOKE NIS waits until a new activation.

If no buffer is available to build a Choke Packet, then the
packet is marked as already processed (intra-node header) and
attached to the Switch Module queue. Then the CHOKE NIS waits
until a new packet enters its queue. Note that in this case the
packet is not tagged, in order to allow a node further along
the path to generate a choke packet.

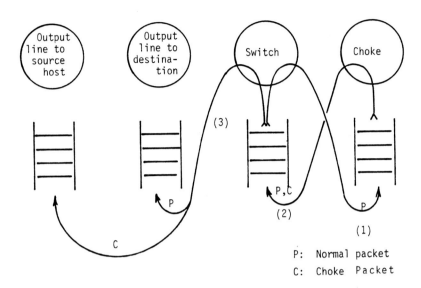

P: Normal packet
C: Choke Packet

Figure 4.4.6.(8)

    - Sequence of operations for generation of a choke packet

c) Host Reaction

Choke packets received by hosts contain, in their   text   fields
(see   figure   4.4.6.(9)),   the indication of the destination to
which congestion was anticipated. In reaction to choke packets,
hosts should reduce the load they offer   to   the   corresponding
destination(s).

Reaction   by   hosts   (rather   than   by the network on behalf of
hosts) is an   essential   feature   which   permits   us   to   adapt
optimally   to a variety of cases, depending on requirements and
capabilities of hosts.

Some hosts may decide to reduce   traffic   only   to   potentially
congested   destinations,   while   others   may   choose   a simpler
strategy by reducing all their traffic to the network.

Hosts may decide   to   reduce   selectively   flows   to   the   same
destination   (e.g.   slow   down   batch   traffic   first   and   let
conversational traffic unchanged).

As an option, the node serving a host may act as a surrogate of the host, in interpreting choke packets and translating them into flow control actions on the transmission line to the host.

In any case the reaction of hosts to choke packets must correspond at least to a defined reduction of the offered load, which will be referred to as the "optimal" host reaction.

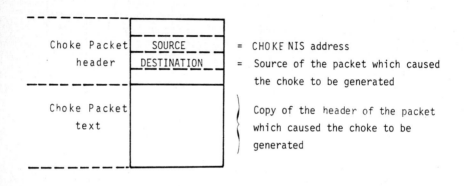

Figure 4.4.6.(9)- Choke Packet format

For the purpose of simulation, a tentatively "optimal" host reaction algorithm has been designed. Although it is probably difficult to implement in a real host, it represents an upper bound to hosts reaction, which allowed us to evaluate the whole congestion control system. This algorithm also suggested some guidelines for further research. To provide full information, it is described in the following as it has been implemented in the simulator.

The optimal reaction of a source host (S) is selective in the sense that it controls independently the traffic load to each destination (D) as described below.

Normally, the receipt of a choke packet causes reduction of the traffic load to the corresponding destination. However, it is assumed that when S receives several choke packets concerning D in quick succession, they are due to the same cause. Thus, in order to prevent the traffic rate reduction mechanism from overreacting, a No-listening Period (NP) is defined. It is a time period after the arrival of the first choke concerning D, during which S will disregard further chokes concerning D (see figure 4.4.6.(10)). The No-listening Period is followed by a Listening Period (LP). Unless a new choke is received, the

traffic rate is allowed to increase again at the end of the LP.
The traffic reduction mechanism is cumulative in the sense that
if during the LP another choke concerning D arrives, the
traffic rate will be further reduced, a new NP started, etc.

More precisely, the reduction mechanism for traffic to D is
specified in the following algorithm where (RL) is defined as a
non-negative integer. RL = 0 represents no reduction and RL is
bound by the Maximum Reduction level (RM) which is a system
parameter.

                        Used symbols

RL = Reduction Level (initial value = 0)
RM = Maximum Reduction Level (system parameter)
LISTENING (i.e. Listening state), is true during LP, false
during NP (Initial value = true)

                         Algorithm

On receiving a choke concerning D,

    begin
    if LISTENING and RL < RM
    then begin RL:= RL+1 ; LISTENING := false end
    end

At end of NP,

    begin LISTENING := true end

At end of LP,

    begin
    if RL > 0
    then begin RL := RL - 1 ; LISTENING := true end
    end

In the simulation, the traffic reduction is performed by
deleting every n-th packet from the stream of packets generated
by S and destined for D. The current value of the reduction
level allows one to determine n as follows : if RL = 0 no
reduction takes place, thus n is infinite ; for RL = 1, 2, RM,
n is set to n = RM-RL+1.

d) Protection against improper Host Reaction

When packets are sent over a path in the Normal State, no
particular actions are taken. When the path is in the Warning
State, hosts are requested by means of Choke Packets to reduce
their traffic until the path load state returns to Normal.
However, if the load keeps increasing, it will enter the Alarm
State. When a node receives a packet which is to be forwarded
over a path in the Alarm State, the packet is dropped. This

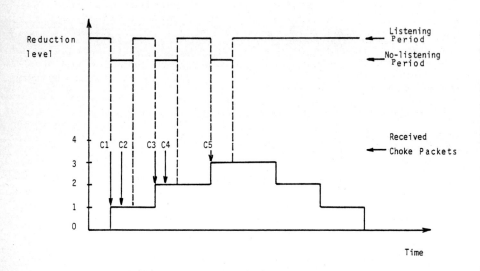

Figure 4.4.6.(10)-Example of traffic reduction level behaviour

action is taken to definitely preclude congestion along this path. No further Choke Packets are issued in the Alarm state since it is assumed that the host or hosts which caused congestion were already notified while the Warning State was in effect.

The propagation of path Load State information to the periphery of the network allows control of improper host reaction by the entry node. Thus, traffic from an ill-behaved host will be dropped immediately, and will not interfere with traffic from well-behaved hosts.

e) Improvements to the initial Traffic Control System

Previous paragraphs present the method originally proposed and simulated. Extensive studies have been conducted in this area and full discussions and results can be found in [IRL77a, GRA78a]. It was found that the basic principles were sound. In addition, a number of simplifications and improvements to the original scheme were introduced. The major results are summarized below.

Double thresholds

Double thresholds on path load were initially introduced to
avoid oscillations between load states, thus reducing the
routing packet traffic. Simulation showed that double
thresholds had little or no effect in practice. It was
therefore decided to use single thresholds which are easier to
implement.

Smoothing constant (ALPHA) and Observation Period (OP)

It was also observed that control mechanisms generally
overreacted. One reason was that the smoothing constant ALPHA
(see heading CHANNEL LOAD MEASUREMENT above in same section)
was set to a low value (originally stipulated to be 1/2). This
caused estimates of channel load to oscillate widely because
too much emphasis was put on the latest sample of the Busy
Channel Flag (BCF). Consequently the thresholds were crossed
and routing packets were generated too frequently.
To provide better smoothing, ALPHA needed to be increased
substantially (up to 7/8). It then turned out that the control
mechanisms did not react quickly enough and that the
Observation Period (OP) had to be increased to compensate for
the new setting of ALPHA. At that point, there did not appear
to be much benefit in varying OP according to the line speed,
particularly when the Update Period (UP) is independent of line
speed. The original scheme has therefore been simplified
further by making OP the same for all lines.

Path load state oscillations

It was observed that an oscillatory phenomenon might be induced
by the path load propagation mechanism when the traffic rate
was just below the threshold level on some channels. An
occasional transition from the Normal to the Warning State
caused routing packets to be sent, which added enough extra
load to force other channels into the Warning State. After a
while, a stable situation was reached. The routing packets
stopped flowing and the load returned to Normal. However, the
change back to the Normal State caused another wave of routing
packets, increased load, etc. This phenomenon was a
self-induced oscillation separated from any oscillation in
traffic caused by host reaction.

It was not clear whether or not this phenomenon had bad effects
in practice. For safety, it was decided, however, to not
include the control traffic when estimating the channel load,
i.e. the busy-free flag is not turned busy when a control
packet is being transmitted over the channel. Instead, the
threshold is lowered to leave a sufficient margin of channel
capacity to safely accomodate the control packets when
required.

Alarm State

As already mentioned, it was observed that the control
mechanisms overreacted due to bad tuning of ALPHA. Another
reason was identified by studying the behaviour of the Alarm
mechanism itself. It turned out that too many packets were
dropped in the Alarm State even under normal load condition. It
was also found that sending Choke Packets in Warning State but
not in Alarm State could cause some problems. If it occurs
that a host does not reduce its traffic drastically enough on
chokes issued in the Warning State and that the Alarm State is
entered, no further chokes will be issued. The host will then
believe that it can resume its higher traffic rate and its
packets will be dropped without further warning. Hence the
control mechanisms may be deadlocked in the Alarm State.

Attempts to tune the thresholds to reduce the Alarm's severity
were unsatisfactory. Yet, when the Alarm State was completely
suppressed (by raising the threshold to 1) throughput increased
significantly. An additional benefit was the reduced overhead
of propagation of the Path Load State changes. With the
elimination of double thresholds, this led us to use a single
threshold between Normal and Warning instead of the four
thresholds of the original scheme.

However, protection against improper host reaction consisted of
dropping packets when the Alarm state was reached. Since the
Alarm state no longer appeared, another protection mechanism,
called the "Tripping Mechanism" was designed.

Tripping Mechanism

The purpose of the Tripping Mechanism (TM) is the same as the
Alarm mechanism, i.e. to relieve congestion if a host or hosts
do not react properly to Choke Packets. The basic principle of
the TM is the following : if the path to a particular
destination remains in the Warning State for a predefined time
interval, called the Tripping Period (TP), any packet entering
the network for that destination is dropped. A Choke Packet is
generated as usual in the Warning State. When the path returns
to Normal State, the action of the TM is automatically
terminated.

In order to avoid dropping packets already travelling in the
network, the TM is implemented only at the first node of the
path (i.e. entry node).

For implementation purposes, TP is specified as an integer
multiple of the Update Period (UP), i.e. TP = TN * UP. A new
variable TC is associated with each destination in routing
tables of a node. Taking into account previously mentioned
simplifications, the Channel Load State update algorithm
(executed each time UP elapses) is revised as follows for
implementing the TM :

Used symbols

CL = current value of the channel load
CLS = current value of the channel load state (i.e.
Normal or Warning)
T   = value of the load threshold between Normal and
Warning states
TC = Tripping Period count (0 when TP has elapsed)
TN = initial value of TC (depending on TP)

Algorithm

```
begin
if CL < T
then CLS := NORMAL
else begin
     comment the new load is in Warning  State.  Check  whether
     the current state is Normal ;
     if CLS = NORMAL
     then begin
          comment  change  from  Normal to Warning : initialize
          tripping count and update state ;
          TC : = TN ;
          CLS := WARNING;
          end
     else begin
          comment  already  in  Warning :  decrease  tripping
          count ;
          if TC > 0 then TC := TC-1;
          end
     end
end
```

Since the Alarm State is suppressed, the Switch Module drops
packets in the Warning State when the Tripping Period has
elapsed (i.e. when TC = 0 in the above algorithm), and only at
the first node of the path. In addition, we must not drop
control packets, in particular routing packets, which allow to
control the network load. Therefore only packets sent by hosts
are subjected to dropping due to the Tripping Mechanism. On
receiving a packet the Switch Module must therefore either
attach it to the best output line queue, or to the CHOKE NIS
queue, or drop it, depending upon various conditions as
specified in the following algorithm :

Used symbols

PLS = State of the path over which the packet is to be
forwarded
TAGGED = TRUE if the packet has been tagged by the CHOKE
NIS
PROCESSED = TRUE if the packet has been processed by the

CHOKE NIS
FULL = TRUE if the CHOKE NIS queue is full
FIRST = TRUE if the considered node is the first of the
path
TRIPPING = TRUE if the Tripping Period has elapsed (i.e.
TC = 0)
HOSTPKT = TRUE if the packet to be switched has been sent
by a host.

Algorithm

```
begin
if PLS = NORMAL
then  comment  attach the packet to the best output line queue;
else begin
    if not TAGGED and not PROCESSED and not FULL
    then comment attach the packet to the CHOKE NIS queue;
    else begin
        if FIRST and TRIPPING and HOSTPKT
        then comment drop the packet;
        else comment attach the packet  to  the  best  output
        line queue;
        end
    end
end
```

f) Implementation in the real network and further research work

The traffic control system described previously has been
simulated. After successful simplification and tuning most of
it has been implemented in the real network. As a result of
simulations the following parameters settings have been used in
the actual implementation :

- ALPHA (Smoothing Constant) = 7/8
- OP (Observation Period) = 500 ms
- T (Threshold between Normal and Warning) = 5/8
- UP (Update Period) = 1000 ms

Simulation has shown that the traffic control technique using
host reaction and the Tripping Mechanism is basically sound and
can be readily tuned so that the throughput is maximized while
the number of packets dropped within the network is minimum
[MAJ78]. It was felt, however, that several aspects of the
technique needed further investigation.

First, it was thought that a Tripping Mechanism driven by
chokes would be more robust than the original Tripping
Mechanism driven by Path Load States. This is primarily due to
the fact that chokes represent more up-to-date information
regarding the load of the network than the Path Load States,
which also need to be propagated through the network.
Furthermore, a TM driven by Choke Packets would allow a more
selective monitoring of host behaviour than a TM based on Path

Load States and time-outs ; chokes travelling back to the
source carry source-destination addresses and therefore can
easily be categorized at the first node of the path. A Path
Load State, on the other hand, reflects the global load of a
path, possibly involving several source-destination flows, and
its influence can only be of a global type. It was concluded
that this choke-driven TM would be more effective, specially to
handle hosts reacting improperly to Choke Packets.

A second area of research concerned the host reaction mechanism
itself. It was proposed to replace the present "optimal" host
reaction by a reaction similar to the new Tripping Mechanism.
It was felt that this had the advantage of an easier
implementation. Further, since both the host and the first node
on the path would react in the same manner, a better control
should be achievable.

Simulation studies have been conducted at the University of
Waterloo (Canada) in order to investigate these questions. The
congestion control mechanisms were modified as proposed, so
that both Tripping mechanism and host reaction were using the
chokes and had similar implementation. Simulation results
indicate that overall the new mechanisms have better
performance than the mechanisms implemented previously. In
particular, they can handle satisfactorily hostile host
conditions (i.e., a host whose reaction mechanism has failed).
The results show that while Tripping Mechanism tends to secure
the network under such conditions, it also tends to do so under
persistant load situations. A detailed description of the
results of this research work can be found in [MAJ78a, MAJ79,
GRA79a, GRA80].

4.4.7. Indirect services

Concepts and principles related to the CIGALE services have
already been discussed in sections 3.1.5. and 4.2.2. Here we
just recall that an indirect service is requested by setting
the corresponding bit in the facility field of the packet
header.

4.4.7.1. Implementation of Services

The indirect services of CIGALE are DIAGNOSTIC, TRACE, ROUTE
and PROBE. DIAGNOSTIC is closely related to DROP and has been
implemented within the DROP NIS for practical reasons. The
DIAGNOSTIC service will therefore be described along with the
DROP service in the section 4.4.8.

TRACE, ROUTE and PROBE are implemented as a single NIS
(Indirect NIS), i.e. there is only one queue and one process
associated to those three services. Each service is actually
processed by a specific subroutine running in that single
process.

4.4.7.2. Basic Principle

As indicated in section 4.4.2, the Switch Module switches packets requesting indirect services (except DIAGNOSTIC) to the INDIRECT NIS queue, thus activating the associated process.

When activated, the INDIRECT NIS process extracts a packet from its queue and successively calls the three routines TRACE, ROUTE and PROBE, which provide the corresponding service (if requested).

Then the facilities flags of the intra-node header of the packet are updated, to indicate to the Switch Module that the requested services have been processed.

Finally, the TRACE packet (if any has been generated) and the packet originally requesting services are attached to the Switch Module queue. The INDIRECT NIS process repeats these actions until its queue is exhausted.

The following paragraphs describe each of the three routines implementing the services of the INDIRECT NIS.

TRACE

If the TRACE service is requested, the TRACE routine tries to get a free buffer in order to build up a TRACE packet. If no buffer is available the requesting packet is switched to the DROP NIS queue (an appropriate error code being put in the intra-node header).

If a buffer is available its source field is set to the INDIRECT NIS address (i.e. node number and NIS number) and its destination field is copied from the source field of the requesting packet in order to send back the TRACE packet to the source of the traced packet.

An exception is to be made if that source is an ECHO NIS : in this case the TRACE packet should be sent back to the real source of the requesting packet, i.e. to the address specified by the destination field of its header.

The text of the TRACE packet is simply a copy of the intra-node header of the traced packet. Detailed information returned in a TRACE packet can therefore be seen in the figure 4.2.3.(2) which gives the packet header format.

ROUTE

If the ROUTE service is requested, the text of the packet is supposed to conform to a particular structure, which is shown in figure 4.4.7.(1). This structure is also intended to be used by the PROBE service and makes it possible to request both

ROUTE and PROBE in the same packet.

The ROUTE subroutine manipulates the following items in the
packet text :

- Route Current Pointer (RCP)
- Route End Pointer (REP)
- Route List (RL)

Each entry of the RL is one octet long and simply contains a
transmission line number.

The ROUTE subroutine then performs the following actions :

Before any processing is done, various consistency checks are
performed on pointers. In case of error, the packet is dropped
(i.e. attached to the DROP NIS queue) with an appropriate error
code set in the intra-node header.

If the end of RL is not yet reached, (i.e. RCP not equal to
REP), RCP is incremented and the next transmission line number
is extracted from the corresponding RL entry. It is then
stored in the output line number of the packet header, thus
forcing the Switch Module to switch the packet to the specified
line (see section 4.4.2).

If the end of RL is already reached, the ROUTE does not do
anything, and the packet is forwarded according to the regular
switching rules (see also section 4.4.2)

PROBE

When the PROBE service is requested, the text of the packet
must agree with the structure shown in figure 4.4.7.(1). The
PROBE routine handles the following items in the packet text :

- Probe Control Byte (PCB)
- Route End Pointer (REP)
- Probe Current Pointer (PCP)
- Probe list (PL)

A new entry is added to PL each time the packet passes through
a node. The figure 4.4.7.(2) shows the structure of a PL entry.
It contains the following items :

REGION number and NODE number are characteristic parameters of
the traversed node;

INPUT LINE number indicates the line over which the packet has
been received by the node. This information is picked up from
the corresponding field in the intra-node header;

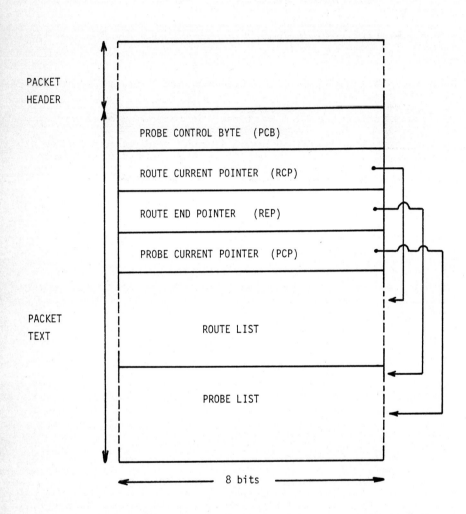

Figure 4.4.7.(1)- Structure of a ROUTE and/or a PROBE packet

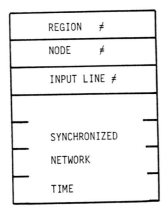

| REGION ≠ |
| NODE ≠ |
| INPUT LINE ≠ |
| SYNCHRONIZED NETWORK TIME |

8 bits

Figure 4.4.7.(2) -   Structure of a PROBE List entry

SYNCHRONIZED NETWORK TIME is the currrent value of the SNT clock in the node (see section 4.4.4).

Since the size of the packet text is limited to 255 octets, it is clear that PL may overflow if the number of nodes traversed is large enough : the purpose of the PCB is to control possible overflow of PL. The PCB contains the two following boolean variables :

LAST is set by the user to specify which policy is to be applied when overflow occurs in PL : LAST is true if the user wants to keep the most recent entries in PL (and lose the oldest), LAST is false in the opposite case;

OVER is set to true by the PROBE subroutine to inform the user that overflow has occured in PL.

When activated, the PROBE subroutine performs the following actions :

If various consistency checks made on pointers fail, then the packet is discarded with an appropriate error code in the intra-node header.

- Subsequent actions are driven by the values of LAST and OVER according to the following table.

                         LAST

          !   !   !
          !   ! FALSE   TRUE   !
          !   !   !
          !------------------------------!
          !   !   !
          ! FALSE !   A   C   !
          !   !   !
OVER   !------------------------------!
          !   !   !
          !   !   !
          ! TRUE   !   B   C   !
          !   !   !

A - No overflow occurred and the user wants to keep the oldest entries : then add a new entry to PL (i.e. update PCP) and set OVER to true if it caused an overflow (i.e. if it reached the end of packet text).

B - Overflow occurred and the user wants to keep the oldest PL entries : do nothing.

C - The user wants to keep the most recent PL entries : then add a new entry to PL (i.e. update PCP). If it caused an overflow (i.e. reached the end of packet text), restart from the beginning of PL (i.e. set PCP to REP) and set OVER to true.

4.4.8. Direct Services

A direct service is requested by sending a packet to the NIS address which provides that service. As previously indicated the NIS process is automatically activated when packets are stored in its input queue. The NIS process then extracts a packet from its queue and processes it (this may generate another packet).

Finally the received packet is released (i.e. returned to the free buffer pool) and the NIS process repeats these actions until its queue is exhausted.

An ON/OFF switch is associated with each direct service in order to provide for more flexible operation. Packets destined to a switched off service are dropped by the Switch Module.

The following paragraphs describe in more detail how received packets are processed by each of the direct services available in CIGALE.

4.4.8.1. DROP and DIAGNOSTIC

Although DIAGNOSTIC service is actually an indirect service, it
has been coupled with the DROP service for   practical   reasons.
DROP   receives   in   its   queue   all   packets   which   are   to be
discarded by the node. There are two types of such packets :

a) the   packet   is   explicitly   destined   to   DROP,   i.e.   the
destination   field   of its header contains the DROP NIS number.
This is typically used to absorb artificial   traffic   generated
for debugging or measuring purpose ;

b) the   packet   was originally destined to another destination,
but the node is unable to forward the packet and   must   discard
it.   The field "error code" of the intra-node header holds the
identification of the   module   which   decided   to   discard   the
packet and the reason why it did.

A sample of reasons are listed below :

output line DOWN
output queue full
traffic overload
unknown destination
maximum transit delay exceeded
ill-formated header
unreachable destination
no buffer available for TRACE packet
unknown source
forbidden destination

The   DROP   service   processing simply consists in returning the
buffer of the packet to be discarded to the free   buffer   pool.
However   this   is done only if the packet is explicitly destined
to DROP or if it does not request the DIAGNOSTIC service.

Otherwise, the DIAGNOSTIC service is provided as follows.

A DIAGNOSTIC packet is built up with the DROP   NIS   address   in
the   source field of the header. Its destination is copied from
the source field of the dropped packet. The same   exception   is
to   be   made here as in the TRACE service, i.e. the destination
field must be copied from the destination field of the   dropped
packet if its source field contains a ECHO NIS address. This is
to   insure   that   the DIAGNOSTIC packet will be returned to the
real source of the dropped packet.   The text of the   DIAGNOSTIC
packet   is   a   copy   of   the   intra-node   header of the dropped
packet. Note that   this   header   contains   various   information
related   to   the   dropping   circumstances   and particularly the
"error code" which specifies the exact drop reason.

In practice the DIAGNOSTIC packet is directly built up   in   the
same   buffer   as   the   dropped packet, thus avoiding additional
buffer handling. Finally, the DIAGNOSTIC packet is attached   to
the Switch Module queue.

4.4.8.2. ECHO

The purpose of the ECHO service is to send received packets back to their source. The ECHO NIS processing is therefore rather simple : it just swaps source and destination fields in the packet header and attaches the packet to the Switch Module queue. The ECHO service is transparent for the packet text : the returned packet contains exactly the same text as received.

4.4.8.3. TIME

Section 4.4.4 describes how the network manages the Synchronized Network Time (SNT). The purpose of the TIME NIS is to make the SNT available to the users of the network.

When the TIME NIS receives a packet in its queue, it builds up a packet destined to the source of the received packet. The source field of this returned packet is set to the address of the TIME NIS.

The text of the created packet contains the current value of the SNT clock which is given both in units of seconds and 1/1600 second. The latter unusual unit has been chosen for practical implementation reasons. The less precise but more usual unit of 10 milliseconds can easily be obtained by a 4-bit shift.

Figure 4.4.8.(1) shows the structure of the packet text returned by the TIME NIS.

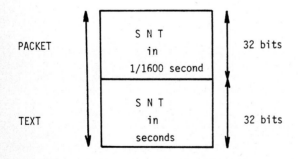

Figure 4.4.8.(1) - Structure of a packet text returned by the TIME service

As in the DIAGNOSTIC service the packet returned by the TIME NIS is built up in the same buffer as the received packet. Then the TIME NIS attaches it to Switch Module queue.

4.4.8.4. TTY

Each CIGALE node is equipped with a teleprinter. The purpose of the TTY NIS is to make it possible to introduce packets into the network from the node teleprinters, to send packets to the node teleprinters and to print their contents. As shown in figure 4.4.8.(2), the TTY NIS is made of 2 parts (i.e. two processes). The IN process is in charge of the input of characters from the teleprinter keyboard. The OUT process prints out the contents of the received packets on the teleprinter.

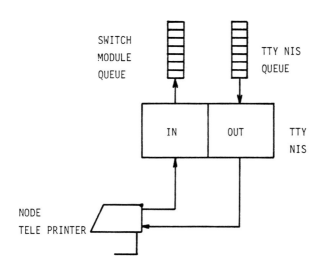

Figure 4.4.8.(2) - The TTY service structure

The functions of each of these processes are examined in the following paragraphs.

a) IN process

The standard MITRA 15 teleprinter provided by the manufacturer operates only in half-duplex mode : thus, the IN process cannot initiate a permanent input on the teleprinter since it would preclude any output. The IN process needs therefore to be explicitly activated by the user when he wants to type characters on the keyboard : this is done by pushing a button on the keyboard which sets an interrupt giving control to the IN process.

When activated, the IN process reads the typed message ; the end of message is indicated by the "carriage return" character. Usual facilities are provided to type messages longer than the teleprinter line, to delete the last character typed, to cancel the line being currently typed, etc. The presence or absence of an escape character in front of the message determines its type.

TEXT MESSAGE (no escape character)

In this case, the message is considered as the text of a packet to be sent. Therefore, the IN process gets a free packet buffer, puts the message into the text field, attaches the packet to the Switch Module queue and waits until a new activation.

The header of the sent packet is copied from the standard header defined with the "H" command (see next paragraph).

An appropriate message is printed out if no packet buffer is available or if the message exceeds the maximum packet text size.

COMMAND MESSAGE (escape character)

The message is not the text of a packet but a local command to the TTY NIS. Each command is identified by the first (after the escape) character of the message. The most important commands are described below :

- H

This command allows one to define the value of each item of a "Standard Header" which is to be used for all packets sent by the TTY NIS. In the absence of modifications to the standard header, consecutive packets created from the same teleprinter will be sent with the same header and therefore to the same destination. This considerably facilitates the dialogue with a fixed destination since only packet texts need be typed. Standard header fields such as sources, destinations, facilities, may be defined by means of the H command. Actually, no restriction at all is put on the standard header definition in order to provide for the most flexible debugging and testing tools.

- ?

This command causes the currently recorded standard header to be printed on the teleprinter.

- C

This allows one to cancel the output of a received packet being printed by the OUT process.

Commands in error (e.g. syntax) are aborted and cause an appropriate message to be printed back on the teleprinter. Once a command has been processed (or aborted) the IN process waits until a new activation.

b) OUT process

The OUT process is automatically activated when a packet is attached to its queue. It then extracts the packet from the queue, prints it on the teleprinter, releases the packet buffer and waits for a new packet in its queue. It is worth noting that the header of the received packet is printed only if its source is different from the destination indicated in the Standard Header : this saves time in avoiding printing headers that the user already knows when exchanging packets with the same destination.

c) IN/OUT processes interaction

Since the teleprinter only operates in half-duplex mode, the IN and OUT processes cannot use it at the same time although they are logically asynchronous processes (this means that the packet traffic that they handle is indeed full-duplex). Both IN and OUT have therefore to consider the teleprinter as a non sharable resource which is to be assigned by means of some mutual exclusion mechanism. This has been achieved by using a classical software "test and set" algorithm and a system event representing the "teleprinter resource".

The IN process must be able to interrupt the OUT process, particularly to allow the teleprinter user to cancel the output of a packet being printed by the OUT process.

Since the teleprinter operates in half-duplex mode the OUT process, while printing a packet, must periodically check whether the IN process has been activated and needs to read some command from the keyboard. In practice, the OUT process checks the IN process activation between each printed line and, if necessary, releases the "teleprinter resource" and waits until the IN process is deactivated. Then, if the packet output has not been cancelled it gets back the "teleprinter resource" and keeps on printing the packet.

4.4.8.5. DEBUG

a) Basic Principle

The DEBUG NIS provides each node with debugging facilities, which are accessible remotely through the network. The DEBUG NIS processing may be summarized as follows. It extracts a packet from the DEBUG NIS queue, picks up the debugging command from the packet text, processes it, and builds up the appropriate answer (possibly an error message). It then prepares a packet buffer by putting the answer into the text field, sets the destination field to the source of the received packet and sets the source to the DEBUG NIS address (as in TIME and DIAGNOSTIC services, the received packet buffer is used to build up the answer packet). Finally, it attaches the answer packet to the Switch Module queue and waits until a new packet enters the DEBUG queue.

b) DEBUG command parameters

The DEBUG NIS is a simple command processor whose basic principles have been borrowed from ARPANET. Received commands contain a list of parameters (separated by commas) followed by one character identifying the command. The parameter list may be empty since implicit parameters are accepted.

Each parameter designates either a memory address or a value. In both cases it may actually be a simple numerical expression in which parenthesis are not allowed. The following operations can be used : + add, - subtract, @ indirection.

The operator @ performs the following functions : the current value of the expression (computed from left to right) is taken as a memory address and the new current value of the expression is set to the contents of that address.

This provides for flexibility in fetching values through various tables. For example, the expression A+4@-5@+3 is equivalent to B in the memory organization shown in figure 4.4.8.(3).

c) DEBUG commands

The following commands are available within the DEBUG NIS :

- P1 /

The answer is the contents of the address designated by the parameter P1. If P1 is not specified, its implicit value is the answer from the last command /, N or <up arrow>. In addition the parameter P1 or its implicit value defines the "Current

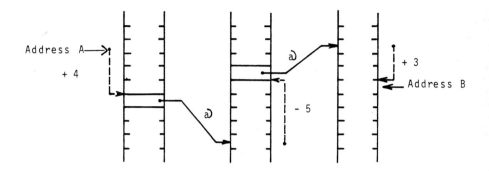

The expression A + 4ⓐ - 5ⓐ + 3 is equivalent to B

Figure 4.4.8.(3)   - DEBUG addressing facilities

Address" (CA).

- P1 <up arrow>

The value of P1 is stored at CA. If P1 is not specified, the CA
contents is not modified. The answer is the contents of the
address preceding CA. This address becomes also the new CA.

- P1 N

Same as the command <up arrow> except that the answer is the
contents of the address following CA which also becomes the new
CA.

- P1 \

No answer. The value of P1 is stored at CA.

- P1, P2 0

The answer is the contents of the memory between the addresses
designated by P1 and P2. The answer may be truncated in order
to fit the maximum size of a packet. The implicit value of each
parameter is its last value specified in an "O" command.

- P1, P2, P3, P4 P

No answer. P4 designates a mask. The bits selected by the mask
in each memory word between the addresses P1 and P2 are forced
to the corresponding bit values of P3. The implicit value of
each parameter is its last value specified in a "P" command.

- P1, P2, P3, P4 S

P4 designates a mask. The bits selected by the mask in each
memory word between the addresses P1 and P2 are compared to the
corresponding selected bits of P3. The answer is the number of
matching words. Ad hoc mechanisms are available to get the list
of these matching words. The implicit value of each parameter
is its last value specified in an "S" or "X" command.

- P1, P2, P3, P4 X

Same as S except that the answer gives the number   of
non-matching words.

- P1, P2 I

No answer. Allows to manipulate interrupts of the MITRA 15 :
e.g. activate, deactivate, validate, invalidate. Both P1 and P2
are mandatory and pertain to the MITRA 15 interrupt system.

- P1, P2 #

No answer. Allows to manipulate system events of the CIGALE
node system, i.e. set them on or off. P1 specifies the event
control block address; P2 specifies its new setting. Both P1
and P2 are mandatory.

- P1 U

The contents of the address P1 is displayed on the upper lights
of the MITRA 15 front panel. It is to be noted that this
display is performed dynamically since   the   lights   are
periodically refreshed from the memory by the clock routine of
the CIGALE node system. If P1 is not specified, then the upper
light display is reset to a predefined implicit address.

- P1 L

Same as U command, except that lower lights of the MITRA 15
front panel are used.

- *DEAD*

In order to avoid mistakes, this command is given a special format. No parameters are needed and no answer is provided. It causes the node to stop functioning and to give control to the boot-strap module called HELP (see section 4.4.9).

A few other facilities are provided in the DEBUG command language. They concern explicit designation of the Current Address in a parameter, decimal-hexadecimal conversion and calculation of a parameter value, and so forth.

4.4.8.6. TRAFFIC

a) Basic principle

The TRAFFIC NIS generates artificial packet traffic from itself to various destinations. Some other characteristics of the traffic to be generated can also be specified. TRAFFIC is particularly used for measurement and testing purposes.

The main functions of the TRAFFIC NIS may be summarized as follows. When activated, the TRAFFIC NIS extracts a packet from the TRAFFIC queue, extracts the command from the text of the packet, and processes it. It then returns the received packet buffer to the free buffer pool or, if necessary, it uses it to build an answer packet to be sent back to the source (the source is the TRAFFIC NIS address, and the destination is the source of the received packet), and attaches it to the Switch Module queue. Finally, it waits until a new command packet arrives in the TRAFFIC NIS queue.

b) TRAFFIC command processing

TRAFFIC is able to process two commands : START and STOP.

The START command allows to start artificial traffic generation. The following parameters must be given in the command :

- traffic generation starting time
- traffic generation duration
- traffic generation period

This last parameter specifies the period of time which must separate the examination of two consecutive entries of the "Traffic Definition Table" (see below).

The specification of a generation starting time makes it possible to start several generations in a time-related manner by sending START commands to different nodes : generation is started by the TRAFFIC NIS in each node when the value of starting time matches Synchronized Network Time (SNT).

The STOP command causes the TRAFFIC NIS to stop generating artificial traffic.

The behaviour of the command processing can be represented by the automaton shown in figure 4.4.8.(4).

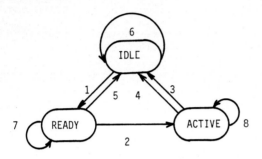

Figure 4.4.8.(4)   - TRAFFIC command processing automaton

Transitions, corresponding events and actions are the following :

1 - START received

Store command parameters and start monitoring starting time. Send answer "STARTED".

2 - Starting time elapsed

Start generating traffic and start monitoring duration.

3 - Duration elapsed

Stop generating traffic. Send answer "OVER".

4 - STOP received

Stop generating traffic. Send answer "STOPPED".

5 - STOP received

Stop monitoring starting time. Send answer "STOPPED".

6 - STOP received

Send answer "NOT STARTED".

7 - START received

Override command parameters (i.e. starting time, duration and
period) and start monitoring new starting time. Send answer
"RE-STARTED".

8 - START received

Send answer ALREADY STARTED.

N.B. In any state, any erroneous command received causes an
appropriate error answer to be sent back to the source.

c) Artificial traffic generation technique

When in the "ACTIVE" state, TRAFFIC generates traffic according
to a TRAFFIC Definition Table (TDT). THE TRAFFIC NIS process
is activated periodically according to the period specified in
the START command.   At each activation, it looks at the next
entry of the TDT. If the end of the table is reached a "Loop
counter" is incremented and the process loops back to the first
TDT entry. Each entry of the TDT corresponds to one packet to
be generated. Figure 4.4.8.(5) shows the structure of a TDT
entry.

The decision about generating a packet corresponding to a given
entry depends upon the value of its "generation gear" : the
packet is generated only if the "Loop Counter" is a multiple of
the "generation gear".

In other words, assuming that : N is the number of entries in
TDT, P is the period specified in the START command, G is the
generation gear of the TDT entry, then, each TDT entry will be
examined every P * N, and the packet corresponding to the
entry i will be generated every P * N * G (i).

When it is time to generate a packet, a buffer is obtained from
the free buffer pool. If no buffer is available the TRAFFIC NIS
records this fact and waits for a new activation. Otherwise,
the number of generated packets is incremented in the TDT entry
and a packet is created. Its destination and text length are
picked up from the TDT. The source field is set to the TRAFFIC
NIS address. No specific information is loaded in the text

Unused
Destination network address

Local destination address

Packet text length
Generation gear

Number of generated packets

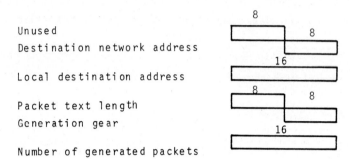

Figure 4.4.8.(5)   - Structure of an artificial Traffic Definition
                     Table (TDT) entry

field of the packet, i.e. it is just left meaningless, which
does not matter for artificial traffic.

The characteristics of the traffic generated by a node can be
simply changed by modifying the contents of the TDT. For that
purpose, both the DEBUG NIS (see section 4.4.8.5) and/or Remote
Load Service (see section 4.5) are usable.

Finally, it is to be noted that the nature of the traffic
generated by TRAFFIC is obviously deterministic. This option
was taken in order to keep the implementation as simple as
possible. However, if more sophisticated random distributions
happen to be needed for lengths and/or inter-packet delays,
they can be approximated by entering precomputed sample values
in the TDT. Clearly, the quality of the approximation depends
on the sample size and consequently on the memory size
available for the TDT.

4.4.8.7. STATISTICS

a) Basic Principle

While running, the CIGALE node software records a variety of
statistical information related to the behaviour of various
system   components.   These   statistics   constitute   an
indispensable tool for debugging, testing, monitoring,
measuring and operating the network.

The purpose of the STATISTICS NIS is to gather a subset of the statistics recorded by each node software module and to send this information to a predefined network address for further processing. In practice, this information is sent both to the Network Monitoring Service (NMS) (see section 4.5).

The STATISTICS NIS process is activated periodically, (every minute), and the following actions are performed at each activation.

The STATISTICS NIS gets two packet buffers from the free buffer pool. If buffers are not available, it waits until the next activation. Otherwise, it builds up two STATISTICS packets (the source is the STATISTICS NIS, the destination is NMS or NMC, and the text contains statistical information) and attaches the packets to the Switch Module queue. Finally, it waits for the next activation.

It is to be noted that there would be no particular difficulty in allowing the STATISTICS NIS to be also activated on reception of packets. It could then send back STATISTICS packets to the requesting sources. However, this facility has not yet been implemented in CIGALE and the STATISTICS NIS has therefore the particular property of not having any input queue.

b) STATISTICS packet structure

The STATISTICS NIS sends information concerning control, node status, line status, NIS status, node statistics, and line statistics.

The line statistics are made of blocks of information, each block concerning a particular transmission line. The number of blocks transmitted corresponds to the actual number of transmission lines connected to the node. In consequence, the length of STATISTICS packets may vary from one node to another, depending on the network topology. Furthermore, provision is made to send a second STATISTICS packet if the first one has been filled up. Figure 4.4.8.(6) shows that the first packet can contain statistics information for up to 7 transmission lines, and that a second packet is required for 8 to 14 lines where 14 is the maximum number of synchronous lines on a MITRA 15.

c) Statistical data

The following data are stored in the text field of the STATISTICS packets (see figure 4.4.8.(6)) :

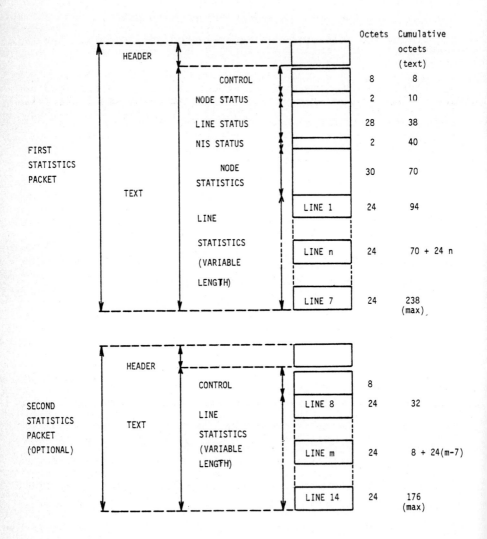

Figure 4.4.8.(6) - STATISTICS packets structure

CONTROL

- Packet type   2 octets
  (e.g. 1st or 2nd STATISTICS packet)

- STATISTICS packet sending time (SNT)   2 octets

- Running CIGALE node software identification   4 octets
  (e.g. version number)

NODE STATUS

- Front panel keys setting   2 octets
  (1 bit per key)

LINE STATUS

This field is broken down into 14 parts of 2 octets each, corresponding to the 14 possible lines. Each part conforms to the following format :

- Physical line status (ON/OFF)   1 bit

- Logical line status (UP/DOWN)   1 bit

- Looped line flag (LOOP/NOT LOOPED)   1 bit

- Unused   1 bit

- Line type (e.g. node-node or node-host)   4 bits

- Line procedure type, (e.g. TMM, BSC, MV8)   4 bits

- Physical number of the synchronous line adapter 4 bits

NIS STATUS

- NIS status (ON/OFF, 1 bit per NIS)   2 octets

NODE STATISTICS

- number of packets processed by the Switch Module   2 octets

- number of deactivations of the Switch Module   2 octets

N.B. The Switch Module is deactivated each time it finds its input queue empty.

- number of dropped packets due to Switch Module
  queue overflow   2 octets

- node CPU cumulative idle time   4 octets

- number of packets destined to a NIS in the node   2 octets

- number of packets having traversed 1 node   2 octets
                                       2 nodes   2 octets
                                       3 nodes   2 octets
                                       4 nodes
                                       more...   2 octets

N.B. this information is recorded only in the last traversed
node

- number of packets having experienced end-to-end
  transit delay from :
                        0   to 0.16 sec   2 octets
                        0.16 to 0.64 sec   2 octets
                        0.64 to 1.28 sec   2 octets
                        1.28 to 5   sec   2 octets

- number of packets dropped due to maximum transit
  delay (5 sec) exceeded   2 octets

LINE STATISTICS

As already mentioned, STATISTICS packets contain one block of
statistical information per line. The following data are stored
in each block :

- number of CRC errors   2 octets

- number of choke packets sent back
  due to line overload (see section 4.2.3.6)   2 octets

- number of times the line status has been
  turned DOWN   2 octets

- number of dropped packets due to full output
  queue   2 octets

- number of transmitted packets whose text length
  in octets was :   from 0 to 15   2 octets
                            from 16 to 63   2 octets
                            from 64 to 127   2 octets
                            from 128 to 255   2 octets

- number of received packets whose text length
  in octets was :   from 0 to 15   2 octets
                            from 16 to 63   2 octets
                            from 64 to 127   2 octets
                            from 128 to 255   2 octets

4.4.8.8. AID

The AID NIS of a given node acts as an intermediate
interlocutor between one of its neighbour nodes and the Network
Control Center during the operation of remote-dump and
remote-load of that neighbour. The AID NIS is indeed an
essential piece of the mechanism involved and for more clarity
its description appears in section 4.5 along with the general
presentation of the Remote Dump and Remote Load Services.

4.4.9. Security and Protection

The aim of the security and protection mechanisms is to protect
CIGALE against a set of potential dangers that are likely to
cause unacceptable degradation in the quality of service. In
general, the choice of appropriate mechanisms determines the
set of dangers that are taken into account. This choice always
results from a compromise between the cost of the mechanisms
implemented and the level of security that they provide. Beyond
this, it is held that penetration of the system is too lengthy,
too complicated, or too expensive and that the probability of
catastrophic failure is reduced to a sufficiently low value.

Problems related to security and protection in computer
networks are still a research field. However, several studies
are already available and an analysis of these questions may be
found in [SHE75, IRI76b].

In CIGALE, it was decided that protection should cope with two
particular types of dangers : node system malfunctions, and
CIGALE service abuse.

a) Node system malfunctions

Protection against node malfunctions is based upon
self-monitoring mechanisms implemented in each node. Some of
these mechanisms are available from the standard MITRA 15
hardware. The others have been implemented in the CIGALE node
software.

In both cases, any trouble detected causes the node to stop
functioning immediately. This approach was taken for the
following reasons.

Stopping the node immediately allows to freeze it in a state
presumably not too far from the failure state. This is of a
considerable help in trouble-shooting of the node system.

Stopping the malfunctioning node causes its automatic isolation
from the rest of the network, i.e. as seen from its neighbours
and from the Network Control Center, it just does not exist
anymore. As a consequence, adaptive routing takes care
automatically of this topological change and keeps the network

functioning.

Keeping the malfunctioning node in operation could cause the whole network to malfunction or even to crash due to propagation mechanisms used in vital functions like adaptive routing, network time management and traffic control.

In addition a node may be forced to stop by an explicit request from an operator. This capability may be used for security reasons but also during regular network operation (e.g. to load a new software release). This explicit stop may be requested either via an appropriate manipulation of the MITRA 15 front panel keys or by using the appropriate DEBUG NIS command (see section 4.4.8).

Upon error detection or stop request the context of the machine (i.e. error code, registers, interrupt level, etc.) are saved in memory. Then the node system is stopped by giving control to a protected bootstrap program called HELP. The HELP program functions are reduced to a minimum set in order to make it as secure as possible. HELP is used to remote dump and/or remote load the node system from the Network Control Center. The mechanisms involved and the HELP functions are described together in section 4.5.2.

The most important troubles causing HELP to be given control are listed below :

- software detection

packet buffer pointer destroyed
queue control block inconsistency
task control block inconsistency
process control block inconsistency
event control block inconsistency
non-existent line number in the intra-node header field
checksum error in characteristic data of the node (i.e. node
    number, region number, hosts connected, etc.)
switch Module queue found full by a background process (while
    its queue is not empty the Switch Module runs with higher
    priority than any background process)
inexistent system service routine called
inexistent interrupt level activated
stop requested explicitly

- hardware detection

power supply failure
privileged instruction used in slave mode
memory protection violation
memory parity error
inexistent memory address accessed
inexistent instruction executed

microprogram error

b) CIGALE services abuse

It is quite obvious that considerable damage could be caused to
the network by inappropriate usage (intentional or not) of some
of the Network Internal Services (NIS) (e.g. DEBUG). The chosen
protection simply consists in controlling access to the NIS at
the network port.

Both direct and indirect services are requested by using either
the destination field or the facilities field of packets
entering   the   network.   Packets   may   enter CIGALE through two
types of entry points : host-node transmission lines and node
teleprinter (using the TTY NIS).

HOST-NODE TRANSMISSION LINES

To   each of the host-node transmission lines of the network are
associated both Indirect Services Access Rights (ISAR) and
Direct Services Access Rights (DSAR). As shown in the figure
4.4.9.(1), each bit of the ISAR and DSAR corresponds to one
service and specifies whether or not that service is allowed to
be accessed.

Each   time   a   packet   enters   the   network through a host-node
transmission line, the facilities field from the packet header
is matched against ISAR.

If   access   to any of the requested services is not allowed the
packet   is   just   switched   to   the   DROP NIS queue with an
appropriate error code set in the intra-node header. Otherwise,
the   destination   of   the   packet is checked for a CIGALE NIS :
this consists in checking both the "Destination PSN address"
and NIS address flag of the "Local Destination address" in the
packet header (see figure 4.2.3.(2) and 4.2.3.(4)). If the
packet   is   destined   to   a   CIGALE NIS, then the bit of DSAR
corresponding to the requested NIS number is checked and, if
access is not allowed, the packet is dropped.

In other cases, the packet is accepted into the network and the
requested services are provided.

At this point, it is to be noted that the system could still be
penetrated   due   to   the   lack   of   checking the source of the
entering packets : assuming that a host is allowed to access
the ECHO NIS it could also access the DEBUG NIS by a simple
trick : send a packet to the ECHO NIS with the source field set
to the DEBUG NIS address.

Therefore source checking is also necessary to guarantee the
correct behaviour of the NIS whenever they have to send packets
back to sources requesting service.

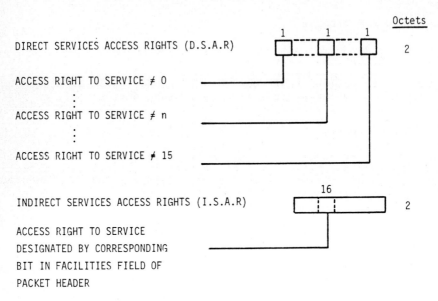

DIRECT SERVICES ACCESS RIGHTS (D.S.A.R)

ACCESS RIGHT TO SERVICE ≠ 0

ACCESS RIGHT TO SERVICE ≠ n

ACCESS RIGHT TO SERVICE ≠ 15

INDIRECT SERVICES ACCESS RIGHTS (I.S.A.R)

ACCESS RIGHT TO SERVICE
DESIGNATED BY CORRESPONDING
BIT IN FACILITIES FIELD OF
PACKET HEADER

Figure 4.4.9.(1) -   Services Access Rights structure

No particular problem arises about source checking since all the necessary information is already known in each node for adaptive routing purpose : to each of the host-node transmission lines of a node is associated the list of the Transport Stations and/or network addresses that are connected through that line. Thus a packet entering the network through a host-node line is accepted only if its source address belongs to the list corresponding to that line. Otherwise, it is just dropped. Note that in this case no DIAGNOSTIC packet is sent back to the source of the dropped packet since the specified source address is meaningless.

Another point is that CIGALE does not discriminate among the sources that share the same host-node transmission line : CIGALE guarantees that an incoming packet comes from the subset of addresses that are allowed to send packets over that line. But this does not necessarily mean that the packet really comes from the source address specified in the header. In other words the proper sharing of a host-node transmission line is the user's responsibility.

NODE TELEPRINTER

Regular users of the network are hosts. They are connected through transmission lines and are therefore all submitted to the protection control described in the previous paragraph. The node teleprinters are supposed to be exclusively reserved for testing, debugging, measuring, and operating purpose. People who are using them are supposed to be both competent and dependable. Therefore, it is essential to provide at least some of those people with totally unrestricted access through node teleprinters (e.g. for maintenance, NIS behaviour or error detection checking). However, unauthorized access to node teleprinters by unqualified persons must be anticipated. Thus, some appropriate protection is still required.

These considerations led to the conclusion that accessing the network through a node teleprinter should be either strictly forbidden or allowed without any restriction, depending on operator qualification. The solution for teleprinter access protection in CIGALE reflects this alternative : a specific key of the MITRA 15 front panel specifies whether or not the use of the teleprinter is allowed. If the key is off, the teleprinter remains blocked and the key has to be switched on to make it usable.

The access control is then based on the fact that the front panel key setting is reported to the Network Monitoring Service in STATISTICS packets (see sections 4.4.8 and 4.5.1) and any key setting change triggers an operator alarm in the Network Control Center. In case of unidentified intervention, the operator calls up the node site for further investigation.

This simple solution has been preferred to the classical password technique which requires considerable management sophistication in a distributed environment.

4.5. The Network Control Center (NCC)

The Network Control Center is not a particular component of the CIGALE network. Rather, this concept designates a particular place where specific resources are made available in order to operate the network. Two types of resources are used in the NCC : the NCC system and the operation team whose activities and structure are described in section 5.1.2.3.

The NCC hardware is a MITRA 15 whose configuration includes card reader, line printer, mass storage equipment and the corresponding software.

In fact, the NCC system is basically a regular CIGALE node in which particular functions needed for the network operation are implemented as additional NIS. In practice, this makes possible to load the NCC system into the hardware of a node for back-up purposes.

In addition, if the NCC system is not too loaded (e.g. in small networks) available resources can be used to perform regular node functions, including host connections.

The purpose of the following sections is to describe the additional NIS that implement the set of functions allowing to operate the network in the NCC system. They are the Network Monitoring Service, the Remote Load Service, and the Remote Dump Service.

4.5.1. Network Monitoring Service (NMS)

As seen in section 4.4.8, the STATISTICS NIS periodically sends a STATISTICS packet to the NMS. This packet contains data about the current state of the sending node (line status, front panel key setting, NIS status, etc.).

By analyzing these data the NMS can continually keep track of the global state of the network. Upon detecting any abnormal condition, it can trigger an alarm and print an appropriate diagnostic message for the NCC operators (see figure 4.5.1.(1)). An alarm triggers a ringing bell and a flashing light. These signals are maintained until acknowledged by an operator.

The following events cause an alarm to be triggered and an appropriate diagnostic message to be issued :

- any change in transmission line status (UP, DOWN)
- any change in front panel key setting
- no STATISTICS packets received from a node for more than 3 minutes
- STATISTICS packet received anew from a previously silent node

In addition to the STATISTICS packets the NMS can receive other packets whose text contain particular commands. The following commands are available :

A : Acknowledge operator alarm.

D : Display the present status of a line, a node, or all network components.

P : Print on the line printer of the NCC all STATISTICS packets received from a node or all nodes.

S : Stop printing received STATISTICS packets.

As any NIS, the NMS uses packets for all external communications. Since the TTY NIS allows the operator to enter any packet, the teleprinter of the NCC system is the basic tool used to operate the network. By convention, the NMS sends diagnostic messages to the source of the last received command packet, i.e. generally to the TTY NIS of the NCC system. However, this simple mechanism makes it very easy to use any other packet source (in particular any other TTY NIS) to operate the network, if the teleprinter of the NCC system is out of order.

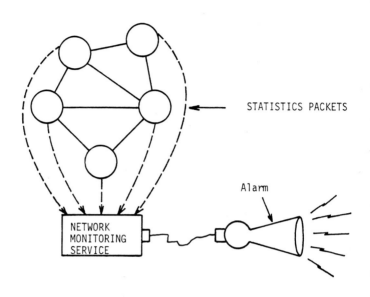

STATISTICS PACKETS

Alarm

NETWORK
MONITORING
SERVICE

Figure 4.5.1. (1)- STATISTICS packet transmission to the
Network Monitoring Service

The NMS´s behaviour is basically the same as that of any other
NIS : it is automatically activated when a packet is switched
into its queue. It then extracts the packet from the queue,
processes it, and waits for a new activation. Depending on the
received packet the following actions are performed.

STATISTICS packet

The received status is matched against the recorded status of
monitored components. If any change, the NMS triggers an alarm
and sends a packet containing the appropriate diagnostic
message (the source is set to the NMS address and the
destination is set to the source of the last command packet
received). Finally, the NMS updates the recorded status of the
components. If printing is requested (depending on its source)
the received STATISTICS packet (see command P packet below) is
printed, and the received packet buffer is released.

Command A packet

The alarm is stopped and the received packet buffer is released.

Command D packet

The received packet buffer is used to set up the following information : the destination is set to the source of the received packet, the source is set to NMS, and the requested component status is copied into the text. The packet is then attached to the Switch Module queue.

Command P packet

The source of the STATISTICS packet to be printed is recorded and the flag requesting printing is turned on. Then the received packet buffer is released.

Command S packet

The flag requesting printing of received STATISTICS packets is turned off and the received packet buffer is released.

N.B. Any erroneous command causes an appropriate error message to be sent back to the source of the received packet.

An additional time-out mechanism allows the NMS to verify that STATISTICS packets are being regularly received from all the nodes. As previously indicated, if no STATISTICS packets have been received from a node for more than 3 minutes, a diagnostic message is issued and an alarm is triggered. A possible reason is that the node system crashed.

However, the coincidence of several failures may cause the network to split into several sub-networks totally isolated from each other (i.e. unable to communicate) and possibly from the NMS. This illustrates the choice of distributing control functions such that each node or each sub-network keeps running properly even when it becomes isolated. This property is also essential to protect the network from NMS failures. Indeed the NMS´s role is normally passive ; each node is equipped with every mechanism judged necessary for its survival.

4.5.2. Remote Load Service (RLS)

Like the Network Monitoring Service, the RLS is implemented as an additional NIS of the CIGALE node system running in the NCC system. The purpose of the RLS is to provide for the capability of remotely loading the software system of any node in the network.

In addition to the RLS itself two other components are actually
involved in a remote load operation : the HELP bootstrap
program, located in the node to be reloaded, and the AID NIS
located in one of its neighbour nodes (see figure 4.5.2.(1)).

A : Node to be reloaded

B : Neighbour of A

C : NCC System

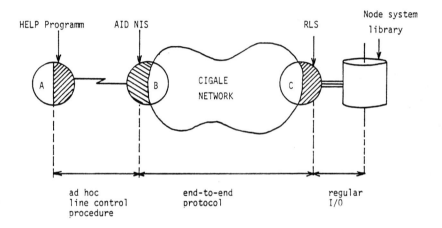

Figure 4.5.2.(1) - Component organisation in a remote load operation

The next paragraph describes the basic principle of a remote
load operation and the actions performed in each of the
components involved.

4.5.2.1. Basic principle

When a remote load operation is triggered (by means of a
request packet sent to the RLS, see RLS description below), the
RLS sends a command to the AID NIS, which sends an
initialization order to the HELP program, waits for the
acknowledgement and sends a report packet back to the RLS. The
purpose of this initialization procedure is to check and set up
the RLS-AID-HELP path before starting the remote load itself.

If everything is all right, the RLS starts to read the system of the node to be reloaded from the mass storage containing the node systems library. Each data block read from the library is put into a packet and sent to the AID NIS.

The AID NIS extracts the block from the received packet and transmits it to the HELP program, which loads it into the node memory. The acknowledgement then transmitted back from HELP to AID causes an acknowledgement packet to be sent back to RLS. The RLS keeps on sending packets until the end of the remote load operation. An appropriate packet is then sent to the AID NIS, forwarded to the HELP program, which transfers control to the newly loaded system.

4.5.2.2. Reliability aspects

Since errors in loading could cause the node to crash or, even worse, to behave inpredictably, particular attention has been given to the reliability aspects of the remote load operation. This concerns particularly the following points :

a)   RLS-AID communication

Both RLS and AID exchange information according to an end-to-end protocol which is comparable to the Transport Protocol used by CYCLADES hosts (see section 3.2) : it provides for error control by means of packet sequencing, end-to-end acknowledgements, and retransmission time-outs. In addition, a checksum is associated with each data block in the system library and transmitted within remote load packets from RLS to AID. Thus, AID performs an end-to-end error check which guards against the possibility of packet alteration happening in an intermediate node memory. (Line handling procedures already take care of errors occurring on intermediate transmission lines).

b)   AID-HELP communication

AID and HELP communicate directly through a transmission line. They use an "ad hoc" line handling procedure conceived to be both very simple and extremely safe : in addition to the classical Cyclic Redundancy Check (CRC), the two following rules are observed.

HELP acknowledges all received orders by sending them back to AID without any change. AID can therefore match the received information against the original and detect discrepancies.

Both the starting address and the length of a data block to be loaded are first sent and acknowledged using the above safety mechanism. Afterwards, the data block is sent and acknowledged separately. This is intended to prevent the destruction of any

memory area that is already correctly loaded, by making sure
that a data block is going to occupy the right place in the
node memory before loading it.

c) HELP program

HELP is given control when the node stops operating after
having detected some trouble. In order to minimize the risk of
HELP program destruction, due to some node system malfunction,
the following actions are taken.

As soon as it is loaded (via the paper tape reader of the node
teletype) the HELP program protects itself using the regular
memory protection system of the MITRA 15. This mechanism traps
most instructions which attempt to access the protected memory
area. When trapped the node system stops and transfers control
to HELP. (Unfortunately some supervisor routines must run
without protection due to a hardware oddity).

A checksum is associated with the invariant part of the HELP
program (instructions and data). This checksum is checked by
HELP each time it is given control. In case of error HELP stops
and must be reloaded from paper tape. This is safer than taking
the risk of unpredictable HELP malfunctions.

4.5.2.3. HELP Program functions

When activated (see section 4.4.9) HELP checks its checksum
(see above) and starts listening to transmission lines of the
node : it is necessary to provide the ability to reload a node
through several lines, i.e. various neighbours. As already
mentioned, HELP receives orders from AID, processes them and
sends them back to AID. The following AID orders are provided.

START

Select the line receiving START for the remote load. This
causes any order received from another line to be disregarded
(except START). A START order overrides at any time any
previously received START order (i.e. a new line may be
selected).

ADDRESS

Record the memory address and block length which define the
area where the data of the next LOAD order are to be loaded.

LOAD

Load the received data into the area defined by the last
ADDRESS order received.

STOP

Stop remote load. This causes any further order received from any line to be disregarded (except START).

GO

End of remote load : transfer control to the newly loaded system.

A few errors (e.g. unknown order, address out of bound) are detected by HELP. They are equivalent to receiving a STOP order. Appropriate error codes are sent back to AID, which forwards them to RLS.

4.5.2.4. AID NIS functions

The AID NIS receives command packets sent by the RLS in its queue. The AID NIS processes the commands received and sends answer packets to the RLS. There are three types of answers transmitted with appropriate parameters : acknowledgements (ACK), negative acknowledgements (NACK), and errors (ERROR). The following commands are processed.

START

The START command indicates which line of the node is to be used for the remote load operation. The AID NIS then instructs the regular line handling process to release that line and then takes it over. A START order is sent to HELP, the acknowledgement is ckecked and an ACK answer is sent back to RLS.

LOAD

This command contains a data block to be loaded. The AID NIS then checks the data block checksum. In case of error it sends back a NACK answer. Packet sequencing is also checked : if duplicated, the packet is dropped and an ACK is sent back. Otherwise, an ADDRESS order with the data block address and length is transmitted to HELP, followed by a LOAD order with the data block itself. Upon acknowledgement from HELP an ACK answer is sent to RLS.

STOP

A STOP order is transmitted to HELP. Acknowledgement from HELP causes an ACK answer to be returned to RLS. The AID NIS then releases the transmission line which returns under control of the regular line handling process.

GO

Same as the STOP command except that a GO order is transmitted
to HELP.

When AID waits for acknowledgement from HELP a time-out is set.
If it elapses, AID triggers the retransmission of the last
order to HELP. When a maximum number of retransmissions is
reached, the remote load is stopped : the transmission line is
released and ERROR answer sent back to RLS. Errors detected by
HELP cause also the remote load to be stopped. The same applies
if an unknown command is received by AID ; then a STOP order is
sent to HELP.

4.5.2.5. RLS functions

The RLS receives packets containing requests related to the
remote load operation in its queue. It extracts packets from
its queue, processes the requests and sends back response
packets to the source. There are two types of responses :
acknowledgements (ACK) and errors (ERROR). There are also two
types of requests : LOAD and STOP.

LOAD

In addition to the identification of the node system to be
picked up from the library, this request indicates   the
neighbour node and the line that must serve to reach the node
to be loaded. The LOAD request causes RLS to send a START
command to the AID NIS of the chosen neighbour node with the
chosen line number. When the ACK answer is received from AID,
an ACK response is sent to the source of the LOAD request. Then
the first data block of the node system to be loaded is read
from the library, and sent to AID in a LOAD command packet.
Retransmission is triggered on receiving a NACK answer from
AID. Receiving an ACK answer causes to read the next data block
from the library and to send it to AID.

When the last data block has been transmitted, a GO command is
sent to AID. On receiving the ACK answer, the RLS sends back an
ACK response to the source of the LOAD request and stops.

If any unrecoverable I/O error occurs in accessing the library,
then a STOP command is sent to AID, and the ACK answer causes
an ERROR response to be sent back to the source of the LOAD
request. The remote load is then stopped.

STOP

The remote load operation can be stopped at any time by this
request. When a STOP request is received, the RLS sends a STOP
command to AID, waits for the ACK answer and sends an ACK

response to the source of the STOP request.

For both LOAD and STOP requests, a retransmission time-out also controls the waiting delay for ACK/NACK answers from AID. If a maximum number of transmissions is reached, then an ERROR response is sent to the source of the LOAD request and the remote load is stopped. The same applies, if any ERROR answer is received from AID.

4.5.2.6. Remote load "in vivo"

A particular parameter of the LOAD request informs the RLS that remote load is to be performed "in vivo". In this case, no line is indicated in the LOAD request and AID does not take over any line. Instead of driving the remote load of the neighbour by means of orders sent to HELP, AID works directly in the memory of the node where it is running. This simple capability allows one to change parts of the node software without stopping its operation. This is particularly convenient to load overlays or to update the artificial Traffic Definition Table (see section 4.4.8).

4.5.2.7. Automatic remote load

The previous paragraphs mentioned that the RLS, like any NIS, communicates with its external environment by means of requests and responses transported in packets. At present, any remote load operation is decided by a human operator and RLS request packets are therefore simply created by using the TTY NIS of the NCC system, or any other if the NCC teleprinter is out of order.

However, the packet interface of the RLS makes it possible to drive it from any NIS or host (assuming appropriate access rights) and particularly from a process capable of making automatically suitable remote load decisions. Obviously, the network monitoring service would be in the best position to do this.

Operating the network in such an automatic mode could make the work of the operation team more comfortable (e.g. during nights and week ends) and could increase the quality of service of the network.

The study of the questions related to automatic remote load has been undertaken and it could be implemented in CIGALE in the future.

4.5.3. Remote Dump Service (RDS)

The purpose of the RDS is to provide for the capability of remotely dumping the memory of any node of the network.

This facility is obviously used for debugging purposes : after a node system crash a remote dump is generally performed before remotely loading the node software.

The mechanisms involved in a remote dump operation are mostly the same as in a remote load. Differences are that RDS has to handle either a dump file or a line printer rather than a node systems library and that some slight modifications to the AID-HELP dialogue are necessary for data to travel in the reverse direction.

All the characteristics described for the remote load in the previous section apply to the remote dump : components (AID, HELP), functions, reliability. Finally, the remarks made about remote load "in vivo" and automatic remote load are also applicable to remote dump "in vivo" and automatic remote dump.

4.6. Software Production and Debugging

The CIGALE node software development began in mid-1973 on the IRIS 80 of the IRIA computing centre. Cross processors and file systems on the IRIS 80 were used to produce MITRA 15 code to be executed on the node machine.

Since the MITRA 15 was at that time a fairly new machine, no high level language cross-compiler was available on the IRIS 80. Thus, the CIGALE software had to be written in assembly language, using a simple-minded - single-pass cross-assembler (the only one available). In order to make it more comfortable, a macro-processor was used extensively to generate automatically system tables, subroutine calls entries/exits, pieces of code, etc.

Other usual processors (text editor, cross-link editor, library manager, etc.) allowed us to produce binary code on the IRIS 80 and to load, execute and debug it on the MITRA 15.

In addition to debugging facilities provided by the CIGALE services themselves (e.g. DEBUG, ECHO, TRACE) some classical debugging tools were implemented in the node system, including snapshots, traps, and of course... dumps.

4.7. Implementation Figures

The figures given in this section are indeed related to a very specific implementation on the MITRA 15. However, they might be useful to interested readers to estimate efforts and resources that might be required to implement a packet switching node system.

The size of a CIGALE node memory is 24 K words of 16 bits. Fixed length instructions are 16 bits long and fit into words. Up to 14 synchronous full-duplex transmission lines can be connected to a node. Figures given below are related to a typical node configuration consisting of 11 lines, including 3 lines operated in MV8 and 8 lines operated in TMM.

Software components	Memory size (in words)
System tables	1 850
System routines (event, queue, clock, time-outs management)	1 930
Utilities and debugging tools	660
Transmissions (11 lines)	5 450
Switch Module	1 070
DROP NIS	110
ECHO NIS	60
TTY NIS	1 560
DEBUG NIS	870
TRAFFIC NIS	580
TIME NIS	60
Indirect services (TRACE, PROBE, ROUTE)	290
CHOKE NIS	70
TIMAN NIS	460
ROUTE NIS	880
STATISTIC NIS	380
Self Monitoring and HELP bootstrap	920
AID NIS	990
TOTAL NODE SOFTWARE SIZE	18 190
Packet buffer size	144

Number of available packet buffers :

(24 K- software size)/buffer size = 44 buffers

Fewer lines are connected to the Network Control Center system
but it is equipped with a 28 K word memory in order to
accomodate additional functions (see section 4.5). Following
figures correspond to a 5-line configuration (2 operated in MV8
and 3 in TMM).

Software components	Memory size (in words)
Regular node software size	18 190
Regular node transmission (11 lines)	5 450
Network Control Centre transmissions (5 lines)	3 830
Network Monitoring Service	3 140
Remote Load service	1 270
Remote Dump service	870
TOTAL NETWORK CONTROL CENTRE SOFTWARE SIZE	21 850
Packet buffer size	144

Number of available packet buffers :

(28 K - software size/buffer size : 47 buffers

4.8. Conclusions

As it must now be apparent to the reader, the software of a
CIGALE node contains rather sophisticated functions, mainly for
network management, supervision, and maintenance. However,
sophistication is in no way detrimental to reliability. On the
contrary, all node functions have been designed and implemented
as autonomous sub-systems, to ease maintenance and to enhance
robustness. As impredictable hardware malfunctions could
destroy software reliability, additional redundancy checks have
been planted wherever it was felt that severe consequences
could occur. As a result, CIGALE is a highly resilient system,
even without hardware redundancy.

CHAPTER 5

CONNECTION OF HOSTS, TERMINALS AND NETWORKS

5.1. Introduction

5.1.1. Project environment

One objective of CYCLADES was to permit extensive experiments in networking in a realistic context. This implied that a sizeable number of applications and services had to be offered on the network to a large population of users.

In order to reach this objective with minimum investment, the strategy chosen for CYCLADES was to use existing hardware and software products as much as possible, while concentrating the effort on specific problems of networking and on the integration of existing systems in the network.

Modifications to existing hardware and software were carefully analyzed, taking into account not only the development effort, but also possible consequences on future maintenance problems. The resulting decision was to use only standard hardware and to modify standard software only when maintenance of the modified version could be guaranteed. Otherwise, interface converters were used to adapt systems to CYCLADES standards.

Later on, when interconnecting CYCLADES with other networks, the same constraint was faced (no modification of the networks) and gateways were used to adapt networks to each other.

Specific implementation choices made for the various parts of CYCLADES are presented in the following sections.

5.1.2. Implementation alternatives

a) Hosts

The simplest case of host connection corresponds to the situation where all host software relating to the network has to be developed, i.e., the overall structure of the host networking software can still be chosen. This was the case for terminal concentrators (see section 5.3) and partly for hosts with new applications to be developed. The usual approach there has been to implement a network access method within the host to handle network protocols (in particular the Transport Protocol and the Virtual Terminal Protocol). This network access method was then used directly by new applications.

The problem of host connection was more difficult when existing products, namely services intended for local terminals, had to be adapted to network protocols. Two major types of solutions were used : the internal adaptation and the external adaptation.

The internal adaptation was used each time it was possible to modify an existing access method, 1) without modifying its interface with application programs, and 2) with the assurance that the new access method could actually be maintained on a quasi-commercial basis. This technique was used in particular for the IRIS 80 (see section 5.2.1) and the IBM 360/67 (see section 5.2.2).

The external adaptation was used each time it was not desirable to modify the host software. This was in particular the case for a number of centres which considered networking only as a part of their activity, which should in no case perturb the rest. These centres very much favoured the external adaptation where the network is connected to the host as a set of local terminals emulated by an interface converter, which looks like a host on the network side, i.e., handles network protocols. In other words, the interface converter pretends to offer services to network users, but subcontracts the work to the host, in pretending to be a set of local users. The implementation of interface converters is presented in section 5.4.1.

b) Terminals

In the CYCLADES architecture, terminals are viewed as specific applications. Like any other application, they have to use the Transport Protocol and the Virtual Terminal Protocol, i.e., a terminal must behave as a host.

Some intelligent terminals have therefore been modified to handle network protocols instead of host specific procedures (see section 5.5).

Dumb terminals have been connected to terminal concentrators which 1) provide users with local assistance (e.g. editing), 2) handle network protocols on the network side, and 3) do the proper mapping between the terminal side and the network side.

Although, in specific cases, some hosts act as terminal concentrators (see section 5.2), the choice was made in CYCLADES to have terminal concentrators implemented in dedicated mini-computers. The rationale for not integrating terminal concentrator software in hosts is similar to the rationale presented in a) above for networking software. In

addition, it was also decided not to integrate terminal
concentrator software in the packet switching nodes, in order
to keep nodes simple, reliable and stable. On the contrary,
some terminal concentrators have been expanded with a
simplified packet switching function for the benefit of local
hosts.

The MITRA 15, already used for nodes, was also used as the
terminal concentrator. Other mini or micro-computers were also
used as well. The implementation of terminal concentrators is
presented in section 5.3.

c) Networks

The interconnection of CYCLADES with other networks raises
problems similar to connecting hosts to CYCLADES (protocol
conversion) plus new problems (e.g., routing). A major
constraint was that these networks, like some hosts, could not
be internally modified. Therefore, gateways were used to
provide external adaptation of other networks to CYCLADES
standards. The similarity of gateway functions with interface
converters functions (see b) above) permitted most of their
respective software to be identical. Therefore, some gateways
were implemented as modified interface converters.
Micro-computers were also used as gateways.

Implementation of gateways is presented in section 5.4.2.

5.2. HOSTS

5.2.1. IRIS 80 - SIRIS 8

5.2.1.1. Semantics of the SIRIS 8 Operating System

The SIRIS 8 operating system [CII72] is a multiprogramming
operating system. It provides users with simultaneous batch
and time-sharing services. The approach chosen to design the
adaptation of this system to network protocols consisted in
describing both the system and the network in terms of logical
entities which model their functioning, and then decide the
mapping between system entities and network entities. We shall
give a description of system entities and then describe the
chosen mappings of these entities onto network entities. In
our description we will adopt conventions used in the data base
field (see figure 5.2.1.(1)).

Service oriented entities and their relations constitute the
functional view of the system as seen from external users.
Then, processing oriented entities and their relations describe
the internal architecture of the system. Then, relations
between entities of these two domains describe how the system
operates to achieve the specific services.

a) Service oriented entities

The system is known to the users as a set of subsystems. SIRIS 8 provides for two subsystems : the batch subsystem (SSBT) and the time-sharing subsystem (SSTS).

A subsystem may present several types of logical I-O devices called entries, each entry being associated with a set of formats and synchronization parameters.

SSTS can be connected through the interactive console (CN) entry. SSBT presents three different entries : the CN entry handles operators' dialogue, the CR entry accepts card-reader-like connections, and the LP entry accepts line-printer connections.

Entries allow users to generate jobs (through SSBT/CN, SSBT/CR, SSTS/CN entries), which are a sequence of job control commands. The SSTS/CN entry allows users to set up sessions during which session commands are processed interactively.

It is a feature of SIRIS 8 that the session commands and the job control commands are the same. This homogeneity means that all derived entities (like catalogs, files, labels) are identical and can be stored by interactive sessions and batch jobs. These jobs produce a set of results to be sent to an output device attached to an LP entry. These results are referred to as op-labels.

From the system point of view a user is associated with a (remote) station identified by a station name. Each op-label may be assigned to a queue, which in turn is associated with the station where the results should go. The assignment of a queue to a station is a system parameter which can be modified by operator control commands.

The diagram in figure 5.2.1.(1) shows the relations between service oriented entities.

b) Processing oriented entities

The processing unit in the SIRIS 8 multiprogramming system is called a task. A task may be a system, user, or foreground user task. Tasks can be created, killed and observed through system primitives.

An intertask communication facility is provided based upon the mailbox entity. A set of mailbox management primitives allows the passing of messages between tasks. System task communication requires initial synchronization which is called a connection. Figure 5.2.1.(2) shows the relations between processing oriented entities.

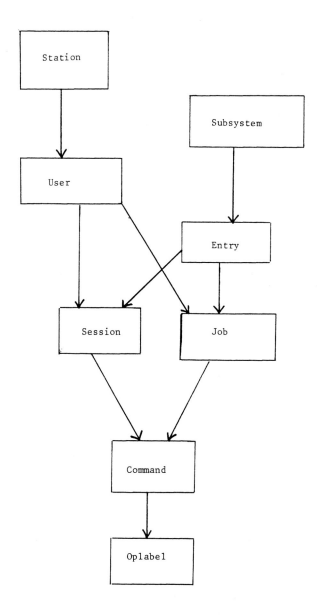

Figure 5.2.1.(1) - Relations between service oriented entities (an arrow corresponds to a 1 : 1 or 1 : n relation)

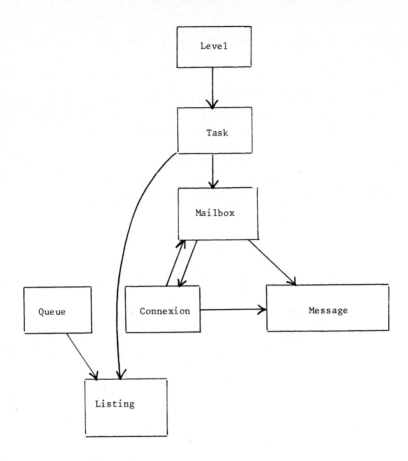

Figure 5. 2. 1. (2) - Relations between processing oriented entities

c) Mapping of service entities onto processing entities

Figure 5.2.1.(3) shows the relations between service entities and processing entities.

The system initiates a number of basic tasks, corresponding to the available subsystems. Each entry is given a mailbox name. The SSBT task accepts users connections to the SSBT/CN entry and creates CR/LP tasks through dialogue on the CN entry connection. The CR task (spool-in) interprets incoming commands and creates job-tasks using the job control language interpreter and scheduler. The SSTS subsystem task accepts users connections and handles corresponding connections, a mailbox being dedicated to this task. The session task interprets messages as JCL commands, accesses catalogs and may produce results and jobs. Each result can be assigned to a queue by JCL commands.

5.2.1.2. Introducing network entities

The goal of the adaptation is to offer to network users access to system functions. In other words, the problem is to map some of the service entities onto network entities (e.g., liaisons, virtual terminals ports). This is the reason for the interest to describe the system in terms of its offered services rather than through its internal structure. As an example the mapping of entry/connection onto port/liaison does not have the same meaning as the mapping of mailbox/task onto port/liaison.

The way in which services concepts are interpreted by network machines makes up a protocol specific to this application. The set of conventions for using a system when the system is accessed through a network must be changed. This is due to the larger variety of physical terminals which may be used on the network.

On the other hand, implementation of the network machines (the transport station access and functions) has to be defined in terms of system processing entities.

a) Interpretation of service entities

Usually users communicate with subsystems by means of terminals. It was then natural that a network user be seen as a cluster of virtual terminals. In the reference structure a virtual terminal is mapped onto a port entity of the transport machine. We have then a first set of relations :

```
one to one    :  SYSTEM      - TRANSPORT STATION
one to one    :  ENTRY       - PORT
one to one    :  SESSION     - LIAISON
m to n        :  COMMAND     - LETTER
one to one    :  ATTENTION   - TELEGRAM
```

The COMMAND-LETTER m to n relation is worth being detailed. The one to one following equivalences have been adopted :

SESSION COMMAND	—	VIRTUAL LINE
SESSION COMMAND GROUP	—	VIRTUAL PAGE
DISPLAYABLE LINE	—	VIRTUAL LINE
CARD	—	VIRTUAL LINE
PRINTABLE LINE	—	VIRTUAL LINE

thus:

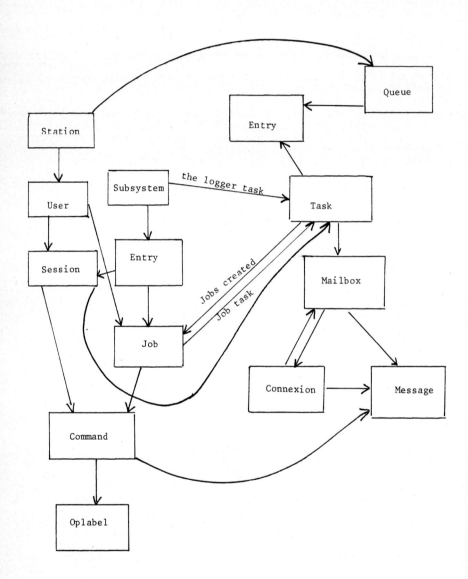

Figure 5.2.1.(3) - Relation between service entities and processing
               entities

```
          PRINTABLE PAGE          -         VIRTUAL PAGE

          JOB INPUT FILE          -         VIRTUAL PAGE

          SCREEN                  -         VIRTUAL PAGE
  thus:
          JOB STREAM              -         VIRTUAL PAGES

          LISTING                 -         VIRTUAL PAGES
```

Note : These entities are specific to SIRIS 8 and are
mentioned here for the benefit of those familiar with the
system.

The above definitions call for some comments :

> There is no network entity corresponding directly to the
> SUBSYSTEM entity since there is no group-of-port entity in
> the network. Actually a subsystem can be identified by its
> CN entry. A connection to a subsystem is obtained by
> connecting to the CN entry. Furthermore, the system
> rejects the connection of a card reader if a control
> terminal has not been connected.

> Similarly, a transport station is a group of virtual
> terminals. On the other hand, a SIRIS 8 STATION is
> represented by a set of ports, thus a transport station.
> In this implementation it is not possible to define
> several STATIONS with the same transport station address.

b) Implementation of the network machines

Two layers had to be implemented, the transport station and the
virtual terminal layer. We also intended to provide user tasks
with access to transport facilities. The m to n relation
between commands and letters implies queueing. Therefore, the
transport machine had to be implemented as an asynchronous task
rather than subroutines. In order to get maximum independence
from the internal construction of the system, the transport
station is a user task. Furthermore, considering the fact that
some asynchronism exists between letters and packets, and
between letters and commands, the transport function and
virtual terminal functions are implemented as asynchronous
processes. Process management and buffer allocation use a
special monitor called SYNCOP [SEG75].

The architecture of the SIRIS 8 network adaptation task, called
CYCLIRIS, is shown in figure 5.2.1.(4). It consists of :

The SYNCOP multiprocess monitor which interfaces SIRIS 8 using
a multiple wait primitive on external events (transmission
events, mailbox events, clock events), and reflects them to
waiting processes.

A set of processes which interface the system mailbox management (access to SSBT and SSTS subsystems), and transport station access, which interprets the subsystem entities (commands, entries, connections) as virtual terminal entities and maps them onto letters, ports and liaisons.

A single process implementing user access to transport functions through user mailboxes. Different user access interfaces have been developed. It was necessary to provide users with assembly language primitives for existing applications such as user subsystems (i.e., SOCRATE [CII77] or STRATEGE [CII76]). On the other hand, it was necessary to provide users (distributed application programmers) with transport primitives available within high level languages.

The following sections detail each part of the implementation.

5.2.1.3. Transport Station description

As a key part of the implementation the transport station was designed to be shared by system and user tasks. It was desirable to provide programmers with a transport access method offering asynchronous primitives. Rather than having the user processes wait on some form of event, we preferred to introduce coroutines specified by the user and called asynchronously by the transport station. This type of interface is independent from the system synchronization tools and therefore constitutes a better approach towards portable specifications. This interface was made available to PL1 programs [DEC77].

a) Description of entities and primitives

A description of entities and primitives appearing at this interface is given below :

```
┌─────────────────┬──────────────────────────────────────────┐
│ entities        │ attributes                               │
│.................│..........................................│
│   port          │   port name                              │
│   site          │   site name                              │
│   liaison       │   local reference, remote reference      │
│                 │   flow control pointers                  │
│   letter        │   reference, length, text                │
│   telegram      │   value                                  │
└─────────────────┴──────────────────────────────────────────┘
```

Transport entities and their attributes

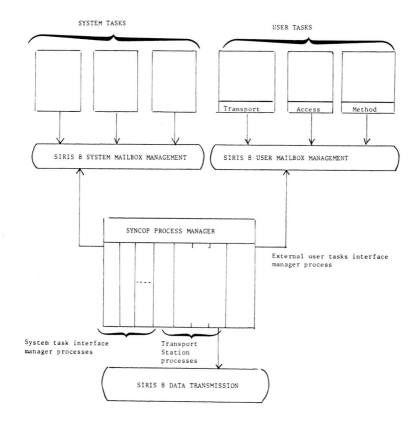

Figure 5.2.1.(4) - Architecture of the SIRIS 8 Network adaptation (CYCLIRIS)

Primitives	Parameters	Associated coroutines and their parameters
OPEN	port	LOGON (local port, remote port)
CLOSE	port	
CONNECT	liaison, local port, remote port, site	RCONNECT (liaison)
DISCONNECT	liaison, reason	RUPTURE (liaison, reason)
READ	liaison, length, reference	RREAD (liaison, reference, letter)
WRITE	liaison, length, reference, letter	RWRITE (liaison, reference)
ACTIV	liaison	RTELEG (liaison, telegram value)
SUSP	liaison	
TELEG	liaison, telegram value	

Transport station interface primitives

For example, the CONNECT primitive introduces user-written
RCONNECT and RUPTURE coroutines (or procedures) to be called
with proper parameters on connection set up or connection

closure. The READ primitive introduces the user-written READ
coroutine called with a "letter" parameter when a letter is
delivered.

b) Implementation

Each interface primitive calls a library routine which encodes
the request as a request-command-block enqueued in a SEND
queue, handled by a SEND process. The request is executed by
several cooperating processes. At termination time
(acknowledgement received or time-out) one of these transport
processes calls the specified termination coroutine.

The list of processes in the Transport Station is given below :

SEND : makes packets from user requests and issues WRITE
packet requests.

RECEIVE : handles input packets and may call user coroutines.

WRITE : handles an output queue to the network.

READ : handles an input queue from the network depending on
the amount of buffers freed by the RECEIVE process.

TIME-OUT : manages time-out events attached to requests.

SURVEY : activated periodically, monitors activity on liaisons
and causes termination when failures have been detected at any
level.

c) Multiprotocol features

Due to the experimental nature of the network, the transport
protocol went through two successive stages of definition, and
other modifications are likely to appear in the future. It
seemed sensible to make our implementation open to new
protocols, provided that the user access to transport service
remained unchanged (or semantically equivalent).

The SIRIS 8 implementation of the transport station allows
several transport protocols to share several transmission
lines, each of which may be connected to different networks but
with the same CIGALE packet format for all, as a temporary
restriction.

The transport protocol is implemented as a pair of processes
(SEND, RECEIVE) while a transmission line is handled by a pair
of READ, WRITE processes. The choice of the output line is
based on the remote address. The choice of the transport
protocol for input packets must be based only on the packet
header. This implied that a protocol be associated with a
single transport station address. Figure 5.2.1.(5) gives an

overview of the transport station architecture. The transport protocol to be used is specified during liaison set up by the user or by transport processes.

The output selector determines the output lines to be used for each packet. This is based on lists of transport station addresses associated with each line. Other parameters such as tariffs, load, speed, could be taken into account. In the present implementation only up-down status is examined. This provides for some kind of alternative routing when transport stations can be reached through separate transmission lines. The list of transport station addresses associated with each output line is fixed before initiation of the CYCLIRIS task.

5.2.1.4. Interface to subsystem tasks

The subsystem task adapter maps entry or connection requests onto transport access primitives, and on the other hand coroutine calls from transport station onto entry connection responses.

Each connection is represented by an individual process associated with a context which maintains equivalence between entities and handles the queue necessary for command-to-letter mapping. Figure 5.2.1.(6) describes the structure of the connection adaptation. The connection context contains the following items :

- entry name
- subsystem name
- connection reference
- liaison identification
- transport protocol type
- virtual terminal parameters
- command format parameters
- connection request queue
- received letters queue

Several connection contexts can be attached to a single entry. An entry context contains the following attributes :

- entry name
- subsystem name
- port name of transport station
- maximum number of possible connections
- connection context list
- actual number of connections

An entry process is created at subsystem initialization. It opens a port and on each call of the LOGON routine creates a connection process.

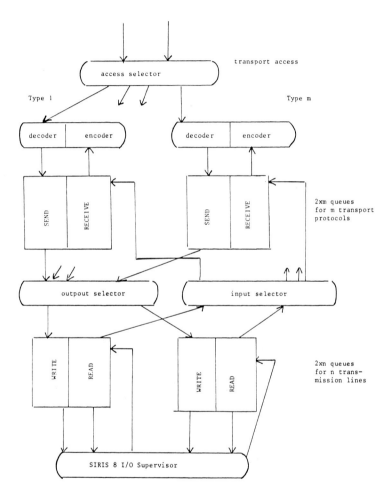

Figure 5.2.1.(5) - Multiprotocol selectors

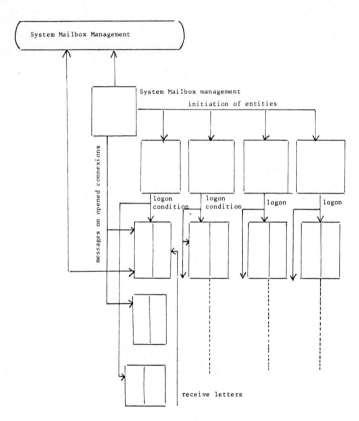

Figure 5.2.1.(6) - Tree structure of system mailboxes to transport adaptator

5.2.1.5. Interface to user tasks

SIRIS 8 was considered mainly as a system offering services (subsystems). However, this view does not cover distributed application capabilities whereby several components of an application cooperate through network communication tools. Although problems of distributed applications had not been extensively investigated, it was our opinion that experiments would develop only if access to network functions were easy to program. This implied that access primitives should be integrated in a high level language. However, it is obvious that transport would introduce asynchronism in a model where it is generally invisible. In order to handle an asynchronous environment some specific tools were necessary. Our approach was to provide within PL/1 the possibility of specifying delayed actions (coroutines) to be triggered at the termination of transport primitives. These actions are described as regular PL/1 procedures.

This approach is similar to event driven programming in real-time or transaction oriented systems. One might argue that a better approach should be based on independent processes and distributed synchronization tools. Although such more sophisticated concepts might prove attractive, they have not yet matured to the point of becoming operational. Techniques adopted within CYCLIRIS are more basic and lead to very simple implementation. This is a practical way to bootstrap real experiments and acquire better insight into distributed synchronization problems.

5.2.1.6. Other implementations on IRIS 80

a) A data base server : SOCRATE

SOCRATE [CII77] is a data-base management system developed by a research team of Grenoble University and marketed by CII-HB and the software house ECA-Automation. SOCRATE is a specific conversational system coexisting with other services on the IRIS 80 ; it has its own local terminal management using the host terminal management system directly. SOCYCRATE (short form for SOCRATE-CYCLADES) is a version of SOCRATE which simultaneously accepts network and local users. For the data base system, SOCYCRATE represents an increase in the number of potential users, without modification of local habits. For the network users, SOCYCRATE represents a new server available from any terminal connected to CYCLADES and operating through the Virtual Terminal Protocol (VTP).

The SOCYCRATE implementation consists in the integration of the VTP as an additional terminal management module. SOCYCRATE uses the transport station external interface available for users like SOCRATE (see section 5.2.1.4). The transport station and SOCRATE are executed by two tasks under the SIRIS 8 system and communicate by a set of mailbox primitives.

The structure of SOCYCRATE is illustrated in figure 5.2.1.(7).

Considered as an experiment, SOCYCRATE is not an operational
product. Nevertheless several demonstrations have proved that
the response time is adequate for the interactive use.

b) A multi-connection concentrator

The multi-connection concentrator (also termed "intelligent
concentrator") allows users to simultaneously access different
servers on the network. Its main function is to multiplex on a
single real terminal several virtual terminals each connected
to a network server. Each connection links a virtual terminal
to a server port. All connections established for one user can
therefore be multiplexed on his real terminal (see figure
5.2.1.(8)). This can be used for instance to monitor batch
processing on one or several servers and simultaneously be in a
time sharing session with another server [FOU78].

The most important problem is that the user must be able to
specify the destination of the commands he sends and identify
the origin of the responses he receives. These distinctions are
made possible by prefixes specifying the active connection.

For this purpose a discriminant identifier is associated with
each connection. It is used to recognize a set of commands and
responses. This mechanism is inadequate for highly interactive
servers, since specifying the server associated with each
message adds too much overhead and inconvenience.

An alternative would consist in dividing the display into
areas, each corresponding to a connection. This mechanism is
possible as long as the areas remain sufficiently large.

5.2.2. IBM 360/67

5.2.2.1. IBM 360/67 Environment

Two operating systems are alternately used on the IBM 360/67 of
the University of Grenoble : an interactive system (CP/67) and
a batch system (ASP-OS/MVT).

a) CP/67
CP/67 is a virtual machine generator. For each user, a virtual
machine simulates the hardware of an IBM 360. Each virtual
machine has its own configuration : core storage, and virtual
units (card readers and punches, line printers, disk drives,
terminals) which simulate real units as seen from an IBM 360.

The configuration of a virtual machine must contain an
operator´s console used to drive the virtual machine. The
standard operator´s console for a virtual machine is the
IBM 1052 which is simulated either on a TTY or an IBM 2741.

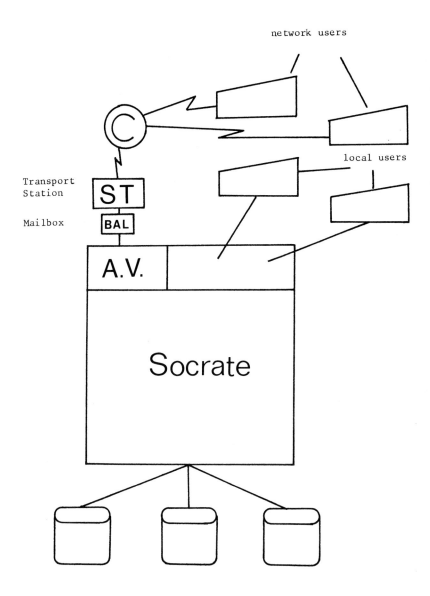

Figure 5.2.1. (7) - SOCYCRATE Structure

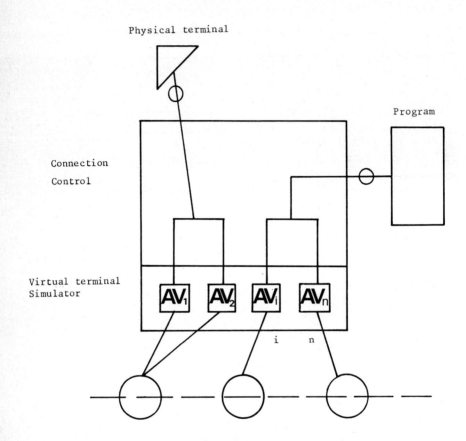

Physical terminal

Program

Connection
Control

Virtual terminal
Simulator

Servers

Figure 5.2.1. (8) - Tne multiconnection   concentrator
structure

Two methods are used by CP/67 to simulate peripheral units   for
virtual machines :

Virtual tape units, line controllers and interactive terminals
are mapped onto real units on a one to one basis, for the   time
they are used by a virtual machine.

A spool is used to simulate card readers, card punches and line printers : I/O traffic from a virtual machine to such a unit is translated by CP/67 into I/O traffic on files representing the virtual units. This is of course not visible from the virtual machine.

The communication means between virtual machines provided by CP/67 uses the spool. The virtual punch or printer of a virtual machine can be dynamically associated by the user with the virtual reader of another virtual machine. Thus, cards or lines written in the spool by one machine can be read by another one on its virtual reader.

Since a virtual machine behaves like the hardware of an IBM 360, each user can load his virtual machine with the operating system of his choice. The most popular system is CMS (Cambridge Monitor System), an interactive uni-programming system.

b) ASP/OS-MVT
OS-MVT (Operating System-Multiprogramming with a Variable number of Tasks) [FOU76] forms the basis of the batch system. The ASP sub-system (Attached Support Processor) running as an OS task manages job submission to OS-MVT as follows :

- it reads jobs from local units and RJE terminals,

- it manages the input job queues,

- it simulates to OS an operator's console and controls the set of local or remote consoles allowing users to access ASP services,

- it requests the operator to mount magnetic tapes or disks necessary for execution of jobs,

- it manages output listing queues and prints them on local units or RJE terminals.

The objective of connecting the IBM 360/67 to CYCLADES was twofold :

- Both services (CP/67 and ASP/OS-MVT) should be offered to remote network users. In other words the IBM 360 should act as a server for the benefit of the network community.

- Users with terminals attached to the IBM 360 should be provided with access to network services. In other words, the IBM 360 should act as a terminal concentrator for local terminals to access the network.

In the long run, the first objective is clearly the most important one. A powerful computer such as the IBM 360 is better used to offer batch or time-sharing services than to drive terminals. But, in the initial phase of network development, the additional usage of the IBM 360 as a terminal concentrator was a simple means to provide the large community of its local users with early access to the network. Terminal concentrators (see section 5.3) implemented on mini-computers have subsequently been used to relieve the IBM 360 of that function.

5.2.2.2. Implementation choices

a) Communications within CP/67

The adaptation of CP/67 to the network uses a gateway-like approach (see section 5.4). A gateway-function is implemented in a "network virtual machine" called NVM, which handles the transport protocol, the virtual terminal protocol and the interface to CP/67. NVM operates as follows (see figure 5.2.2.(1)).

Cards received from a remote reader are written on the NVM virtual punch. The first card received contains the name of the user virtual machine. It is used to associate the NVM virtual punch and the virtual reader of the user virtual machine.

Output to the remote printer from the user virtual machine is read on the NVM virtual reader. The first line designates the network address of a remote printer.

A program running in NVM simulates the operator´s console for the user virtual machine. This console is viewed as a new type of terminal, called 1052X.

In order to allow easy development of new applications, virtual machines must have access to the transport service provided by NVM. Since no efficient communication means was available in CP/67, we had to develop one. It was the paging mechanism : a page of the virtual machine can be copied into a page of another. With this new mechanism a specific interface has been developed whereby any virtual machine can send requests to the transport station in NVM and get responses back.

ASP/OS-MVT

For this system [ANS76], all network software is implemented as an OS task running concurrently with the other tasks. Communication between the network task and ASP makes use of standard ASP services already used by the time-sharing option of OS (TSO), and a new facility added to ASP for that purpose.

Standard services allow any OS task (e.g., TSO or the network task) to send a job stream interpreted and stored in ASP´s job queues as any other job. When a job has been executed by OS-MVT, ASP sends back the output listing to the OS task which originated the job. These services make use of the channel to

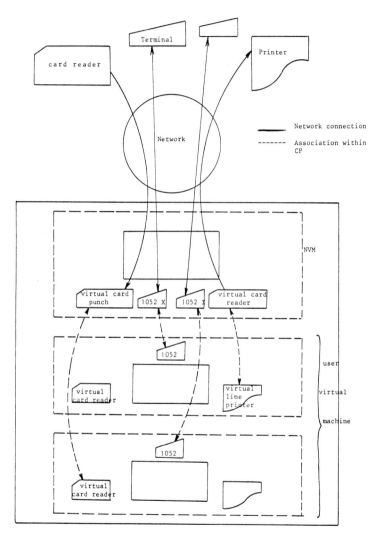

Figure 5.2.2.(1) - NVM Operation

channel adapter, or a simulation of it when ASP and OS run in the same machine.

The communication mechanism added to ASP makes use of virtual consoles declared in ASP. On these consoles, ASP can start input-output operations and signal them to OS tasks, through a specific supervisor call. OS tasks can terminate the operation when data related to the I/O operation have been transferred.

b) Network control monitor

In both CP67 and ASP-OS/MVT, the same network control monitor called SYNCOP is used. This permits portability of network software from one system to the other (see section 5.6.2).

In CP/67 this monitor is used as the operating system of the network virtual machine. With ASP/OS-MVT, it is used as a sub-system running in the network task. In both cases, the organization of the network task and the network virtual machine are similar (see figure 5.2.2.(2)).

```
┌────────────────────────────────────────────────────┬───┐
│      S Y N C O P      monitor                      │ L │
│                                                    │ I │
│ │ │ │ │ │ │     │ │ │ │                            │ N │
│ │ │ │ │ │ │     │ │ │ │                            │ E │
│                                                    │   │
│  using the services of      Transport station     │ H │
│  the transport station      processes             │ A │
│                                                    │ N │
│                                                    │ D │
│ │ │ │ │ │ │     │ │ │ │                            │ L │
│ │ │ │ │ │ │     │ │ │ │                            │ E │
│                                                    │ R │
└────────────────────────────────────────────────────┴───┘
```

Figure 5.2.2.(2) - General structure

SYNCOP provides the following services :
- process management,
- interprocess communication and synchronization,
- memory management,
- time management,
- input-output operations,
- debugging facilities.

5.2.2.3. Transport station implementation

The transport station structure is the same in both systems. It is made of four processes (see figure 5.2.2.(3)) :

. P-LINE   handles the transmission line to CIGALE
. P-RECEIVE   processes incoming packets
. P-SEND   generates packets to be sent
. P-INTERFACE   processes subscriber requests

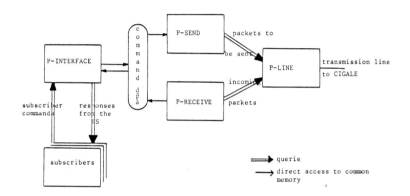

Figure 5.2.2.(3) - Transport station structure

P-INTERFACE is responsible for interaction with subscribers. Suscriber processes pass command blocks to P-INTERFACE through queues. P-INTERFACE processes these commands and updates the common data area (CDA) accordingly. For each command it delivers back a response block to the subscriber process through queues.

The CDA contains the context of each active port and liaison :

- queues of letters and telegrams to be sent,
- number of credits,
- reference of next letter to be sent,
- reference of last letter acknowledged,
- reference of last letter received,
- queue of free buffers for letters to be received,

- queue of letters already received.

P-SEND produces packets containing transport commands (fragments of letters, acknowledgements, etc.) and passes them to P-LINE. CDA is updated accordingly. A scheduling algorithm in P-SEND caters to fair sharing of packet transmission between liaisons/ports.

P-RECEIVE processes transport commands contained in incoming packets and updates the CDA accordingly.

P-SEND and P-RECEIVE use the time-management service provided by SYNCOP to set up time-outs. Delayed actions associated with time-outs are thus triggered by SYNCOP. They consist mainly in updating counters in the CDA and activating P-SEND.

P-LINE handles the line control procedure (BSC). Packets in the queue from P-SEND are sent to the CIGALE node, while packets received from the CIGALE node are put in the queue to P-RECEIVE.

In an initial implementation, P-INTERFACE was responsible for interfacing all subscriber processes. In a later version, subscriber processes running under SYNCOP make use of subroutine calls to perform the same function while subscriber processes located in another virtual machine or another OS task still use P-INTERFACE.

5.2.2.4. Server decription

Access to CP/67 or ASP/OS-MVT is provided by a network server. Both the CP67 and ASP/OS-MVT servers have the same internal structure, consisting of cooperating processes (see figure 5.2.2.(4)).

Communication with remote devices relies on the transport service (liaisons with error and flow control) and the virtual terminal protocol.

A permanent process P-CONTACT is waiting for connection requests on three well known ports, one for each kind of remote device. It is prepared to handle interactive terminal or console, card reader, or line printer.

On receipt of a connection request on one of those ports, it creates a process dedicated to driving the remote device :
- a P-TERM (CP/67) or P-CONS (ASP/OS-MVT) process for each remote interactive terminal or console,
- a P-READER process for each remote card reader,
- a P-PRINTER process for each remote line-printer.

When a P-CONS or a P-TERM process has been created by P-CONTACT, it opens the liaison with the remote device. Then, both ends exchange letters according to the virtual terminal

protocol. Virtual lines contained in incoming letters are sent
to the system through a virtual console (ASP/OS-MVT) or a 1052X
(CP/67). Lines received back from the system through these
virtual units are mapped into virtual lines formatted according
to the virtual terminal and sent in letters on the liaison. The
P-CONS and P-TERM process is suppressed when the remote user
closes the liaison.

Access to batch services raises a specific problem : ASP/OS-MVT
accepts only one job stream at a time and delivers back only
one listing at a time. In order to allow remote card readers to
work in parallel, the server makes use of a private spool on
disk to queue incoming jobs streams. In the reverse direction,
each listing produced by the system is stored in the spool
until it can be sent to the destination line printer.

With CP/67 it should have been possible to use several virtual
punches and virtual readers to pass jobs streams and listings
between the server and the system. However, we decided to use
the same organization as in the ASP/OS-MVT server, in order to
provide independence between the number of remote users and the
number of communication paths to CP/67.

A permanent process, P-SPOOL, handles the spool on disk for the
benefit of processes.

A permanent process, P-OUTPUT, receives lines to be printed on
remote printers through a virtual card reader (CP/67) or from
the CROS service (ASP/OS-MVT). These lines are formatted
according to the virtual terminal protocol and written in the
spool. Each file in the spool contains a listing with its
destination address in the network.

For each connection request received from a remote printer,
P-CONTACT creates a P-PRINTER process which opens the liaison
and reads (through P-SPOOL) the files destined to the remote
printer.   Records are just sent within letters (one record per
letter). This process is suppressed when the remote user closes
the liaison.

For each connection request received from a remote card reader,
P-CONTACT creates a P-READER process which opens the liaison.
Letters received from the remote device are written by P-READER
into the spool through P-SPOOL. P-READER is suppressed when the
remote user closes the liaison.

The card files in the spool are sequentially read by the
P-INPUT permanent process. P-INPUT gets card images contained
in the VTP messages and writes them on the virtual card punch
(CP/67), or passes them to the IJP module of ASP (ASP/OS-MVT).
With CP/67 the first card is used to associate the virtual
punch with the virtual reader of another virtual machine (see
section 5.2.2.1).

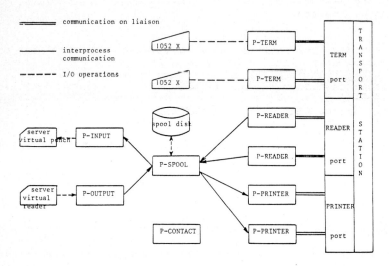

Figure 5.2.2.(4) - The CP/67 server

5.2.2.5. The terminal concentrators

Two terminal concentrators are available on the IBM 360/67 :
one for interactive terminals, the other for RJE terminals
[FOU76].

The interactive terminal concentrator drives IBM 2741 and TTY
or TTY-like terminals. The structure of this concentrator is
very simple. One process is associated with each active
terminal and converts it into a virtual terminal (see section
5.3).

The RJE terminal concentrator handles all terminals directly
connected to the IBM 360/67. These terminals were previously
directly handled by ASP, by means of the HASP multi-leaving and
BSC procedures. In order to modify neither software nor
hardware in the terminals, the concentrator uses the same
procedures. The various devices in each RJE station are viewed

as being independent i.e., the console can be connected to one
or several batch or interactive servers, the card reader to
another server and the line printer to another one. Each device
can also be simultaneously connected to several servers. There
is in fact one virtual device for each connection but the
mapping of the virtual devices into real devices depends on the
kind of the device :

- On the console, messages sent or received on different
liaisons can be mixed. They are just prefixed with the name of
the destination or of the origin.

- Only one virtual reader at a time can be associated with the
real one by the terminal operator. The other virtual readers
are in an idle state.

- All virtual line printers can be simultaneously active.
Incoming lines are stored in the spool. The resulting files are
then sequentially sent to the corresponding real printer.

The internal organization of the RJE terminal concentrator is
the following (see figure 5.2.2.(5)).

One permanent process is associated with each real (R) device
(R-CONS, R-READER, R-PRINTER) and one process is dynamically
created for each virtual (V) console or printer (V-CONS,
V-PRINTER). For each terminal, a permanent process (P-LINE)
handles the line control procedure.

A switch SW indicates which virtual reader context C is
associated with R-READER.

P-LINE controls the line and multiplexes outgoing messages and
demultiplexes incoming messages according to the multi-leaving
format. It uses queues to pass messages to the associated
R-CONS and R-READER processes and to get messages for the
terminal (in multi-leaving format) from R-CONS and R-PRINTER
processes.

R-CONS analyzes and processes messages received from the
console. These messages carry the following commands :

- CONNECT DS : connects device D to server S. On receipt of
this command, R-CONS opens a liaison with server S and
creates :
      - a V-CONS process if D = CONS
      - a V-PRINTER process if D = PTR
      - a C context if D = RDR

- DISCONNECT DS : R-CONS closes the liaison between D and S.
The V-CONS, V-PRINTER or C associated with this liaison is
suppressed.

- TRANSMIT S MSG : transmits message MSG to server S. The
message is delivered to the V-CONS process associated with

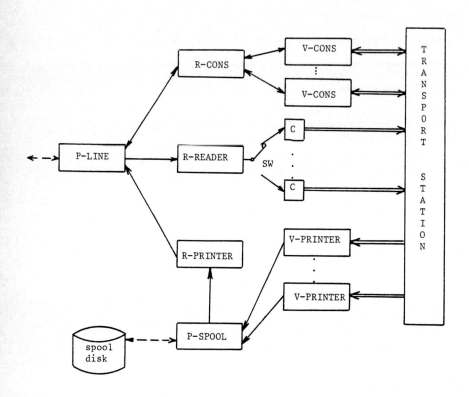

Figure 5.2.2.(5) Processes involved in one RJE terminal

server S.

- START S : indicates the destination S of the next deck of
cards to be read at the terminal. This command moves the switch
SW to the C context corresponding to server S.

R-CONS transmits to P-LINE the messages received by V-CONS from
its remote server. R-CONS prefixes each message with the name
of the corresponding server.

V-CONS receives on the liaison the VTP messages from its server
and passes them to R-CONS. V-CONS receives messages from R-CONS
and sends them in VTP format on the liaison to its server.
V-CONS performs translation from and to VTP formats.

R-READER receives cards from P-LINE, translates them into VTP format and sends them on the liaison corresponding to the C context pointed by SW.

V-PRINTER receives lines from the server in VTP format and writes them into the spool with the indication of the terminal they have to be sent to.

R-PRINTER reads from the spool the files (one file at a time) to be sent to its associated terminal. Lines contained in VTP messages are passed to P-LINE by R-PRINTER in multileaving format.

5.2.3. Other Host Implementations

5.2.3.1. The T1600 Front-end

The T1600 front-end to CYCLADES was implemented by the "Ecole des Mines de Saint-Etienne" [CHA76]. Their objective was : 1) to allow their local terminals to access network services available on CYCLADES, 2) to allow their local computers (DEC PDP 11/40, Philips P 1175) to provide services to remote terminals on CYCLADES.

A mini-computer (SEMS T1600) was chosen to achieve this goal. On one side it is connected to a CIGALE node, while on the other side it is connected to the local computers. In addition, it supports local terminals on the campus.

The main function of this network front-end is thus to permit interworking between terminals and computers offering services. To perform this task it acts both as : (1) a terminal-concentrator (see section 5.3) handling local terminals and mapping them into virtual terminals, and (2) an interface converter (see section 5.4) allowing local host computers to handle virtual terminals on the network.

Acting as a terminal-concentrator, the T1600 front-end supports a variety of devices (interactive terminals, card readers, line printers, etc.) allowing users to access in the same manner conversational or batch services provided by local computers as well as remote computers on CYCLADES.

Acting as an interface converter, the T1600 front-end emulates terminals known by the local computers and performs the mapping between the virtual terminal protocol and the terminal handling protocols specific to local computers. Through this network front-end, local computers appear as standard CYCLADES services.

A special purpose operating system has been designed for the T1600 front-end, to permit the various functions performed by the front-end to be clearly separated with well defined interfaces. In addition to facilating debugging of the

front-end itself, this modularity has allowed other CYCLADES
participants to re-use some of the front-end functions in other
implementations.

5.2.3.2. CII IRIS-50

Several centres equipped with CII IRIS-50 were candidates for
connection to CYCLADES. They all already had local customers to
whom they were providing services on a regular basis.
Therefore, they were not prepared to admit any modification of
SIRIS-3, the standard operating system of the IRIS-50. Moreover
the network activity necessarily had to run in parallel with
regular local user jobs.

The telecommunication access method in SIRIS-3 allows each
telecommunication task to be decomposed into several processes.
Each process is normally attached to a line or a terminal, but
additional processes (not attached to any line or terminal) may
also be created. All processes within the same
telecommunication task may communicate through shared variables
and message queues.

The IRIS-50 transport station is implemented as a set of
cooperating processes within a single telecommunication task to
which the transmission line to CIGALE is assigned, using the
same structure as for the IRIS 80 (see section 5.2.1) and the
IBM 360/67 (see section 5.2.2).

A first set of users of the transport station is made up of
processes running in the same task as the transport station
itself and interfacing with it through internal queues.

In order to provide all user jobs with a network access method
(i.e., access to the transport station), another interface has
been developed, making use of inter-task message queues
(mailboxes) provided by SIRIS-3. This interface is very similar
to the one developed for the IRIS 80 (see section 5.2.1).

Both interfaces can be used for developing distributed
applications.

The internal interface is used in particular by a terminal
concentrator program (consisting of one process per terminal)
providing local terminals with access to CYCLADES.

In addition, SOCRATE, the Data Base System of the IRIS-50 has
been made available to CYCLADES terminals, also using the
internal interface to the transport station. This was very much
facilitated by SOCRATE being built as a set of processes under
the same telecommunication access method of SIRIS-3 already
used for the transport station. Thus SOCRATE processes were
easily included in the transport station task. They had to be
partly modified in order for them to handle virtual terminals
through the transport station, rather than directly handling

real terminals.

5.3. The Terminal Concentrator (TC) for Simple Terminals

5.3.1. General requirements

Terminal access is a prime function of any computer network [NAF76c]. In most cases, users will need to access the available services with simple terminals. Network access points should be readily available in areas where a large number of users exists. Access should also be available via switched lines, leased lines, or dedicated local lines at various speeds.

Since the existing simple terminals lack the necessary processing capability to include the network protocols, some external machine should be installed in order to perform the functions defined in the reference model : namely, the Virtual Terminal protocol, the Transport Station, and the Transmission Interface. Another important function is also performed by this machine : the Terminal Handling function which drives the physical terminal and interacts with the operator who is the network end-user. This machine is called the Terminal Concentrator (TC) in CYCLADES. As explained in section 5.3.1, terminal concentrators have been implemented in hosts in some specific cases, but the general choice was to have them in dedicated computers.

In the following we will describe two implementations. One is based on a minicomputer (MITRA 15), the other is built on a multi-microprocessor.

5.3.2. The minicomputer approach

5.3.2.1. The hardware

The TCs in CYCLADES were built on MITRA 15 minicomputers, which are identical to the CIGALE nodes. This minicomputer has a microprogrammed CPU, 800 ns cycle time, 16-bit word length and 32 levels of interrupt. It includes also 32 asynchronous line-adapters, and 14 synchronous line-adapters. Terminals may be connected through leased or dedicated lines, and via the public switched telephone network [DEN75a]. Different speeds can be used : 110, 150, 300, 600, 1200 bits/sec, for asynchronous ports, and up to 48 Kbs/sec for synchronous ports. The main memory can be expanded to 64 K octets by adding boards of 4 K octets.

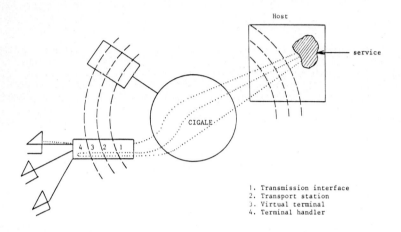

1. Transmission interface
2. Transport station
3. Virtual terminal
4. Terminal handler

Figure 5.3.1.(1) - Terminal Concentrator

5.3.2.2. The software

The principal design decision was to build the system around the basic software of the CIGALE switching node. The following reasons lay behind this choice :

The CIGALE node contains all system mechanisms for cooperating processes, which are needed in the TC.

The TC must perform the function of switching packets between external and internal transport stations. This function is performed by the node.

Internal transport stations representing the services offered by every node in CIGALE (ECHO, TIME and DEBUG) are very useful in the TC.

Lastly, a compatible program in the TC permits the Network
Control Center (NCC) to supervise both the nodes and all the
TCs (remote-loading, remote-dump, measurements, etc.).

The architecture of a TC is shown in Figure 5.3.2.(1). It
consists of :

- A supervisor part which performs queueing management and
process synchronization.

- Immediate tasks for handling the lines. The line control
procedure is TMM-UC. These tasks are attached to interrupt
levels that are triggered by external events (line adapter,
clock).

- Permanent tasks attached to interrupt levels triggered by
software. These tasks are :
    - the packet Switch,
    - the Transport Station (TS),
    - the letter switch performing the switching of messages
    between terminals and transport station. Terminals
    attached to one concentrator exchange messages
    (Lettergrams) locally without passing through the network.
    - the connection control for supervision of liaisons,
    - the terminal adaptations performing the mapping between
    real terminals and virtual terminals,
    - Terminal Handling (TH). Great care has been given to
    this function because it interfaces with human users. The
    interface with the user is given in the following section.
    - Terminal Emulation (TE) applies when connecting to a
    host, (see interface converter).

5.3.2.3. User Interface

As previously said, the TC enhances the functional capabilities
of simple (asynchronous) terminals so that they appear to
applications as virtual terminals. The virtual terminal is also
made visible to the terminal user who can trigger the VT
functions by means of the terminal keyboard according to
conventions defined between the TC and the user.

These conventions are very flexible, in order to take into
account physical terminals characteristics and human user
wishes.

Having added this value to the physical terminal, it is
desirable to provide a number of local facilities to help the
user in the operation of the terminal (e.g., correction of
typing errors) and to simplify the use of the network (e.g.,
provide default parameter values).

The dialog between the user and the application is conducted
through a local user to TC dialog and a TC (emulating the VT)
to application dialog. The conventions of the user to TC dialog

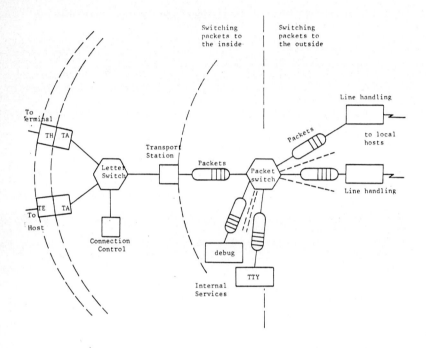

Figure 5.3.2.(1) - Terminal Concentrator Software Organization

define the TC to user interface [WEB77, WEB77a].

Since the main objective of the TC is to allow the human user to talk to applications as conveniently as possible, the user to TC dialog conventions have been designed in such a way that the TC becomes invisible to the user, once the application to user connection has been established, unless the user escapes and enters a "command mode" in which he interacts with the TC.

The dialog between the terminal concentrator and the user at the terminal consists of an exchange of commands and responses. Commands are composed by the user and executed by the TC. Three classes of commands can be distinguished :

a) Editing commands to help the user in the composition of the other commands (e.g., delete the previous character, delete the command text being constructed, and stop the current output).

b) Network commands corresponding to keystrokes on the virtual terminal keyboard. This class is composed of :

   - connection control commands to set up or close a connection (action on the connection control device of the VTP),

   - commands to send text messages, as well as qualified interrupt dialog control messages, to the application. Text messages consist of graphical symbols, addressing functions (New Line, New Page) and control information (qualified End Of Message, Your Turn indication).

c) Local commands to establish or change user interface parameters (e.g., terminal key to command assignments) as well as commands to interrogate the status of the interaction with the TC (e.g., parameter status, connection status).

To ensure flexibility in the command composition conventions, the concept of a "Local Virtual Keyboard" is introduced, similar to the one described in the VT model.

This keyboard consists of :

- a set of keys producing the VTP graphical symbols,

- a set of control keys producing the VTP functions associated with text, i.e., End Of Message qualifier : (EOM1),...(EOM4), Your-Turn indication (YR-TURN), addressing functions : (NL),(NP),

- a transmit control key (TRANS) used to terminate a command composed by means of keys of the two classes above,

- Attention control keys (A1), (A2), which trigger a "Send Attention" command,

- a Please control key (PL) which triggers a "Request Turn" command,

- a set of local editing control keys (EC) to trigger the editing commands,

- One and possibly two Escape control key(s) (ESC) to distinguish between command classes.

When no connection has been established with a remote application, commands to the TC can be entered by composing a text message terminated with the (TRANS) control key or by pressing one of the (EC) keys. The text of the command will then be interpreted by the TC as a command name with the associated parameters, e.g.,

> CONNECT 482,3 (TRANS) is interpreted as a request to set up a connection with the addressed subscriber (Local command).

When a connection with a remote application is active, the text of the commands and the asociated VTP functions are implicitly considered as belonging to a message to be sent to the application. It is then transparent to the TC, which formats the message according to the VTP conventions and forwards it into the network. Two different means may be used for sending commands to the TC. One is to press a control key which triggers a defined command, another is to start the command with an (ESC) key in which case the following text is interpreted as a command name with the associated parameters, e.g.:

> (ESC) DISCONNECT (TRANS) is interpreted as a request to disconnect the established liaison.

The formal definition of the command syntax is the following :

```
<COMMAND> ::= <COMMAND TEXT><(TRANS)>|<(A1)>|<(A2)>|<(PL)>|<(EC)>
<COMMAND TEXT> ::= <TEXT><VTP CONTROL>|<(ESC)><TEXT>
<TEXT> ::= Displayable characters string
<VTP CONTROL> ::= VTP functions associated with Text (translated
```
only when belonging to a message to be sent on a liaison, otherwise ignored).

The virtual keys are mapped onto the real terminal keys (usually control or function keys). In most cases, the user prefers to associate several usual VTP functions such as (EOM) + (YR-TURN) + (NL) with a single keystroke, and it is a convenient user interface facility to assign some of the real terminal keys to such combinations of elementary virtual keys.

It may happen that the real terminal keyboard includes fewer keys than the virtual one. In this case, only a subset of the virtual keyboard may be used, leaving some of the uncommonly used or unessential keys unassigned. Another possibility is to trigger some commands through the extended command syntax, e.g., (ESC) ATTENTION 1 (TRANS) command would have the same effect as pressing the (A1) virtual key.

The mapping between virtual and real keys is a user interface parameter which can be modified dynamically by the user himself, by means of a special command. Specific values may be set for real terminals connected through dedicated lines. Standard default values are assigned for all other means of connection.

Character echoing is handled by the TC software. It may be turned off on application request (HIDE VTP function). The echo of a control character is a sequence of characters (possibly empty) which can also be modified by the user.

In the same way that the terminal keyboard is shared to input text to the remote application or the TC itself, the presentation unit is shared for printing (or displaying) responses originating from two sources : the TC itself and the remote application.

In order to avoid mixing messages from both sources on the presentation unit, TC virtual terminal commands do not induce any response from the TC itself unless something goes wrong, e.g., the message cannot be sent due to a lack of TC resources. This leaves the presentation unit clear for the display of the elements of the dialog between the application and the user, i.e., the TC also remains transparent for output on the presentation unit. Only local commands trigger explicit responses from the TC commands, but they rarely are invoked in the course of the user to application dialog.

The dialog is an alternating exchange of commands and responses, except for VTP commands which can be input until the (YR-TURN) control key has been pressed ; responses coming from the remote application are then output on the presentation unit until the TURN comes back from the application.

A type ahead facility is offered to allow the user to prepare his commands in advance. Such commands are buffered and the echo of the characters delayed until the TC is allowed to take them into account (e.g., the TURN is back from the application).

5.3.3. The multi-microprocessor approach

The terminal concentration function can be divided into four main parts : terminal handling, virtual terminal, transport station and transmission interface. All these sub-functions are independent and can be performed by dedicated tasks cooperating through simple and well defined interfaces.

Since the advent of microprocessors and LSI memories [NAF77], it became evident that implementing those tasks in separate microprocessors running in parallel, could offer to users a very cost-effective and flexible method to access the network. One possible architecture is to assign the procedure handling the transmission network interface to one processor, and to implement the others in another processor controlling a cluster of terminals.

In CYCLADES, a multi-microsystem called MLV (Multiplexeur de Liaisons Virtuelles) has been built. It concentrates a cluster of four teleprinter oriented terminals. The MLV uses two INTEL 8080 microprocessors.

One microprocessor performs the TMM line control procedure with 1.5 K octets of PROM and 1 K octet of RAM. The other microprocessor performs the other tasks with 3.5 K octets of PROM and 4 K octets of RAM. The PROM is divided into 2 K octets for transport station, 0.5 K octet for virtual terminal and 1 K octet for terminal handling.

The user of a terminal attached to an MLV can open a liaison with another MLV and indicate the mode of operation at the terminal level : transparent or virtual. The transparent mode is used for connecting terminals whose functions fall outside of the capabilities of VTP (e.g., graphics). More details on MLV can be found in [NAF76a].

5.4. Interface converters and gateways.

5.4.1. Interface Converters

5.4.1.1. The modular interface converter

It was mentioned in section 5.1.2 that in order to connect a non standard informatics system (terminal, host) to a network without making any modification to its hardware or software, one needs to adapt their behaviour to network protocols by means of "converters" inserted between the system and the network. When connecting hosts as terminal servers, the only host-dependent function in the converter is the Terminal Emulation (TE).

In order to minimize the effort required to connect a variety of hosts, the common part of all converters, i.e. the handling of network protocols, is developed only once and complemented with different specific TE "boxes" to accomodate various hosts as required. This approach is referred to as the "modular interface converter" (see figure 5.4.1.(1)).

The same modular interface converter is also used to connect terminals to the network by adding a Terminal Handling (TH) "box" to the network protocols module in the modular interface converter, thus providing a terminal concentrator function.

Different terminal emulation boxes were studied and developed corresponding to the following line configurations and control procedures (see also figure 5.4.1.(2)) :

- Multipoint-asynchronous RTC IBM 360/65

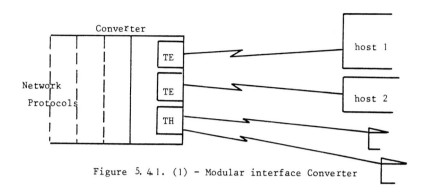

Figure 5. 4. 1. (1) - Modular interface Converter

  - Multipoint synchronous MSV1 UNIDATA 7730

  - Point-to-point asynchronous PDP10, PDP 11, etc.

  - Point-to-point synchronous HASP IBM 370

The main advantages offered by this unified approach are :

a) The modularity of all interface converters simplifies maintenance and further development.

b) The network accomodates various types of terminals or hosts. The only specific piece of software to be developed is located within the interface converter.

c) Since the interface converters perform dedicated tasks, their implementation within multi-microprocessors systems working in parallel will greatly improve their performance. In the following sections, this approach will be illustrated by the different interconnection products developed within CYCLADES.

Three classes of Terminal Emulation modules were considered corresponding to different line configurations :
- Polled terminal emulation corresponding to multidrop lines,
- Point-to-point terminal emulation corresponding to non-multiplexed point-to-point lines,
- Multiplexed point-to-point terminal emulation corresponding to multiplexed point-to-point lines.

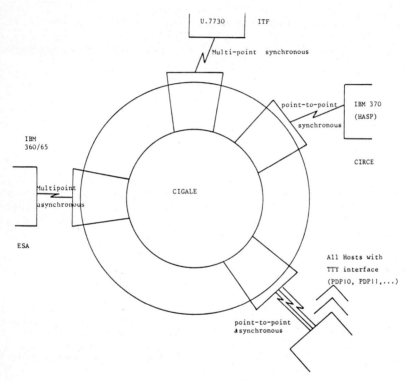

Figure 5.4.1 (2) -   The Interface Converters in CYCLADES

5.4.1.2. The terminal emulation in the Interface Converter (IC)

a) Polled terminal emulation

The IC emulates a teleprinter oriented terminal and must perform the following tasks :

- handle the line control procedure supported by the Host,
- assign "polled addresses" to transport station "Ports",
- maintain a composite path constituted of the "data link" handled by the line control procedure, and the "port-to-port liaison" handled by the transport protocol (see figure 5.4.1(3)),
- map the messages exchanged over the composite path by converting the transport commands : Liaison Initiation (LI-INIT), Liaison Termination (LI-TERM), Send and Receive Letter and Telegram, into commands of the polling procedure. For example, a select command received from the host is converted into Send Letter to the distant transport station. A Letter received from the distant transport station will be an answer to the next poll received from the host. If no letter has been received, a "negative" answer to the Poll is sent back to the host. No polling commands cross the network.
- convert between host specific text messages and commands, and virtual terminal text-items and control-items (see section 3.4).

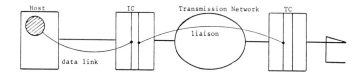

Figure 5.4.1 (3) - The Composite Path

Two host systems were connected to CYCLADES with such a multidrop line interface : the first is the IBM 360/65 of the European Space Agency located at Frascati (Italy). The line control procedure used is called RTC. The second is the UNIDATA-7730 (Siemens) of the Institut Textile de France located at Boulogne (France) which uses the MSV1 line control procedure of SIEMENS.

The major problems encountered in these two cases concern the last two tasks mentioned above i.e- : transport mapping, and virtual terminal mapping.

Problems in transport mapping result from the fact that services offered by the transport protocol on a liaison cannot match exactly services offered on the data link by the line control procedure. For example, the RTC procedure lacks error control and flow control, which are performed by the transport stations. Thus messages can be lost between the IC and the host, or discarded by the IC if they are received from the host while not enough buffers are available. This exemplifies the possible unreliability of the external adaptation solution when emulating a primitive line control procedure.

In the case of MSV1, matching transport protocol and procedure logic is easier. Error control applies independently on each segment of the composite path. Flow control is performed without anticipation. Figure 5.4.1.(4) shows a typical diagram of commands and messages exchanged between terminal and host across the IC.

Problems encountered in virtual terminal mapping relate in particular to dialogue mode. The virtual terminal protocol operates normally in alternate mode controlled by the exchange of YOUR-TURN indications. Most interactive servers also operate in the same mode, controlled either explicitly (e.g., with an End of Message indication) or implicitely (i.e., the operator is supposed to know from the context when he may send a message, e.g., receipt of a specific prompt character depending on the specific software subsystem being run).

The explicit EOM indication can easily be mapped into the YOUR-TURN indication, but the implicit one cannot be traced by the interface converter. This led us to augment the virtual terminal protocol to let it also operate in "free running mode" where the right to send a message is not controlled by the protocol, and orderly dialogue depends on proper behaviour of both the operator and the application program. The mapping between real terminal commands does not raise any problem when VTP functional capabilities include all important real terminal characteristics.

b) Point-to-point terminal emulation

This method can apply to the connection of any host system which can handle start-stop terminals attached via point-to-point lines operating in character mode (n asynchronous host ports are linked to the IC). The value of n will depend on the maximum number of simultaneous data paths that the host wishes to maintain with other network processes (usually terminals) (see Figure 5.4.1.(5)).

The same problems as were mentioned in the above sub-section will be encountered in this type of emulation. The same solutions adopted for the virtual terminal mapping problem can

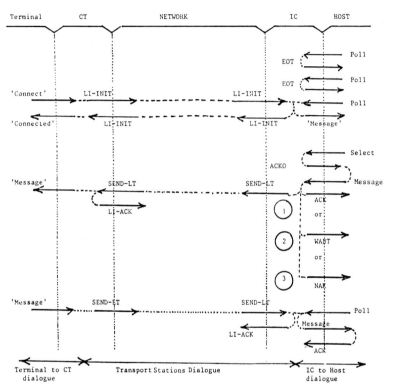

1. Queue not full, credit available
2. Queue full, or no credit
3. Terminal has disconnected

Figure 5.4.1.(4) - Examples of dialogue in multidrop
line Terminal Emulation

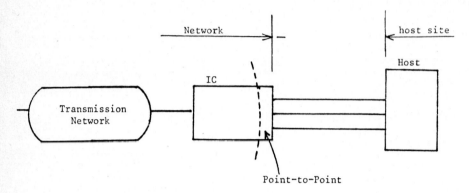

Figure 5.4.1.(5) - Point to point terminal emulation

apply here.

With regard to transport, the problems are more complicated since the asynchronous transmission procedure lacks any error control and recovery. The quality of the transport service is no longer guaranteed when a physical link is stitched with a liaison. The resulting quality relies primarily on the quality of the asynchronous physical link, which may be particularly poor.

In order to improve the quality of the transmission over the link between host and IC, one can bring the IC interface nearer to the host, by putting an Intelligent Processor at the host site, and linking this processor to the IC via a dedicated line handled by a line control procedure with error control and recovery. This was achieved in CYCLADES by designing a microprogrammed system, called MUMI, described in section c) below.

c) Multiplexed point-to-point terminal emulation

Two types of multiplexed point-to-point terminal emulation were developed : 1) The MUMI (Multiplexeur Microprogramme) interface, which multiplexes flows of asynchronous ports at the host onto a synchronous link to the interface converter, and 2) The HIC (HASP Interface Converter), which multiplexes streams of batch peripheral units onto a synchronous link.

The MUMI interface

The MUMI is linked to the IC via a dedicated line. The exchange of blocks is controlled by the TMM-UC procedure with error and flow control. It is also linked locally to the asynchronous

host ports through a standard modem interface (RS 232 C or
V 24), (see figure 5.4.1.(6)). The MUMI performs statistical
multiplexing of the flows from asynchronous host ports over the
synchronous link. Data received from a host port are sent as an
item in a block of information exchanged over the synchronous
link. The multiplexing scheme is block oriented and is shown in
figure 5.4.1.(7). The port number is indicated in the header.
When no information is available at one port, the corresponding
item is not present in the block. At the other end of the
synchronous link, the multiplexing is performed in software by
the IC, which assigns a "Port" and a "Liaison" to each active
host port.

The scanning of host ports is done continuously by the MUMI.
The decision as to when to package the information received
into one item is based on two criteria : inter-character timer
and full buffer. The values of the timer and the buffer size
are chosen according to the speed of the asynchronous ports
(for 300 bits/s ports typical values are 100 ms for the timer,
and 30 characters for the buffer). The MUMI was built around
the Motorola 6800, with 2 K octets of RAM and 4 K octets of
PROM. All details about MUMI software and hardware can be
found in [NAF77b].

In addition to the advantage of having more reliable
transmission between the host and the network, the MUMI
approach permits a saving in the line cost. At the time the
MUMI was developed, its cost was half the price of traditional
TDM multiplexer.

Many hosts such as the PDP-10, PDP-11, and IBM 370 were
connected to CYCLADES using this approach.

The HASP Interface Converter (HIC)

The function of the HIC [QUI78] is to connect an IBM batch
service to the network, without any modification in the
hardware or software of the IBM machine, providing that the IBM
machine is able to handle RJE terminals following the HASP
multi-leaving conventions.

The HIC is connected to the network like every host : its line
to CIGALE is controlled by the TMM-UC procedure and it contains
a transport station. At the upper level a batch server is
implemented, allowing the connection of three types of virtual
devices : consoles, card readers and line printers. As seen
from the IBM system, the HIC is a set of RJE terminals,
emulating the IBM 360/20.

A conversion is done between both sides (see figure 5.4.1.(8)).

A short description of HASP multi-leaving will allow us to
define the conversion. Between an RJE terminal and the IBM
system, data are exchanged within blocks following the BSC line

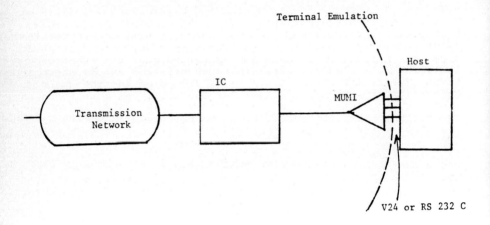

Figure 5.4.1.(6) - The MUMI interface

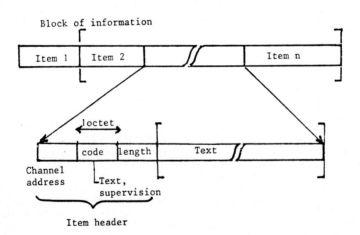

Figure 5.4.1.(7) - Multiplexing scheme

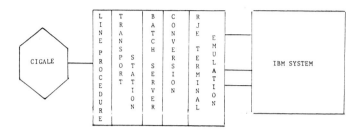

Figure 5.4.1.(8) - The HIC logical structure

control procedure. Each device of an RJE terminal communicates
with the host through a virtual link called a stream, provided
with error and flow control mechanisms. The operator´ consoles
use two streams : one for each direction. In the streams, data
are structured in records and strings. A record corresponds to
a line or a card and is made of string descriptors representing
sequences of characters. This structure of strings allows data
compression. In front of each record a byte identifies the
stream the record belongs to. Several records can be
multiplexed in one block.

The conversion is done by using the following correspondences
between the network and the multi-leaving entities :

1) Liaisons are associated with streams. In both protocols
these entities are the links used to communicate with the RJE
devices.

2) A letter on a liaison corresponds to a sequence of records
on a stream. Letters and records are the basic entities
exchanged on liaisons or streams.

3) A virtual line corresponds to a record.

4) A VTP item corresponds to a string. They are the basic
elements of a VTP letter or a record and the functions they
perform are identical.

The HIC has been implemented on a mini-computer (SFENA ORDO
400) running under control of its standard operating system,
called METEOR. Due to the limitations of METEOR, the HIC has
been designed with a reduced number of processes. The structure
of the transport station is similar to those of other machines
on the network. Its peculiarity is that it realizes only the
minimum of the transport protocol required by the virtual

terminal protocol : in particular there is no fragmentation or
reassembly, since virtual terminal and applications exchange
only one-fragment letters.

On each line connecting the HIC to the IBM System, an RJE
terminal is simulated. Each simulated RJE terminal corresponds
to a network batch station connected to the HIC. Therefore the
number of batch stations simultaneously accessing the service
is limited to the number of lines on the IBM side. The
implementation is described in figure 5.4.1.(9).

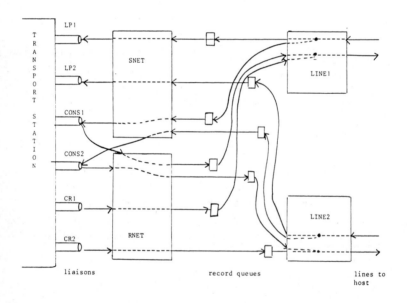

Figure 5.4.1.(9) - HIC Implementation

Each line to the IBM machine is handled by a LINE process
performing the BSC procedure. The received blocks are analyzed
and the records they contain are enqueued. There is a queue for
each stream. The records to be sent are dequeued and
multiplexed in blocks before transmission on the line.

The liaisons to the remote network devices are handled by two
processes.

The SNET process gets records from the queues, converts them
into the VTP format, put them into letters sent on the liaisons
corresponding with the stream.

The RNET process performs the reverse functions. Letters
received on the liaisons from the remote devices are analyzed.
The virtual lines they contain are reformatted into
multi-leaving records. These records are put into the queues
associated with the streams.

5.4.2. Gateways

5.4.2.1. Basic principles

The layered type of network architecture chosen in CYCLADES and
now adopted for most computer networks is primarily intended to
facilitate design, implementation, and evolution of individual
networks (see section 2). Layering also facilitates
interconnection of separate networks [POU77g, GIE79a, POU80].

Indeed, let us take an example of two computer networks in
which the virtual terminal protocol and the transport protocol
are identical, but using different transmission systems. Then,
they may be modelled as in figure 5.4.2.(1).

Since protocols apply end-to-end, terminals attached to one
network would access applications in the other network, if it
were not for the gap between transmission systems. It is clear
from this model that the interconnection problem boils down to
the interconnection of two different transmission systems, so
that messages exchanged in the transport layer be properly
routed and delivered to their destination.
Most internetworking problems may be analyzed in terms of
typical basic configurations [SUN75, SUN77]. A set of basic
cases are examined in the following.

a) Substitution of a layer

A practical situation could be the replacement of a private
packet net by a public packet net, all other components
remaining unchanged. In the network model a certain layer (L)
is replaced with a new one (L1) offering a different interface
(see figure 5.4.2.(2)).

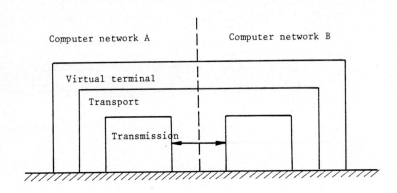

Figure 5.4.2.(1) Two quasi-identical computer networks

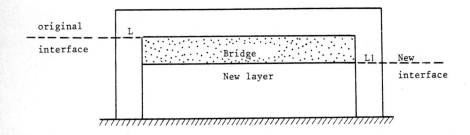

Figure 5.4.2 (2) - Substition of a layer

As long as the service provided by Ll is "similar" to the one
provided by L, it is feasible to map interface L onto Ll
through an interface converter often called a bridge. There is
no good measure of similarity between L and Ll. The complexity
of the bridge, and the characteristics of the service should be
assessed.

When the original and the new service are functionally very
different, it is not always clear that a substitution is
possible without impacting higher layers. E.g., replacing a
transmission system using leased or switched circuits by a
packet network may require the replacement of higher layers,
because transit delays cause their performance to detoriate.

The foregoing example illustrates the delicate balance designers have to strike when layering a system. In principle, layering is intended to prevent the propagation of modifications throughout the entire system. However, this is only effective to the extent that potential future characteristics have been more or less anticipated. Occasionally, new technologies based on new concepts require major changes in the overall system architecture.

b) Interconnection within one layer

A practical situation could be the interconnection of two computer networks with identical protocols, but using different transmission systems, N1 and N2.

In the model, one layer is made up of two distinct components, as illustrated in figure 5.4.2.(3).

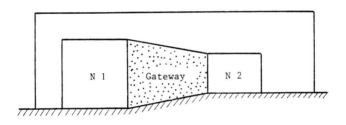

Figure 5.4.2 (3) - Interconnection within one layer

Interfaces with the upper layer may be different but this is immaterial, as long as protocols are identical.

An adapter is necessary between N1 and N2. This is often called a gateway. Typically gateway functions may be placed in either of two categories :

MAPPING
When entities and functions within N1 and N2 are in one-to-one correspondence, it may be convenient to map them onto each other. E.g., each message passing from N1 to N2 is reformatted. This is the case when N1 and N2 are two variants of the same design.

BRIDGING
In other cases, it is not possible to establish a satisfactory one-to-one mapping. An alternative solution is to cross the obstacle within the next higher layer, which by definition is

the same in both computer networks.

Thus, the gateway appears to N1 and N2 as a common higher layer (see figure 5.4.2.(4)). Since the protocol is common, messages passing through the gateway need no further conversion.

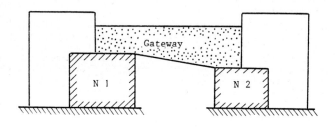

Figure 5.4.2 (4) - Gateway in a higher layer

c) Interconnection of two similar networks

It is assumed that networks are built on the same model, and that protocols are "similar". Again similarity is a vague concept. An actual criterion is the complexity of the adaptation.

Interconnecting two similar networks consists in interconnecting separately each layer (see figure 5.4.2.(5)).

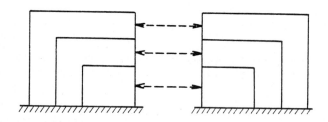

Figure 5.4.2 (5) - Two similar computer networks

Functionally, this would result in as many gateways as there are layers to interconnect. As we have said, a mapping gateway within one layer requires strong similarity, otherwise a bridging gateway should be in the next higher layer.

Thus, it may happen that the only layer where similarity is strong is an outer layer, e.g., the virtual terminal (see figure 5.4.2.(6)).

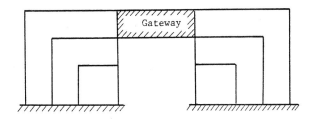

Figure 5.4.2 (6) - Gateway in the virtual terminal layer

d) Interconnection of two dissimilar networks

Even when networks are built on the same model, the mapping of corresponding layers may be too cumbersome. A worse case is networks based on different models, or too intricate to be modelled at all. Then, it is not even possible to identify corresponding layers. A solution is to resort to an outer layer that always exists, namely device handling. Every application program communicates with some kind of real or virtual device : terminal, magnetic tape, file, etc. Thus a gateway may appear to mimic some device attached to each network (see figure 5.4.2.(7)). It may be convenient that emulated devices be identical, e.g., a teleprinter, but this is not necessary, as long as the gateway ensures a mapping between them.

5.4.2.2. The CYCLADES/EIN gateway

The architecture of EIN [BRB76, SED76] is very similar to the CYCLADES architecture : CIGALE and the EIN packet network offer both a Datagram type of service and both networks have a transport layer and a virtual terminal layer with similar protocols. The gateway between CYCLADES and EIN provides interconnection at all three levels : Packet, Transport and Virtual Terminal.

a) Interconnection at Packet level

Both networks use the same Datagram format, but some network services and the line control procedures are different.

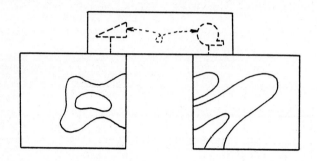

Figure 5.4.2 (7) - Dissimilar networks

Therefore it was not possible to directly interconnect a CIGALE node and an EIN node. A gateway had to be developed. Its functions are :

- Exchange packets with CIGALE using an ECMA frame and a specific line procedure.
  N.B. ECMA frames are character oriented. The layout is as follows : SYN, SYN, DLE, STX, text, DLE, ETX, checksum, SYN, SYN.
- Exchange packets with EIN using an HDLC frame and a specific line procedure.
  N.B. HDLC frames are bit oriented. The layout is as follows : Flag, address, control, text, checksum, flag.
- Filter out or convert requests for network services.

There is no need for name mapping in the gateway, since both CIGALE and EIN use a hierarchical name space containing a network name.

This interconnection makes CIGALE and EIN appear as a single network for packet transmission. It is a perfect application of the CATENET approach [POU74g].

This gateway was developed on a MITRA-15 already used as switching node in both networks. The effort consisted in integrating parts of networks nodes software and adding the mapping function.

The resulting compound packet network was used by CYCLADES hosts participating in the EIN project to interwork with other EIN centres according to EIN higher-level protocols (see figure 5.4.2.(8)).

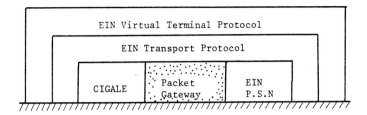

Figure 5.4.2.(8) - Interconnection of CYCLADES and EIN at packet level

b) Interconnection at transport level

Both CYCLADES and EIN transport protocols [EIN76] are very similar, but : 1) Some control fields are larger in the EIN transport protocol, (e.g., the numbering cycle is longer), and 2) Telegrams (i.e., interrupt messages) are acknowledged in EIN, but not in CYCLADES.

The mapping of letter numbers is straightforward, since letters are in one-to-one correspondence. So are messages which open and close liaisons.

Messages originating from EIN for parameter negotiation are intercepted by the gateway, and answered in a predefined manner.

Interrupt acknowledgements sent from EIN are also intercepted by the gateway. Since they consume interrupt credits, i.e., the right to send one interrupt, the gateway returns one credit per acknowledgement, in order to keep the credit status unchanged.

This transport gateway function was implemented in the same computer as the packet gateway function, providing users of CYCLADES and EIN with a compound transport function on top of which common protocols have to be used (see figure 5.4.2.(9)).

c) Interconnection at virtual terminal level

The two virtual terminal protocols are similar [EIN77]. All messages are in one-to-one correspondence. Differences appear in the coding of some control fields, which are translated by the gateway. An odd discrepancy results from a CYCLADES feature allowing a condensed coding of message lengths. Since this feature does not exist in EIN, the letter length may increase when mapping from CYCLADES to EIN. When the new length happens to overflow the maximum length agreed in opening the liaison, an extraneous letter is generated by the gateway. This must be

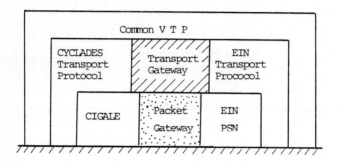

Figure 5.4.2 (9) - Interconnection of CYCLADES and EIN at Transport level

balanced by the gateway taking away one credit from the next EIN allocation.

This virtual terminal gateway function was also implemented in the same computer as the preceeding ones, providing users in each network with access to services in the other network.

The complete gateway with conversion functions at all three levels is illustrated in figure 5.4.2.(10).

5.4.2.3. The CYCLADES/TRANSPAC gateway

CYCLADES initially used only CIGALE for packet transmision. It was decided that TRANSPAC, the French PTT packet network, should replace by the end of 1979 the part of CIGALE using PTT circuits. TRANSPAC offers only a virtual circuit service through an X.25 interface. Asynchronous character mode terminals can be attached to TRANSPAC through an X.28 interface to a Packet Assembler Disassembler (PAD) which interacts with hosts according to the X.29 protocol.

In order to use TRANSPAC, computers on CYCLADES must be provided with an adapter (a bridge) mapping a datagram interface into a virtual circuit interface. Bridges are intended for several modes of adaptation, as illustrated in figure 5.4.2.(11) :

a - allow communications between CYCLADES computers (A, B, C) and with terminal concentrators (D),

b - allow communications between CYCLADES computers (A, B, C) and computers attached directly to TRANSPAC through an X.25 interface (E),

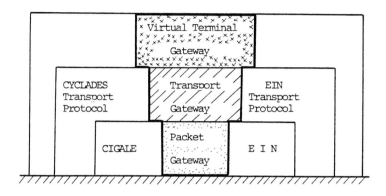

Figure 5.4.2.(10) - Interconnection of CYCLADES

and EIN at all levels

c - allow communications between CYCLADES computers (A, B, C) and terminals attached to TRANSPAC through an X.28 interface (F).

Each mode (a, b, c) corresponds to the mapping of a different layer. Mode (a) maps the transmission layer, i.e., datagram/virtual circuit. It is modelled as shown in figure 5.4.2.(2).

Mode (b) maps the transport layer. CYCLADES protocols explicitly include a transport layer. Computers attached directly to TRANSPAC may be provided with only an X.25 interface, i.e. the minimum required. The choice made for the mapping is to consider level 3 of X.25 (the one handling virtual circuits) as a pseudo transport layer for TRANSPAC computers. Then, the mapping applies between CYCLADES logical links (called liaisons) and X.25 virtual circuits. The model is as shown in figure 5.4.2.(3).

Mode (c) maps the CYCLADES virtual terminal protocol into commands required by X.29, for handling asynchronous terminals through TRANSPAC. The model is as shown in figure 5.4.2.(6).

A diagrammatic representation of the functional layers of the CYCLADES-TRANSPAC bridge is shown in figure 5.4.2.(12).

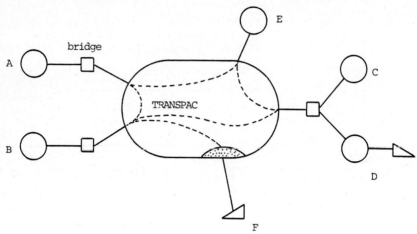

Figure 5.4.2 (11) - CYCLADES and TRANSPAC

Virtual Terminal	C	X-29
Transport	b	X-25
Line Procedure	a	

Figure 5.4.2 (12) CYCLADES/TRANSPAC bridge

The CYCLADES/TRANSPAC gateway is implemented in a specific multi-microprocessor manufactured by CSEE. It contains all three gateway functions described below:

a) Packet gateway functions :

When communications take place between CYCLADES machines, only mode (a) is used. Its functions are :

- exchange datagrams with CYCLADES computers through one of the synchronous line procedures in use,

- exchange packets with TRANSPAC through an X.25 interface,

- place datagrams into packet sequences, with appropriate X.25 headers,

- extract datagrams from packet sequences and strip off X.25 headers.

Bridges use permanent or switched virtual circuits. This choice is a matter for further trade off since corresponding costs are dependent on traffic structure. There is only one virtual circuit between any two bridges.

No difficulty arises at this level, because the transmission layer in CYCLADES is assumed to be a simple packet carrier, which does not guarantee the delivery of every packet. Thus, transmission integrity still relies on the transport protocol.

b) Transport gateway function

The variant of X.25 implemented in TRANSPAC does not contain any end-to-end control functions. It is only a local interface. Consequently, it is not possible to maintain end-to-end control between a CYCLADES computer and a TRANSPAC computer using only X.25. The end-to-end transport protocol terminates in the bridge, and cascades into a virtual circuit, as shown in figure 5.4.2.(13). Therefore, there is no longer guarantee of transmission integrity through TRANSPAC.

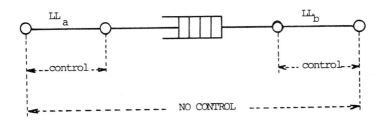

Figure 5.4.2.(13) Control cascade

Opening a liaison in CYCLADES translates into opening a virtual circuit in TRANSPAC. Interrupt messages must be limited to 8 bits (due to X.25). There is no mapping of error and flow control. Mode (b) acts simply as a buffer between two independent logical links.

c) Virtual terminal gateway function

The virtual terminal protocol in CYCLADES consists of coded messages carrying text or control information. It is designed for handling a hypothetical message terminal. Physical terminal handling is delegated to terminal concentrators, so that application programs are unaware of the specific characteristics of the real terminal (half or full-duplex, line length, delays, control keys, etc.).

The X.29 interface consists of packet formats reflecting closely the functions of an ASCII character mode terminal. The physical characteristics of the terminal are not hidden. On the contrary, they are explicitly visible as a set of 16 parameters, which may take different values.

In order to accomodate a variety of physical terminals, without destroying the principle of the virtual terminal, mode (c) of the bridge contains a set of standard parameter values applying to various classes of real terminals.

The mapping between X.29 packet format and virtual terminal messages is rather straightforward. However, there is a "turn" problem, because there is no dialogue control in X.29. A control character is used to control the "turn" between the gateway and the user at the terminal (Bell from gateway to user and usually CR from user to gateway). Since the PAD has no concept of "turn" or alternate dialogue, it always (or never) echoes characters typed on the terminal, therefore the user may not type ahead as he often does when connected to CYCLADES terminal concentrators. Also, passwords requested from applications programs will print in clear on terminals, when echoing is done by the PAD.

d) Complete gateway

To sum up, the CYCLADES-TRANSPAC bridge is actually 3 gateways in one box. Each of the modes (a, b, c) is exercised for a specific class of adaptation. Users may buy only the modes they need. This example illustrates the case of two networks structured in well defined layers, but layers differ in number (3 in CYCLADES, 2 in TRANSPAC), and they are not functionally equivalent.

5.5. Intelligent terminals

Two examples of intelligent terminals directly handling network standard protocols are given in this section : TIPAC, a microprogrammed cluster of displays and printers [NAF78], and MRBS, a Multiple Remote Batch Station [QUI78a].

5.5.1. The TIPAC system

5.5.1.1. General characteristics

The TIPAC [NAF75a, NAF76b, NAF78] is a microprogrammed system which is directly linked to CIGALE like a host, via a dedicated 4800 bps line. TIPAC can handle liaisons simultaneously with three different applications (see figure 5.5.1.(1)).

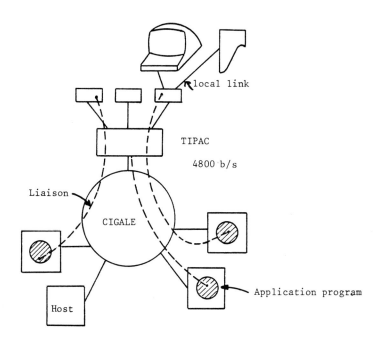

Figure 5.5.1(1) - The TIPAC system in CYCLADES

Each alphanumeric terminal has its own CRT screen, a 96-key keyboard and a 132-column printer. It can operate in two different virtual modes : Scroll or Data-Entry (see section 3.4).

In Data-Entry mode, data to be displayed are organized into fields, each field being defined by an attribute character (see figure 5.5.1.(2)).

The attribute indicates whether the field is protected or not protected (only unprotected fields may be entered by the operator), alphanumeric or numeric (only numeric characters are

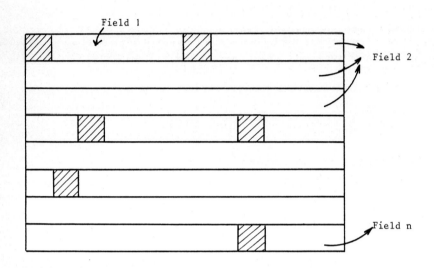

Attribute character

Figure 5.5.1.(2) - The display image

accepted in numeric fields), and displayed normaly, intensified
or in reverse video.

Hardware

The heart of the system is the TVT 500, a Thomson-CSF
microprocessor based on TTL technology, without interrupt
capability. It has a 500 ns cycle time and micro-instructions
of 16 bits length. Its LSI memories consist of 16 K octets of
PROM (Programmable Read Only Memory), 256 octets of scratchpad
RAM (Random Access Memory) and 8 K octets of RAM organized as
follows : one block of 2 K octets for packet buffering, and
3 blocks of 2 K octets, one for each of the three local
displays.

Network functions

The TIPAC system performs the same system network functions as
any other host, viz.:

a) Transmission interface : handling of the datagram interface
with CIGALE.

b) Transport Station : handling of the the end-to-end transport
protocol with other hosts.

c) Virtual Terminal control : handling of the Virtual Terminal
Protocol,   thereby   permitting   interaction   with   distant
applications either in scroll-mode or in data-entry mode
[NAF76, NAF78a] .

5.5.1.2. Design concepts and choices

The internal   architecture of TIPAC is based on a top-down
design by successive decomposition of functions.

A - First level of decomposition

TIPAC is first decomposed (see figure 5.5.1.(3)) into the three
main functions described above, i.e. Transmission, Transport
and Virtual Terminal. Interfaces between these functions are
well defined and consist of : a) Letters and telegrams between
the Virtual Terminal and the Transport Station, and b) Two FIFO
queues between the Transport Station and the Transmission
function.

B - Second level of decomposition

The three functions above are again decomposed into simpler
functions which correspond to processes of the system. Each
process has its own internal structure and a well defined
interface with other processes. The transmission interface is
divided into 3 processes : HANDLER, PROC, and INET. The
Transport Station is divided into 2 processes : TSEND and
TRECV.   The Virtual Terminal control is divided into 2
processes : SIUSER and DEVICE. The TIPAC processes functions
are described below :

a) Transmission interface functions

These functions are illustrated in figure 5.5.1.(4)

HANDLER (Line handler)
This process sends and receives characters over the line in
transparent mode (double DLE). The characters are defined in
commands such as : Send Sequence (for line initiation and
acknowledgment of a block), Receive Sequence, Send block
(containing text), Receive block. All these commands are
defined in a communication table whose contents identify the
type of the command and parameters such as buffer address or
sequence of control octets to be sent. HANDLER computes CRCs
(16 bits) for text blocks to be sent, and checks received CRCs.

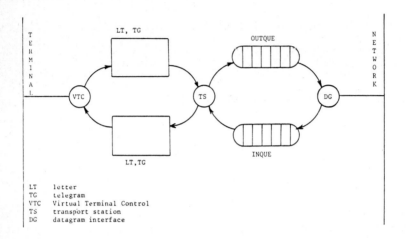

Figure 5.5.1.(3) - First level of decomposition of TIPAC

PROC (Line control procedure)
This process sends and receives blocks of text and control
sequences according to the logic of the TMM-UC procedure. PROC
uses HANDLER for sending and receiving sequences and text
blocks containing packets. PROC interfaces with INET through
two communication tables which contain addresses of packets to
be sent or addresses of received packets.

INET (Network interface)
This process handles 2 FIFO queues (INQUE and OUTQUE). It
extracts packets from OUTQUE for transmission by PROC. When
there is no packet to be sent, it generates an empty packet for
transmission. INET places correctly received packets (not
empty) into INQUE. Commands exchanged between the three
Transmission Interface processes are shown in figure 5.5.1.(4).

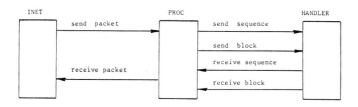

Figure 5.5.1.(4) - Transmission Interface Processes

b) Transport Station functions

These functions are illustrated in figure 5.5.1.(5).

TSEND (Sending Transport Station)
This process initiates the Liaison upon request from SIUSER, by
generating a LI-INIT command in which it indicates the maximum
length of the letters to be received and the additional
services requested : Error and Flow control. TSEND is also
responsible for transmitting letters. No anticipation is
performed by TSEND. The credit value is always set to one.
TSEND fragments letters if needed. It creates packet headers
for fragments and inserts the corresponding packets in OUTQUE.
It retransmits the same letter if it is not acknowledged after
a certain amount of time.

TSEND interfaces with SIUSER through a communication table in
which SIUSER indicates the type of command to be executed by
TSEND : Send-Letter, Send-Telegram, Open-Liaison,
Close-Liaison. Another table is used for communication with
TRECV.

TRECV (Receiving Transport Station)
This process handles the receiving part of liaison initiation.
It also reassembles packets from INQUE into letters to be
delivered to the user. It asks TSEND to acknowledge letters
correctly received. Received acknowledgments and liaison
initiation or termination commands are passed to TSEND.
Interfaces between Transport Station processes and the other
processes are shown in figure 5.5.1.(5).

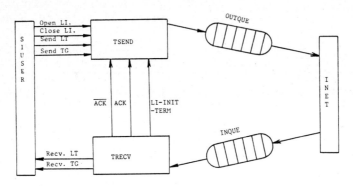

Figure 5.5.1.(5) - Transport Station Processes

c) Virtual Terminal Control

SIUSER (User interface)
This process transfers text characters from the line buffer in which packets are received into the display memory, and executes the Virtual Terminal conversion. When moving characters from the display memory back into the line buffer, SIUSER performs a prefragmentation : the first text character is placed in the 26th position of the packet buffer, leaving 8 octets for the fragment header, 12 octets for the datagram header and 5 octets for the TMM-UC header, (thus, a 25-octet header).

SIUSER also passes requests for opening or closing a liaison from DEVICE to TSEND, and passes back answers from TSEND to DEVICE.

DEVICE (device handling)
Responds to local commands, editing commands, and network commands entered at the keyboard.

Editing commands consist of erasing, tabulation, repeat and cursor positioning functions, which assist the user during data entry.

Network commands permit the user to open or close a liaison and to transmit a letter or a telegram. This part of the user interface has been designed with great care. Some keys on the

keyboard were dedicated to these functions : when the OPEN key
is pressed a special form is automatically generated on the
screen. The operator is invited to introduce the Network
address, the Transport Station address and the Port address of
the destination. The Virtual Terminal mode is set previously by
pressing a single dedicated key. The last line on the display
(the 25th) unavailable to the VT or the Application is divided
into fields where the DEVICE process permanently displays the
state of the terminal (scroll, and data-entry), the state of
the liaison (open, closed), and the state of message exchange
(LT received, LT sent, TG received, TG sent). Functions like
PLEASE (ask for the TURN), and telegrams (TG1-TG7) can also be
generated by pressing dedicated keys. The meaning of TG1-TG7 is
user-application dependent.

d) Summary of TIPAC processes

TIPAC processes and their relations are summarized in figure
5.5.1.(6).

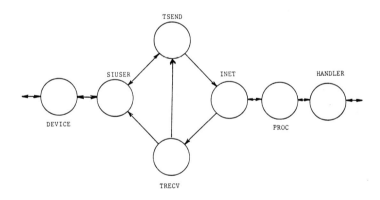

Figure 5.5.1.(6) - TIPAC processes and their relations

C - Third level of decomposition

A simple executive routine causes at most one segment belonging
to each process to be executed each time all the processes are
polled. Since no priority is assigned to any process, the
segment must be quick enough in execution to ensure that real

time events are properly handled. Each process may be in one of three states : blocked, ready and active.

The CPU time distribution is dictated by the most frequent real time event, i.e., the exchange of characters over the communication line (4800 b/s or 600 Characters per second). This yields 230 microseconds as the critical quantum of time per process. Interaction between processes is done through a block/wake-up mechanism controlled by binary semaphores. Each process has its own status byte. The first bit gives the value of the associated semaphore, and the others give the restart address of the process in ready state. The executive uses a process selector to poll processes sequentially. HANDLER, PROC and INET are common to all users. The remaining four processes are shared between the three users. Therefore, the executive maintains user indicators to keep track of which user is being serviced by each of these processes (see figure 5.5.1.(7)).

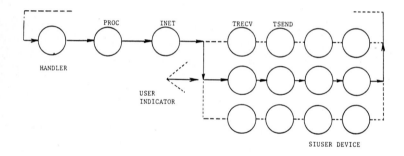

Figure 5.5.1.(7) - Activation of TIPAC processes

5.5.1.3. Implementation

Each process is implemented as a finite state automaton described by a state transition diagram. One transition between two states constitutes a segment and requires less than the critical quantum to be executed. The whole program is therefore structured in the form of small sequential segments (see figure 5.5.1.(8)). Each segment has one and only one entry point (An) and one and only one exit point (Bn).

The whole micro-code was written in 7000 instructions of 16 bits. Figure 5.5.1.(9) gives the volume of micro

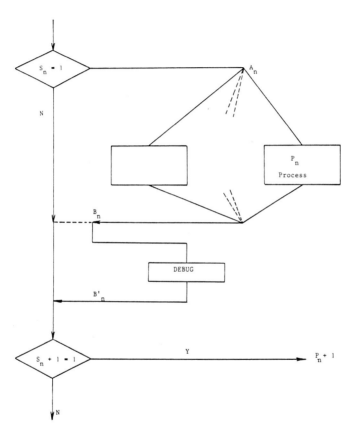

Figure 5 . 5.1. (8) - TIPAC programs structure

instructions corresponding to the different program modules. It took 12 man-months to design and test the whole system.

Monitor	120	General
System Initialization	100	470
General Subroutines	250	
HANDLER	600	Transmission function 1 300
PROC	500	
INET	200	
DEVICE	1 650	Virtual Terminal Control 3 540
SIUSER	1 890	
TSEND	625	Transport station 1 625
TRECV	1 000	
Total : 6935	instruction of 16 bits	

Figure 5.5.1.(9) - TIPAC Microprogram

Buffer management

The TIPAC hardware includes only one block of 2 K octets for packet buffering. This block is divided into a pool of 7 buffers of 272 octets each. One buffer can contain a Fragment text (247 octets), a Fragment header (8 octets), a Datagram header (12 octets), and a TMM block header (5 octets).

Only two processes request buffers : SIUSER, when it has to move a letter from the display memory to the line buffer, and INET, when it requests PROC to receive a block on the line. SIUSER will obtain a buffer only if at least one buffer exists for INET.

It is clear that 7 buffers of 272 octets are not sufficient as such to attach three display stations of 2 K octets each. Due to this hardware constraint, two decisions were made : 1- the display memory is used for retransmission during the end-to-end error recovery, and 2- fragments received in sequence are immediately delivered to SIUSER, which moves them to the display memory. However, if the letter is not completely received, SIUSER erases the part of the text which has been displayed with anticipation.

Debugging

The internal structure of TIPAC permitted us to create two debugging tools : DEBUG for selective testing, and LINE SPY for displaying data in real time.

DEBUG is placed as needed at the exit point (Bn) of a segment (see figure 5.5.1.(8)). When active, DEBUG automatically generates the image of the scratchpad memory containing all parameters and data. The contents of memory locations can be changed, the line buffer can be printed or a jump to the Executive can be forced.

LINE SPY is used by the HANDLER process. During each state transition, when a character is received or transmitted, a special subroutine is executed. It displays received characters in intensified mode.

The use of these tools considerably reduced the debugging time of the 7000 instructions program. The line control procedure was debugged in two weeks. Two more weeks were subsequently needed to debug the other processes.

5.5.1.4. Impact of TIPAC

The implementation of TIPAC proved that microprogrammable terminals could be connected directly to packet switched networks, and could incorporate high level protocols such as a Transport Protocol and a Virtual Terminal Protocol.

Following this experiment, several other implementations and studies have been conducted for TRANSPAC and EURONET [NAF77e].

5.5.2. The Multiple Remote Batch Station (MRBS)

A mini-computer (SFENA ORDO 400) has been used to develop a multiple batch station for CYCLADES [QUI78a]. The objective was to allow users to simultaneously access several batch services on the network. The MRBS configuration can include several devices, up to : 1 console, 2 card readers (CR), and 2 line printers (LP). Magnetic tapes can also be attached by simulating CRs and LPs.

The mapping of virtual devices into real ones is done as follows : a) each real card reader or line printer is used for emulating a virtual one, (no multiplexing can be done, since there is no secondary storage capability), b) the operator´s console is used for emulating several virtual consoles.

It is useful if not necessary to have a virtual console connected to each server to which another device is connected. Thus the MRBS has to provide several virtual consoles. However, the dialog between a batch service and a remote console is characterized by very little activity. Therefore this solution (sharing the real console) has been chosen, in order to reduce the cost of the system, (see also section 5.2.1.6).

Each virtual device can be connected independently of the others, i.e., each virtual device can be connected to a different server.

In order to keep commpatibility with SFENA products, the standard operating system (METEOR) was used.

The constraints imposed by the operating system led us to minimize the number of processes. The transport station and the line handler were borrowed from the HASP interface converter (see section 5.4.1.2). This TS does not impose any correspondence between liaisons and processes, i.e., one process can handle several liaisons, and one liaison can be handled by several processes. Using this characteristic, the number of processes involved in the MRBS has been reduced to 3 (see figure 5.5.2.(1)).

The CONS process handles the console keyboard and accepts two types of commands.

a) Local commands allow the user to control the MRBS. The most important local commands are used for connection and disconnection of virtual devices.

2) Remote commands are addressed to a server to which a virtual console is connected. They are translated into VTP format and sent to the server on the liaison.

The RECV process receives letters incoming through any liaison. VTP messages in letters are analyzed and the lines they contain are printed on the device associated with the liaison. Lines printed on the console are prefixed by the identifier of the virtual console to which they are addressed.

The SEND process handles the card readers. Cards read are encoded into VTP format, put into letters, and sent on the liaison associated with the card reader.

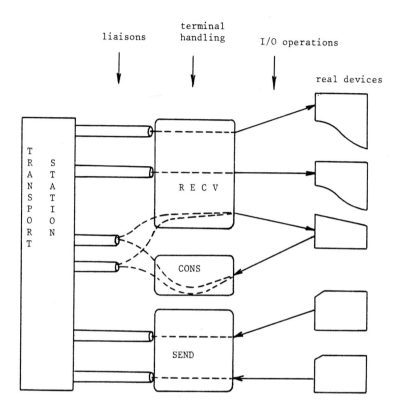

Figure 5. 5. 2. (1) - Structure of the MRBS

Testing this software was made easy by the availability of a
server software on the same computer : the HASP interface
converter was used as server for the first connections of the
MRBS. Controlling both ends of each liaisons very much
simplified the testing of the various layers.

5.6. Conclusions

This previous chapter presents only a relevant sampling of interconnection problems and experiments performed during the CYCLADES project. Many other implementations were carried out using similar principles. As it turns out, computer networks architectures and protocols depart considerably from traditional structures based on a central host and plain circuits. Interconnecting the past and the future is a massive task, at times cumbersome. As it is demonstrated in this chapter, solutions can be found, with technical elegance and cost effectiveness. However, one should keep in mind that interconnection bears intrinsic limits and deficiencies as mentioned in various occasions. Mapping natural objects as protocols relates to mapping a horse into a cow.

As we know, standardization only applies to the future, thus some other techniques have to be devised for the past. The descriptions presented here resort mainly to clever engineering and craftmanship. For a substantial progress to occur, it would be necessary to create tools allowing a formal description of existing systems.

CHAPTER 6

NETWORK OPERATION AND SERVICES

6.1. Operation environment

The CYCLADES network, although it was defined at the beginning as an experimental project, progressively became more than a prototype only used by its creators. The connection of various hosts increased the interest of a great diversity of users in networking. Rapidly, the CYCLADES network came to be considered as a common tool by a still-growing community of users. This evolution led us to extend the coverage of the network and the number of access points, to set up an operational structure, to develop specific tools for monitoring maintenance, and to clarify the relations between users and the network authority.

6.1.1. Topology

Figure 6.1.1.(1) shows the CYCLADES topology as it existed in 1978. CYCLADES nodes, network access points for host connection and access points for terminals (by means of concentrators or multiexors) are located at :

        Paris
        Grenoble
        Rennes
        Lyon
        Toulouse
        Nancy
        Nice
        St-Etienne

The whole network is composed of six nodes, ten terminal concentrators and around twenty host computers.

CYCLADES was also connected till 1980 to other networks such as the National Physical Laboratory network (NPL), the European Informatics Network (EIN) or the European Space Agency network (ESA).

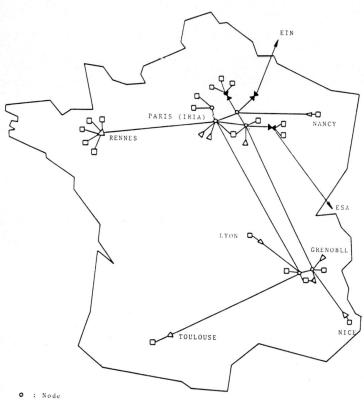

EIN

PARIS (IRIA)

RENNES

NANCY

ESA

LYON

GRENOBLE

TOULOUSE

NICE

o : Node

Δ : Concentrator

M : Gateway

□ : Host   Figure 6.1.1(1) - CYCLADES topology (1978)

The host computers are of various kinds. These are given below together with their location :

Institut de Recherche d'Informatique et d'Automatique (IRIA), Rocquencourt	Mitra 15
	Mitra 125
	Iris 80
Direction Generale des Impots (DGI), Versailles	Iris 80
Institut de Recherche des Transports (IRT), Paris	Iris 80
Centre Inter-universitaire de Traitement de l'Information (CITI-2), Paris	PDP 10
Universite de Paris VII, Paris	PDP 11
Institut Textile de France (ITF), Paris	Unidata 7730
Federation du Batiment (CATED), Paris	IBM 370/158
Universite de Lyon, Lyon	Mitra 15
	Iris 80
Universite de Grenoble, Grenoble	Mitra 15
	Iris 80
	IBM 360/67
Institut de Recherche d'Economie Politique (IREP), Grenoble	Mitra 15
Universite de Toulouse, Toulouse	Mitra 15
	Iris 80
Centre d'Etude et de Recherche de Toulouse (CERT), Toulouse	Iris 80
Universite de Rennes, Rennes	Mitra 15
	Iris 80

Institut National des Sciences Appliquees, Rennes	T1600
Ecole Superieure d´Electricite, Rennes	Iris 50
Centre Commun d´Etudes de Television et	
de Telecommunications (CCETT), Rennes	Iris 80
Ecole des Mines de Saint-Etienne, Saint-Etienne	Philips 1100
	T1600
Universite de Nancy, Nancy	Iris 80
Universite de Nice, Nice	Iris 80
Agence Spatiale Europeenne (ESA), Frascati (Italy)	IBM 360/65

6.1.2. Operational structure

In a first stage, the CIGALE subnetwork was operated by the team in charge of its implementation. With the evolution of the services required by network users, it became evident that this work had to be assigned to a dedicated team. In July 1975, the IRIA computer center was appointed to operate the CIGALE subnetwork in order to provide the best possible service to its users [GRA76a].

In a network, problems encountered are essentially due to the geographical distribution of users, servers and network components, the diversity of network equipments and the complexity of their inter-relations. It was thus necessary to determine the boundaries of responsibility precisely, to define the activities of the operation team clearly and to adopt a structured organization for it.

6.1.2.1. Boundaries of responsability

In section 3.1 CIGALE is described as the packet switching network of CYCLADES (also called the communication subnetwork). In this strict definition, nodes and lines are the only components which have to be taken care of. Terminals, however, are not directly connected to CIGALE nodes : they need concentrators to access the network. In some cases, the linking of a computer requires some additional equipments such as a gateway or a front-end, which implement the conversion to network protocols. Since users are concerned only by offering or accessing data processing services, it seems normal that the responsibility for the whole communication facilities be handled by only one organization.

To determine the exact boundaries of responsibility it is necessary to list the various components used within the network. Figure 6.1.2.(1) shows the various ways of connecting a data processing machine to CIGALE :

- Simple terminals are connected through terminal concentrators by leased or switched telephone lines. In some cases, multiplexors are used to share a leased line between remote terminals.

- Intelligent terminals can be directly connected to a CIGALE node.

- Hosts are either connected directly to a CIGALE node or via the "host-port" of a concentrator, or by means of specific gateways (see section 4.5).

- Other networks are connected by means of gateways.

These components (concentrators, multiplexors, gateways, nodes, lines) can be shared among users belonging to different organizations, which raises problems of responsibility.

When CYCLADES operation started, the operation team was responsible for CIGALE only, i.e., nodes and lines between nodes. After a few months, experience led to a re-examination of this way of operating, as users were not satisfied with the quality of service provided by the network access components, which were under the responsibility of each individual network participant. CIGALE itself ran smoothly.

It was then decided to extend the responsibility of the CIGALE operation team to a greater number of network access components. In figure 6.1.2.(1) this is represented by the domain inside the dotted line [DGQ77].

6.1.2.2. Activities of the CIGALE operation team

The activities of the CIGALE operation team [GRA75b], located at IRIA, can be divided into two parts : the first one is specifically oriented towards daily operation and the second one is concerned with the evolution of network services.

a) Network operation

Providing the best possible quality of service is an essential objective, which implies permanent supervision of all components [GRA76b]. Operational control has been centralized in a network control center located at IRIA (see section 6.2), which keeps track of the global state of the network and performs all necessary functions to recover from any abnormal condition (e.g., line failure, node breakdown). Some tools are available for detection of faulty components. If a failure cannot be repaired, the component supplier has to be called.

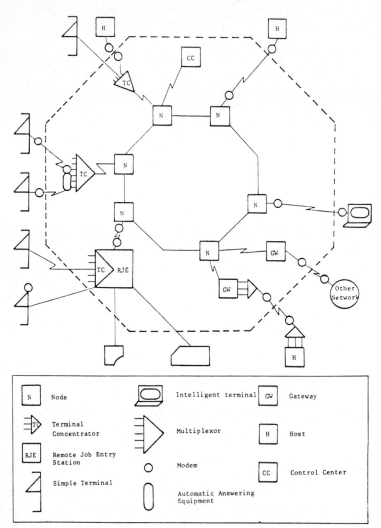

Figure 6.1.2.(1) - Network Components

This implies that well-defined maintenance contracts be negotiated with these component suppliers (e.g., PTT, computer manufacturers, software houses)

b) Network evolution

A network like CYCLADES is constantly evolving. This evolution takes various aspects : modification of existing hardware, addition of new components, connection of news hosts or new terminals, and changes of software versions.

The design and implementation concepts of CYCLADES facilitate these changes. However it is necessary to define strict rules in order to minimize risks of trouble when a change is made. The operation team has to plan these changes according to operational and user constraints.

c) User assistance

Three types of assistance can be distinguished :

1) Accessing the servers through the network needs instructions [COM75, WEB77, WEB77a] for terminal use, concentrator connection procedure, server connection procedure, network access points and accessible servers.

2) Using a specific service is possible only by means of adequate documentation, usually provided by the servers. However, at network level one has to indicate available services, where documentation can be found, administrative conditions of use and so forth.

3) If something does not work well, users must have the opportunity to complain directly to the network operation authority.

6.1.2.3. Operation team structure

The structure of the operation team is illustrated below :

                    Network operation manager

      Network control manager   User assistance manager

Control center   Regional centers   Hardware intervention
(4 operators)   (liaison officers)   (engineer)
                        (1 per center)

The control center team is in contact with correspondents located in each regional centers where nodes or concentrators are located (see figure 6.1.(1)). The network is in operation 24 hours a day, 7 days a week. However, the control center team is reachable only from 8 am to 8 pm on working days.

This network operation team is a part of the IRIA computer center and acts under the control of a network users committee composed of the different organizations supporting the network.

6.1.3. Users and services

Users and servers connected to the CYCLADES network do not all have the same motivations. For some users the network gives the opportunity to access services not available locally. This is the case, in particular, for data bases which were previously available only locally or through specialized networks. Other users find processing power at lower cost through the network. For some computer centers, it is a good opportunity to offer specialized services, to do business or to acquire experience in the computer network field. For multi-computer centers, the network brings new tools to provide uniform access to various heterogeneous local computers.

Services available on CYCLADES can be grouped into five categories :

- Standard computer center services : Time-Sharing and Remote-Job Entry (on CII-HB Iris 80, IBM 360 and DEC 10 computers)

- Specialized services such as :
. AGORA : a "poste restante" message service
. PIAF : an interactive system for French text analysis
. IMAGII : a computer aided design system for electronic circuits.

- General information retrieval systems :
. MISTRAL (CII-HB Iris 50 and Iris 80)
. RECON (IBM 360) at the European Space Agency

- Specific information retrieval systems :
. ARIANE : civil engineering information (IBM 370)
. TITUS : textile information (Unidata 7730)
. THERMODATA : Thermodynamic information (IBM 360)
. HEMOPHILIE : Medical information (IBM 360)
. CIDA : Chemical information (PDP 11)
. BIAM : Medical information (PDP 10)

- Data base systems :
. SOCRATE (CII-HB Iris 80, Iris 50, IBM 360)
. SYMBAD (Mitra 15)
. SYNTEX (Iris 80)

Users can also be divided into 4 types :
- research people working in the field of computer networks
- programmers and analysts implementing systems or

applications
- engineers and researchers of various disciplines using specific tools
- information retrieval specialists.

The optimal organization of users and servers on a computer network is still a topic for research, as well as the nature of the tools required to make life easy on a network.

6.2. Network Control Center

6.2.1. Centralized control

Since CIGALE nodes are computers, we could have operated the network by operating each node individually as a single regular computer. Practically this would have led us to have an operator at every node. Although this solution could seem attractive, it involved some serious drawbacks as shown in following paragraphs.

The practical activity of operators is reduced to a simple monitoring function (high node reliability, no peripheral units). The geographical distribution of components makes it more difficult to detect, localize and repair failures. A global view of the main network components is to be provided in order to monitor and understand as fast as possible what is happening in the network. Decentralizing the network control function does not meet this requirement.

Some operations (e.g., new system releases, topology changes) may be complex and/or delicate and they may need coherent and synchronized actions by the whole network. Assuming decentralized control along with numerous possible decision points, these operations are made considerably more difficult to organize.

The decentralization of operating personnel also means the dispersion of the operating responsibility. This would certainly affect both delay and efficiency of decisions regarding the operation of the network and cause a corresponding degradation in the quality of network service.

Consequently, it was decided to centralize the operation and control functions of CIGALE in a Network Control Center (NCC) [GRA77]. The NCC is made of a computer (CII Mitra 15) connected to the network and of an operation team in charge of operating the network with the help of the NCC machine.

One basic function of the NCC is the close monitoring of the network behaviour with the aid of a very simple mechanism (see section 4.2) : each node periodically ·sends a control packet to the NCC machine, containing data about its current state, such as : queues lengths, telephone line status, front panel

keys, clocks. By analyzing all these data the NCC machine can
continually keep track of the global state of the network and
automatically trigger an alarm upon detection of any abnormal
condition (e.g., line failure, unexpected front panel key
change, silent node).

Following an unfortunate coincidence of several failures it may
happen that the network breaks down into several "sub-networks"
totally isolated from each other (i.e., unable to communicate)
and possibly isolated from the NCC as well. In order to make
the network capable of continuing to function in spite of such
a degraded state, the following basic characteristics are
required :

   - The NCC does not perform any function which could be
   considered as vital for the node's operation (e.g.,
   routing).

   - The node system must as much as possible continue to
   function in presence of various troubles : transmission line
   failures, isolation from some nodes, from all the other
   nodes, from the NCC, etc.

6.2.2. Monitoring

In order to detect transmission troubles as fast as possible,
each CIGALE node closely monitors telephone lines. In addition
the "line status" is periodically reported to the NCC
indicating whether the line is "UP" or "DOWN" (see section
4.2).

Various failures (nodes, lines, hosts) may cause accidental
topology changes. Since mesh networks provide some path
redundancy, CIGALE should adapt automatically to these changes.
The adaptive routing function computes and dynamically sets up
the best path towards each destination (see section 4.2).

In addition to the path "cost", nodes compute a path "load" in
order to monitor and control the amount of traffic travelling
through that path (see section 4.2). Each CIGALE node also
monitors its own behaviour. In case of severe hardware or
software failure, control is passed to a "rescue" program which
puts the node into a ready state for "remote loading" from the
NCC. This function of remotely reloading the node software is
performed by the NCC, through any neighbour of the distressed
node (see section 4.2).

Most of the failures are automatically detected thanks to some
of the mechanisms listed above and described in sections 3.1
and 4.2 (node self monitoring, line monitoring, NCC report,
etc). However, it remains to determine the exact cause of the
trouble as fast as possible. Additional tools are used for that
purpose.

6.2.3. Hardware operation

The CIGALE network has been in operation since early 1974 and, from this experience, various considerations may be brought out about operating a distributed packet switching network. First, although it was not specifically designed for packet switching, the Mitra 15 mini-computer appeared to be reasonably convenient for that purpose in the CIGALE network case. In particular, in spite of some concern we initially had, it turned out that the CPU power stolen by the present transmission adapter microprogram is rather significant since 40 microseconds per octet can be considered as an average value. Actually this was acceptable in the CIGALE network where there were only a few high speed lines. The node system reliability has been measured over a long period of time (more than 4 years) and the MTBF (including both hardware and software failures) is about 1 month per node. The proportion of software failures is almost negligible and transient failures of power supply are responsible for 50 % of hardware failures. A pretty good value is obtained for the MTTR since the average figure per node is a few hours.

As far as transmission lines are concerned, it should be noted that they are provided by the French PTT and that their technical characteristics are quite variable in CIGALE : length (from a few kilometers to a few hundreds of kilometers), modulation (classical, base band), rate (from 4.8 to 48 Kbits/s). The measured MTBF per line is about 1 year but the failure distribution is both very dispersed and very stable; in other words, some lines tend to always fail, while others tend to never fail. The most sophisticated lines (long distance, high rate) are the least reliable. The MTTR per line is rather long, being a few days. Other than a number of "mini" failures (fixed up in a few seconds or minutes) most of the failures need at least 48 hours to be repaired.

The global network service level is computed on a weekly basis by computing the availability rate of a path between any two hosts in the network. All transmission line failures are taken into account in this availability rate, a node failure being equivalent to the simultaneous failure of all the lines connected to that node. The measured availability rate generally oscillates between 90 % and 100 %. This rather wide variation of the availability rate essentially appears because, for budgetary reasons, the topology did not provide the network with a very high path redundancy. Consequently, the availability rate is very sensitive to any line or node failure.

6.3. Measurements and performances

6.3.1. Introduction

The independence of the various CYCLADES layers and components is reflected in the structure of the measurements which have been conducted on the network at many stages during its development and operation [GIE78a]. The main measurements concerned the behaviour and performance of individual components of the switching machine (CIGALE) (e.g., lines, modems, switching nodes), the switching machine itself (e.g., routes, queues, packet traffic), higher level components (e.g., transport stations, terminal concentrators), and the global service as seen from a CYCLADES user (e.g., user level traffic).

Some aspects of these measurements, using various techniques, and hardware as well as software tools, are presented here, along with results obtained at the time they were performed.

6.3.2. Propagation delays over CIGALE links

The characteristics of CIGALE transmission lines vary to a large extent from one to another : distances range from a few meters to hundreds of kilometers, signal modulation can be of the classical types or of the base band type, and line capacity ranges from 4.8 to 48 Kb/s. Measurements of propagation delays over the various elements of a link, i.e., modems and telephone lines, aimed to compare the influence of those characteristics on link performance [GRA76c].

Definitions

- Propagation delay is defined as the delay for a signal to cover the distance between two given points on a transmission link (see figure 6.3.2.(1)).

- Modulation Delay (MD) is the propagation delay from A to B or from D to C, i.e., the delay due to crossing a modem from the junction side to the telephone line side.

- Demodulation Delay (DD) is the propagation delay from C to D or from B to A, i.e., the delay due to crossing a modem from the telephone line side to the junction side.

- Line Delay (LD) is the propagation delay from B to C or from C to B, i.e., the delay to travel through the telephone line.

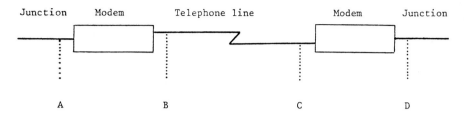

Junction   Modem   Telephone line   Modem   Junction

A   B   C   D

Figure 6.3.2.(1) - Link structure

- Junction to Junction Delay (JJD) is the propagation delay
from A to D or from D to A, i.e., the delay to traverse the
overall transmission link.

$$JJD = MD + LD + DD$$

Measurement method

The method used for measurement of propagation delays is based
on hardware tools (see figure 6.3.2.(2)).

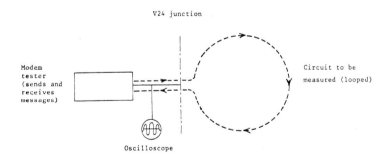

Figure 6.3.2.(2) - Measurement method

The oscilloscope is used to measure the delay between the
transmission on the circuit of the first bit of a message and
the reception of the first bit of the same message, coming back
from the looped cicuit. This delay represents the propagation
delay across the circuit.

Propagation delay across modems (MD + DD)

The circuits measured in this case are composed of looped modems. Some of the results obtained are the following :

MODEM	MD + DD (Mean)	Number of bits that can be transmitted during MD + DD
Classical Modem (V24) 4800 b/s	29.25 ms	14
Base Band Modem 19200 b/s	0 58 ms	1
Base Band Modem 48000 b/s (V35)	0 49 ms	2

Table 1

The last column of the table shows that delays to cross modems (MD + DD) are negligible compared to transmission delays of CIGALE packets, which contain typically at least one hundred bits.

Propagation delays across telephone lines (LD) and between junctions (JDD)

An example of the results obtained for two different lines between Paris and Grenoble (600 km) is given below :

Configuration	JJD (MD+LD+DD)	LD (JJD-MD-DD)	Nb of bits that can be transmitted during JJD
Classical Modems 4800 b/s	10.1 ms	7.175 ms	48
Base Band Modems 48000 b/s	3.45ms	3.4 ms	166

Table 2

This example shows that overall propagation delays between nodes (JJD) are not negligible compared to transmission delays. Indeed, it can correspond to the transmission of 10 to 20 octets. Therefore, these propagation delays must be taken into account in network models or simulations intending to provide quantitative information. They should also be taken

into account in network clock synchronization mechanisms if the
required precision is better than 10 ms.

6.3.3. Performance of line control procedures

As seen previously (see section 4.2) several line control
procedures can be used on CIGALE links. Measurements have been
conducted to evaluate their maximum throughput [GRA78]. Results
presented here concern total throughput for two procedures :
TMM and MV8.

TMM (Transmission Mode Messages) [POU73g] is a CII-HB line
control procedure that is used primarily to connect CII-HB
computers to CIGALE. MV8 (Multi Voies 8) [PAY75] is basically
derived from the IMP-IMP protocol of the ARPA network and is
used as the node-to-node control procedure within CIGALE.

Total throughput expressed in Kb/s includes packet text and
overhead, i.e., control characters, packet header,
acknowledgments. It represents therefore the physical
utilization of the line.

These measurements involved two MITRA-15 node computers
including an artificial traffic generator and interconnected by
a local telephone line of 19.2 Kb/s (see figure 6.3.3.(1)).

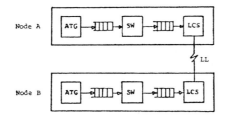

ATG = Artificial Traffic Generator

SW = Switch module

LCS = Line Control Software

LL = Local telephone Line (19.2 kb/s)

Figure 6.3.3.(1)- Line procedure measurements

Artificial traffic generation

Each of the laboratory node generates packets addressed to the other one and discards packets received from it. In all experiments artificial traffic generation is used to generate fixed length packets at the maximum possible rate in both directions, i.e., as fast as line control will accept them. In practice, the generation rate is set to a value ensuring that the line control queue is kept saturated. Overflowing packets are discarded. In order to prevent perturbation of measurement, modules exchanging control packets (e.g., route and time propagation) are not activated. In addition, the short length of the line allows us to make sure that no transmission error occurs, thus avoiding uncontrolled retransmission of erroneous or lost packets.

TMM throughput measurement

First results concern TMM performance under balanced traffic conditions, i.e., packets generated in both directions have the same length. Balanced traffic is the most favourable case for the TMM procedure, since no line bandwidth is lost due to packet length difference (see section 4.1). Three throughput curves are plotted in figure 6.3.3.(2) :

a) throughput in packets/second ranges from 50 to less than 8 for the maximum packet size,

b) total thrughput in Kb/s includes packet text and overheads, i.e., control characters, packet header, acknowledgements. Depending on packet length, total throughput varies from 13.2 to 18.3 Kb/s. Corresponding line utilization rates are about 69 % and 95 %,

c) useful throughput in Kb/s includes only packet text. The maximum value of 16.2 Kb/s is reached for the maximum packet size. In this best case, user data, i.e., packet text, uses about 84 % of the available line bandwidth.

Other measurements have been performed in order to study TMM performance under unbalanced traffic conditions, i.e., when packet lengths are not the same in both directions. Curves presented in figure 6.3.3.(1) give total throughput in Kb/s for A-B and B-A, (A and B being the two ends of a line). Figure 6.3.3.(3) represents a series of curves showing throughput values vs. A-B packet text length for various fixed values of B-A packet text length.

All these curves have a similar shape. A remarkable point is the A-B and B-A curves intersection. This corresponds to the balanced traffic case, i.e., both A-B and B-A packet lengths are equal. TMM protocol behaviour is basically dissymmetrical on each side of this point :

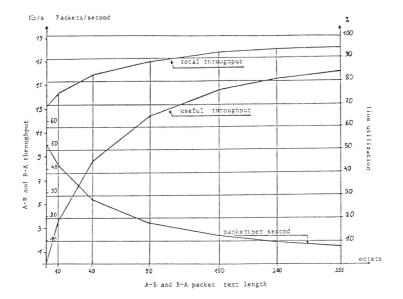

Figure 6.3.3. (2) - TMM Troughput for balanced traffic

When A-B packets are shorter than B-A packets, B-A throughput
is higher than A-B throughput and remains stable while A-B
throughput increases linearly.

This can be explained by looking at the TMM functional
behaviour (see section 4.1) : long B-A packets use almost the
total line capacity while short A-B packets waste a portion of
the line bandwidth because they have to wait for
acknowldgements. However, when A-B packet length increases,
waste of bandwidth decreases, thus improving A-B throughput.

When A-B packets become longer than B-A packets, A-B throughput
gets higher than B-A throughput and keeps slightly increasing
while B-A throughput collapses drastically. A-B throughput
increases because the fixed portion of the line capacity that
is lost between each message, due to software overhead, becomes
more and more negligible as compared to the capacity used to
transmit packets. On the other hand, while A-B packet size
increases, B-A packet acknowledgements are more and more
delayed, thus causing B-A throughput to decline.

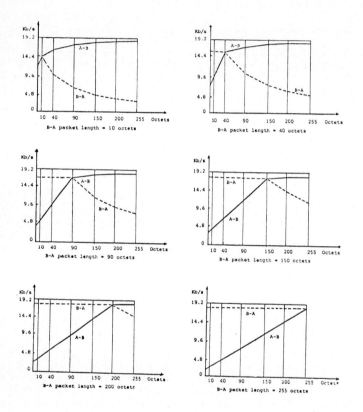

Figure 6.3.3.(3) - TMM total troughput vs. A-B packet text

MV8 maximum throughput measurement

MV8 channels are designed to allow "anticipation". While waiting for acknowledgement of one packet transmitted on one channel, other packets can be sent on other channels, thus improving line bandwidth utilization. MV8 measurements have been performed in order to study this anticipation mechanism behaviour and performance.

In order to facilitate comparisons with TMM, results presented here have been obtained for the same line speed (i.e., 19.2 Kb/s). Figure 6.3.3.(4) shows total B-A throughput vs. A-B packet length for various values of B-A packet length. It can be observed that all plotted curves have about the same shape : when A-B packets are short B-A throughput remains stable. However, when A-B packets get longer, B-A throughput drops down more or less abruptly depending on B-A packet length. In general, B-A throughput is better when B-A packets are longer. With the maximum packet length the throughput reaches 18.4 Kb/s, i.e., 95 % of the line capacity. However, some discrepancies can be observed when A-B packet size increases, e.g., 16-octet B-A packets have much less throughput than 15-octet packets and even less than null length packets.

Figure 6.3.3.(5) helps to understand this phenomenon. It gives B-A throughput in packets/second vs. A-B packet text length for various B-A packet text lengths. Again B-A throughput remains constant until it starts to collapse when A-B packet length reaches a given value. In addition, B-A throughput for short packets is much more sensitive than for long packets.

In order to explain these phenomena, let us consider curves L(0) in both figure 6.3.3.(4) and 6.3.3.(5) where throughput begins to decrease when A-B packet text is about 90 octets long. Let us look at what is happening when A-B packet text length is 100 octets (B-A packet text length being 0 octet) : due to added control characters, 126 octets are transmitted for each packet in A-B direction and 26 octets for each packet in B-A direction. Ratio between message lengths in both directions is therefore about 5. Figure 6.3.3.(6) represents the transmission diagram in this case and shows how B-A packets are acknowledged.
It can be seen fron figure 6.3.3.(6) that a portion of the line capacity is not used by B-A : while anticipation is exhausted by using all available channels (0-7), acknowledgements are delayed by long A-B packets. This explains why throughput curves decrease. However, when A-B packets are short, anticipation still allows to compensate for acknowledgement delays and therefore to keep the line busy : this is illustrated by the flat and high portion of throughput curves. Actually, key figures are the ratio between message lengths in both directions and the anticipation factor, i.e., the maximum number of packets that can be transmitted consecutively without receiving acknowledgement.

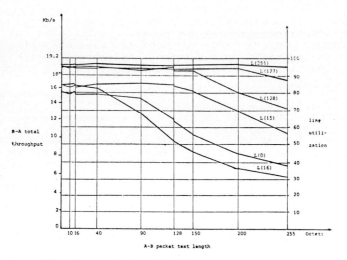

L(X) is the curve obtained when B-A packet text is X octets long

Figure 6.3.3.(4) - MV8 B-A throughput in kb/s

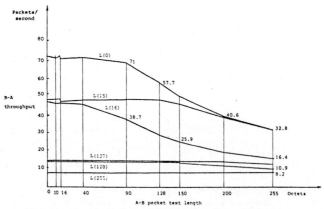

L(X) is the curve obtained when B-A packet text is X octets long

Figure 6.3.3.(5) - MV8 B-A throughput in packets/second

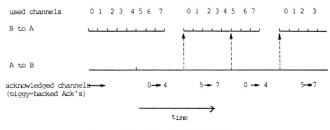

used channels   0 1 2 3 4 5 6 7   0 1 2 3 4 5 6 7   0 1 2 3

B to A

A to B

acknowledged channels⟶   0⟶4   5⟶7   0 ⟶ 4   5⟶7
(piggy-backed Ack's)

time

A-B packet text length = 100 octets
B-A packet text length =   0 octet

Figure 6.3.3. (6) - MV8 Transmission diagram

Clearly, the anticipation factor in MV8 is the number of usable channels. In other words, the anticipation factor value is 8 for short packets, 4 for medium packets and 3 for long packets. This explains why some discrepancies appear in figure 6.3.3.(4) where 16-octet packets have considerably less throughput than 15-octet packets. Throughput improvement obtained by increasing the packet size by 1 octet is almost negligible compared to throughput degradation due to reduction of the anticipation factor from 8 to 4.

This phenomenon appears clearly in figure 6.3.3.(7) in which a series of curves show total A-B and B-A throughput vs. A-B packet text length for various values of B-A packet text length. Particularly when B-A packets get longer, A-B throughput collapses when A-B packet length crosses class limits (i.e., 15-16 and 127-128 octets) corresponding to different anticipation factors.

6.3.4. CIGALE route measurements

Measurements campaigns were conducted from a host computer on CIGALE, to evaluate the performance of some predefined routes [EYR77]. These measurements focused on maximum throughput and mean transit delay under different load conditions.

Measurement configuration

The routes studied belonged to a subset of CIGALE represented in Figure 6.3.4.(1). Characteristics of each "hop", i.e., line control procedure and line capacity, are also mentioned in this figure.

A packet generator in the host was used to send fixed size packets to CIGALE. These packets were received by the same host after a trip within CIGALE following a predefined route.

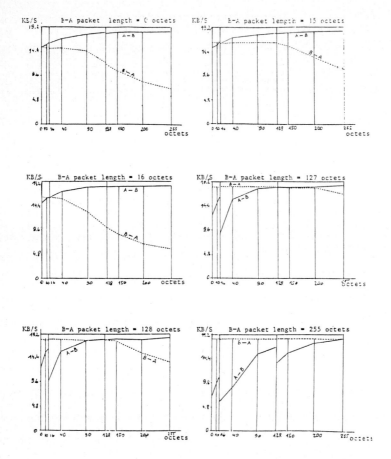

Figure 6.3.3.(7) - MV8 Total throughput VS A-B packet text length

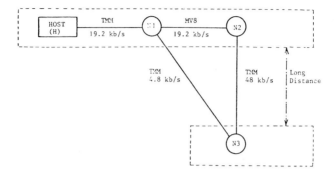

Figure 6.3.4.(1) - Route measurement configuration

Two traffic conditions were studied in detail. First, packets were sent as fast as possible (maximum throughput), akin to traffic generated by a file transfer. Secondly, packets were sent only when previous ones had been received back, akin to transaction oriented traffic.

Some of the results obtained are summarized in the following paragraphs. Maximum throughput is limited by the capacity of the slowest line. Results obtained here are consistent with those discussed in [GRA78], i.e., the maximum useful throughput that can be reached when operating the TMM line control procedure is about 80 % of the available bandwidth.

When using a line control procedure like MV8, it may happen that transmission errors cause packets to be desequenced. Indeed, packets are transmitted and acknowledged independently of each other on MV8 logical channels. While a packet in error is waiting for retransmission on one channel, subsequent packets can still be transmitted over other available channels.

Figure 6.3.4.(2) shows the ratio between the number of desequenced packets and the number of received packets, for different packet sizes. For each studied route, packets were generated at maximum rate. Of course, only routes with MV8 links can cause packet desequencing. The desequencing ratios appear to be independent of packet sizes and their mean value is about 1.2 %.

It should be noted that, because routes are predefined, there is no desequencing introduced by adaptive routing.

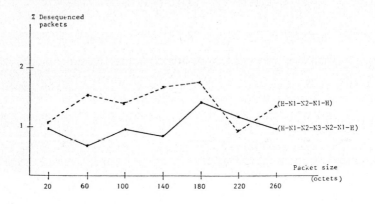

Figute 6.3.4.(2) - Packet desequencing

Number of packets in transit

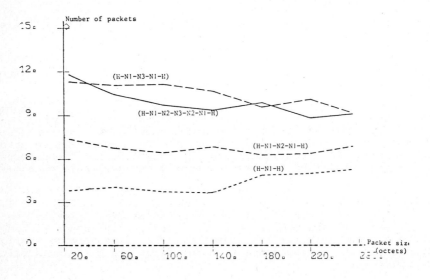

Figure 6.3.4.(3) - Number of packets in transit

Figure 6.3.4.(3) shows the mean number of packets in transit on each route studied, when packets are generated at the maximum rate. In other words it represents the capacity (in number of packets) of each of these routes, for different packet sizes.

As can be seen from figure 6.3.4.(3), the number of packets in transit is independent of packet size. Packets are generated from the host at maximum rate (over a 19.2 Kb/s line). In a CIGALE node, packets to be transmitted over a line are stored in an output queue whose maximum capacity is 5 packets. An output queue may start filling up when the packet arrival rate exceeds the output line capacity. Because of MV8´s anticipation capability, the maximum throughput achieved with MV8 is higher than with TMM for the same line speed.

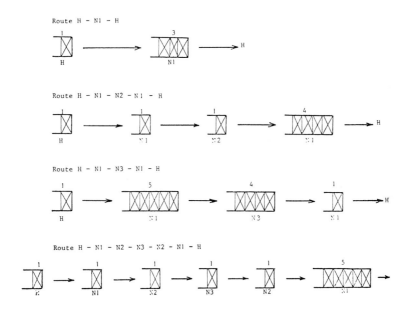

Figure 6.3.4.(4) - Distribution of packets in transit within nodes

From the above considerations, and taking mean values of the results plotted in figure 6.3.4.(3), we can deduce the distribution of the packets in transit within each node (see figure 6.3.4.(4)).

Transit delays

Results obtained and plotted in figure 6.3.4.(5) represent mean
values of round trip delays for packets of different sizes,
transmitted on some of the routes studied. These values,
obtained for a minimum load on the network, vary from 150 ms up
to 700 ms. The curves are essentially linear. Variations may
result from queues containing regular traffic, i.e., CIGALE
control packets or bursts of CYCLADES host-to-host traffic
during the measurement period.

Under the measurement conditions the influence of the number of
nodes on the route is not very significant, especially for
short packets.

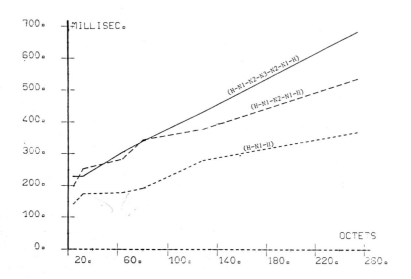

Figure 6.3.4.(5) - Mean round trip delay

Figure 6.3.4.(6) represents some distributions of measured
round trip delays for short and long packets. These diagrams
show a very tight distribution of delays.

However, it is to be noted that 5 % of full packets experienced
a round trip delay of 3.5 seconds when using the route

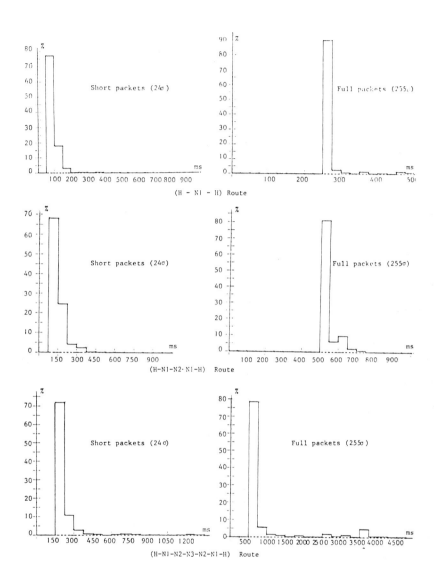

Figure 6.3.4.(6) - Round trip delays distribution

H-N1-N2-N3-N2-N1-H.   This can be explained by errors occurring
on the 48 Kb/s line,   which   caused   erroneous   packets   to   be

retransmitted after a time out of 3 seconds. As a consequence,
these results led us to reduce that particular time   out   value
to 200 ms.

If   we   look   at round trip delays when generating packets from
the host at maximum throughput (i.e., 19.2 Kb/s), we find   that
mean   values   vary from 200 ms up to 1.5 s for routes where the
traffic load can be carried. On the H-N1-N3-N1-H route the mean
round trip delay can go up to 5 seconds for full packets.   Such
a value results from two factors : the low speed of   the   N1-N3
line   (4.8 Kb/s)   and   the   packet generation rate (19.2 Kb/s),
which fills up node queues.

Distributions of round trip delays at maximum   generation   rate
are not so sharp as at low rates, due to the fact that one line
error   on   any   line   can fill up some of the node queues, thus
creating a delay for all packets.

6.3.5. User traffic

As seen in section 2, an end-to-end   transport   protocol   above
CIGALE   provides   CYCLADES   users (i.e., terminals, application
programs, time-sharing or remote job entry services, data   base
systems),   with   an   inter-process communication facility. This
facility allows users to establish liaisons with   other   users,
on which they can exchange letters with error and flow control.
Measurements have also been conducted at this level of service.
The partial results given below concern some characteristics of
the   traffic   exchanged   between   the   time-sharing system on a
CII-HB IRIS-80 machine in   Grenoble   and   its   users accessing
CYCLADES   through   terminal   concentrators   or   intelligent
terminals [BEN77].

Letter length

Figure 6.3.5.(1) represents a distribution   of   letter   lengths
for   time   sharing   users   of   the Grenoble IRIS-80 (the length
excluding the 12-octet packet   header).   Each   slice   of   the
abscissa   represents   letters   having lengths within an 8-octet
range, e.g., letters having lengths ranging from 8   through   15
octets are all represented within the same slice.

The   dotted   line   represents   the   distribution   of lengths of
letters received by the host, the solid line represents that of
transmitted letters.

The mean length of received letters   is   23   octets,   that of
transmitted letters is 50 octets.

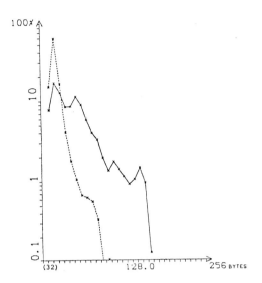

Figure 6.3.5.(1) - Distribution of letter lengths

Round trip network delay

We call here "round trip delay", the interval between the first transmission of a letter from a host and the reception by the host of the acknowledgment for this letter. This delay, which provides a measure of the effective rate at which user data may be transmitted, includes outward and inward network delays (whose measurements have been mentioned earlier), distant station response time, and delays incurred in the host network access method.

Figure 6.3.5.(2) is a histogram that displays the distribution of round-trip delays for distant Terminal Concentrators (TC) located in Grenoble (TC1), Lyon (TC2), and Paris (TC3) and an intelligent Terminal (T) located in IRIA near Paris.

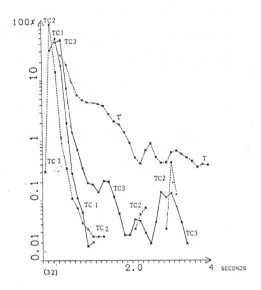

Figure 6.3.5.(2) - Round trip network delay

6.4. Conclusions

It would not be justified to draw general conclusions from the
real measurements presented in this chapter. Nevertheless, they
confirmed design intuitions that a simple packet switching
technique based on datagrams would provide for a stable and
efficient service. This is demonstrated by the various charts
introduced earlier. The stability of transit delays is actually
better than could have been expected in a context of stochastic
variables. The proportion of packets arriving out of sequence
remains too small to have a practical effect on performance
figures and buffer occupancy.

We also understood better why full duplex transmission
procedures were subject to significant interferences between
traffic going in each direction. This is difficult to predict
precisely by simple deduction. In addition, measurements at
user process level confirmed that efficiency is better served
by fast error handling in CIGALE, rather than by perfect error
recovery. Delays incurred within a packet network in order to
eliminate all possible packet losses work counter efficiency at
higher level. It would be useful to investigate from an

economic point of view what is the best balance of resources in
handling error recovery at various layers of a network
architecture. This could be a subject for further research.

In the following chapter analytical and modeling techniques are
used to investigate other aspects of network performance. They
are complementary to real measurements, and bring some
additional insight.

CHAPTER 7

SIMULATION AND MODELLING

7.1. Introduction

Modelling and simulation are well known disciplines, intended
for rigorous description, assessment and evaluation of complex
systems. The goals are identical but the means are different.
For the time being and for the particular context of computer
networks, it seems that the main difference between modelling
and simulation lies in the fact that simulation can be used as
it stands [MCD70], whereas modelling has found in computer
networks an incentive to develop new mathematical techniques
[KLE76].

As a matter of fact, many analytical models of computer
networks depend on assumptions that are sometimes far from
reality, e.g., infinite storage or transmission capacities,
perfectly reliable environments, Poisson arrival rates, no
time-out mechanism, etc. Analytical models have been proposed
only recently, which consider limited capacity nodes, but
mainly for tandem queueing systems. General models can be
found in various papers where different approaches are studied.
On the other hand, although simulation models seem to be more
easily adaptable to distributed systems analysis, they are also
more costly to utilize and they require great care and skill in
order to avoid misinterpretation. In CYCLADES, modelling and
simulation have proved to be extremely helpful on the following
counts :

- complete understanding of complex system behaviour,
- logical validation and debugging of system specifications,
- assistance in devising new designs,
- performance evaluation of proposed or hypothetical systems in
  environments conceivable a priori,
- assessing the efficiency limits of a mechanism, through
  performance evaluation in a full range of contexts,
- avoidance of useless trials and erroneous implementation
  effort (may rank very high).

In the following, emphasis is put on results rather than on the models themselves. Interested readers are referred to existing documents indicated throughout this chapter.

7.2. Internode protocols

7.2.1. Internode traffic

Reliability and efficiency are required at the transmission level. Physical transmission between adjacent packet nodes may be performed by using general data link control procedures called internode protocols. However, in the case of internode traffic, the following points are worth noticing :

1) since packets carry both origin and destination addresses, one could imagine the application of a traffic regulation based on criteria such as source-destination pair, traffic class, dominant flows, etc.

2) internode traffic is difficult to predict ; resources involved are CPU cycles, buffer space and line capacity ; static and dynamic allocation strategies consist of different trade-offs in the utilization of these resources ; should one of those resources be forgotten, optimization could just be a dream.

Because of remark (1), several existing internode protocols are based on the virtual channel concept as used in the Arpanet IMP-IMP protocol [MCQ77] and the MV8 protocol (see section 4.4) ; virtual channels are simplex and operated through an alternate scheme intended for the detection of duplicates. All simulations described here relate to that type of virtual channel based protocols.

7.2.2. Scope of the simulation studies

In CIGALE, buffers containing copies of in-transit packets are released upon receiving matching acknowledgments. The problem is to trade buffer space utilization against increased transmission and processing overhead. Different acknowledgment strategies are analyzed in section 7.2.3.

The protocol MV8 includes a static pre-allocation scheme for virtual channels. Dynamic allocation may be suggested ; is it simple and cheap ? And how much better is performance with dynamic schemes ? Solutions and results are given in sections 7.2.4 and 7.2.5.

7.2.3. Acknowledgment strategies

Two acknowledgment strategies have been simulated; they are
described in [DAN75] and [DAN75a]. In the following they are
referenced as protocols P1 and P2.

Protocol P1 : acknowledgments may be piggybacked with the
reverse direction traffic, special frames being used only when
there is no data packet to be sent.

Protocol P2 : acknowlegments are sent prior to normal packets
and exclusively within special frames.

Results show a strong sensitivity to traffic balance. When
traffic is not symmetrical (relative ratios of 2 or 3 in terms
of bits/sec), then protocol P1 is more efficient ; transmission
delays and waiting times before transmission are smaller and
less buffer space is required than with protocol P2 ; the
advantage of protocol P1 increases as line utilization
increases.

However, these results must be interpreted carefully, because
another simulation model showed that the opposite conclusions
hold in the case of balanced traffic for reasonable line
utilization ratios (in the range of 60 %).

In conclusion, it can be said that, for line utilization ratios
under 65-70 %, protocol P2 can be recommended because excess
line capacity can be used in order to save on buffer space,
although savings are relatively small ; on the other hand, for
higher line utilization ratios, P2 should be definitely avoided
if the goal is good utilization of buffer space.

As a consequence, only P1-like acknowledgment strategies are
recommended, and only this type of strategy is used within
CIGALE.

7.2.4. Performances in a specific environment

A specific configuration of CIGALE has been simulated,
including two nodes to which various hosts are connected. A
different approach to the same problem is described in section
7.2.5. The important results are given below.

Sensivity to transmission errors

One experiment has been conducted for which the internode link
is error-free. In another experiment, random errors are
generated at the rate of 1 bit in 100,000. Random link errors
(at the rate tested) do not cause any significant degradation
in network performance ; the only measure that is subject to
appreciable change is standard deviation of transit delay
[IRL76a].

Variations of the MV8 protocol

Two variations of the MV8 protocol have been considered. The
first one, called MV8S, dispenses with the three classes of
packets (short, medium and long). Instead, only a single queue
of packets is formed and transmitted on a
first-come-first-served basis.

The second modification, called MV8P, retained the concept of
three classes of packets, but it allowed all of them to use
every channel. However, short packets are always sent ahead of
medium packets, which in turn are transmitted before the long
ones. Within each class the first-come-first-served discipline
holds.

Results reported in [IRL76a] show that :

a) link utilization changes very little,
b) the average queue length is smallest for the MV8P protocol,
largest   for MV8S,
c) MV8S causes a substantial increase in average transit delay.
While the delay differences between MV8 and MV8P are small,
they favour MV8P.

Another simulation showed that short packets are favoured by
MV8, MV8P coming a very close second. Large packets are least
penalized by MV8S. Considering that short acknowledgement
packets should be given very fast service due to the probable
requirements of any end-to-end protocol, MV8S must be deemed
undesirable. The tradeoffs between MV8 and MV8P are quite
close ; MV8P is preferred because it provides considerably
better service for medium length packets, while degrading full
length packet service only a little.

7.2.5. General evaluation of internode protocols

Another heuristic approach may be adopted for simulating
internode protocols. Instead of evaluating performances for a
specific topology, the goal is to produce results applicable to
many environments. For that purpose, the simulator input is
defined as a specific set of proportions of internode traffic
mix (different cocktails of short, medium and long packets). It
remains to be investigated which real traffic conditions and
network topologies correspond to those simulated traffic mixes.

A variant of the MV8 protocol has been simulated. It adapts to
traffic variations and it is called the MV8 channel stealing
protocol (MV8-CS) : the same preallocation scheme as in MV8 is
used, but free channels can be stolen from one category for
another one if that latter category is predominating. Stolen
channels are immediately returned to their "owner" when a
packet of its category has to be transmitted. This protocol
should be simple to implement.

A third protocol has been evaluated. It is identical to MV8S
described in section 7.2.4 and referenced as FIFO procedure.
For this simulation, the propagation delay on the line was
given a non-zero value, which seems more realistic than the
opposite assumption usually made. Measurements confirmed that
this was a sound choice (see section 6.3).

RESULTS

Results are taken from [LEL76]. The three protocols perform
identically if link utilization is kept below 50 %. Above that
ratio, MV8 and MV8-CS provide a stable transmission delay for
short packets in all cases, which FIFO does not achieve. For
some traffic patterns, MV8 introduces artificial limitation,
because of the static channel allocation scheme ; this does
not translate into a significant throughput degradation but
into larger waiting times for medium or large packets, and
thus, into larger buffer utilization. For instance, buffers
may be kept busy up to three times longer with MV8 than with
MV8-CS. When using MV8-CS, these undesirable effects
disappear ; the only limiting factor is line capacity itself.

Considering these results, it may seem attractive to recommend
a simple protocol for internode traffic handling ; such a
protocol could manage two packet categories only, each being
served FIFO : a short packets category and a category for other
packets, the first one being scanned first. Obviously, this
would perform efficiently as far as the subnetwork itself is
concerned. But the consequences of such a choice for the higher
levels in the network must be evaluated. In particular, it may
be necessary to provide the transport network level with the
same priority scheme because short Letters or acknowledgment
Letters impact host resource utilization ; such letters may be
classified as medium-packets at the subnetwork level. What is
then really needed is not a FIFO scheme mixing large and medium
packets, but a MV8-CS-like scheme.

On the other hand, it should be noticed that MV8 and MV8-CS
protocols introduce more packet desequencing than FIFO-like
protocols ; if sequenced delivery is required at the user
level, then the trade-off is between utilization of buffer
space at the receiving end and potential switching capacity.

7.3. Buffer management and transit delay

In CIGALE, if a packet arrives at a node while all its storage
is occupied, the packet is destroyed. Simulation and modelling
have been used to assess the acceptance of such a policy by
determining packet drop rates for various traffic loads ;
these rates also depend on the buffer management policy being
used.

A complete network (7 packet nodes and 34 hosts) was simulated and modelled. The model chosen for this simulation corresponds to an early prototype of CIGALE. In particular, transmission was half-duplex and packet transit delay was dominated by a constant overhead due to modem controls ; consequently, these delays were almost independent of packet length. Therefore, the following results do not apply to newer versions of CIGALE. Detailed results may be found in [IRL75a]. They are summarized below.

7.3.1. Dropped packets

Below 90 % utilization of the busiest link, very few or no packets are dropped, and the average total delay is acceptable. Somewhat above 90 %, the percentage of lost packets becomes prohibitive. It might be surprising that as high as 90 % utilization could be reached without major degradation of network performances. This is understandable, however, because of the point mentioned above, that is almost constant packet delays. As is well known, the average queue length, and hence the probability of packet loss, is a function of both link utilization and variance of the service time. Small variance results in smaller queue lengths.

On the other hand, it can be reasonably expected that when the large constant transmission overhead is reduced, the transmission time variance will increase and the maximum link utilization that still allows adequate network performance will lie somewhere between 70 % and 80 %. Of course, with faster links the network throughput will increase anyway.

7.3.2. Buffer management policy

It is observed that packets that are dropped by a congested node are not necessarily intended for the highly utilized link ; they may be going onto a link that is under-utilized when all buffers in the node are monopolized by the busy link queue. For example, the queue for the busiest link averages 17.5 to over 18.5 packets (out of the total 20 in the node) for the three highest loads offered. This observation suggests that a buffer management policy should be introduced so as to prevent buffer monopolization by a single link. In order to get a better insight into the internal behaviour of a node, a mathematical model has been built [IRL75] ; it gave the following results.

7.3.3. Analysis of buffer and line management

Under same conditions, the number of packets successfully processed by the node may decline when more traffic is applied. Improvement in throughput has been shown possible.

The policy is to allow each output queue to grow, at most, up to a certain predefined maximum length, and to drop any excess packets. This policy implicitly favours packets destined to less utilized links over those destined to highly utilized ones. The maximum queue size (assumed common to all output queues in the node) that provides for best throughput depends mainly on the total traffic into the node from all its input links ; it could be set as a table look-up parameter once it has been precomputed from the model.

The single node model has been extended to cover the entire network, and analytical results confirm the shape of the throughput curve obtained by simulation.

In interpreting raw simulation results one would like to be able to explain this or that behaviour of some observed parameters. If, for instance, simulation results indicate existence of bottlenecks in the system, as they usually do for sufficiently high traffic levels, it is desirable to determine their causes, and perhaps identify the most critical one. This may be very difficult to do, for several different factors often interact, limiting the observed system performance. Some of these factors may actually result from interaction of the system with its environment, rather than constitute part of the system proper.

For example, it was observed that the curve representing delivered traffic vs. offered traffic declines above a certain level of offered traffic (see figure 7.5.1.(1)). Bad buffer management can cause this. However, environmental reasons were also identified.

One reason is saturation of interfaces connecting hosts with CIGALE. This environmental factor not only limited the amount of traffic actually entering the network, but also, in some simulation runs, changed the structure of the traffic flowing through the network. The two limiting factors in the network proper are buffer starvation and link saturation. One of the objectives of good network design is, of course, proper balance between buffer supply and link capacities, so as to avoid wasting expensive transmission resources because of insufficient buffer storage. Buffer management techniques, such as the one mentioned above, are also useful in improving network throughput without adding extra hardware.

The relative influence of buffer capacity and link capacity is illustrated in figure 7.3.3.(1). A specific CIGALE configuration was simulated [IRL75a, IRL75c]. All links have nominal speed of 4.8 Kbits/s except links 37 and 79 that are 19.2 Kbits/s. Each packet switch has 20 buffers shared between all input and output queues. A buffer contains exactly one packet (of any length). One would normally expect a bend in a utilization plot for a server with finite waiting room and loss discipline to occur well below the 95 % level shown for links 37 and 79. The linear growth shape is explained by: - virtually

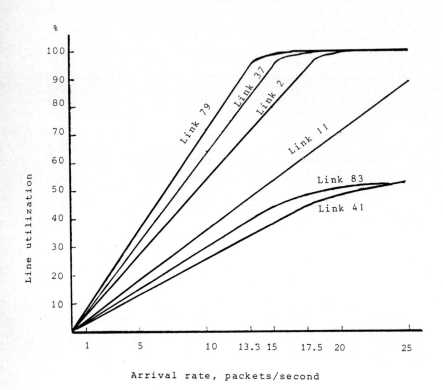

Figure 7.3.3.(1) - Line utilization of selected links

constant service time on these links, which reduces buffer
requirements, - low level of traffic on other links leaves 20
buffers almost exclusively available for these link queues,
making them appear as infinite storage systems. Links 41 and
83 do not have this advantage and their utilization curves bend
earlier. Links 2 and 11 are from hosts with infinite waiting
room, thus, the utilization plots are straight lines. Results
presented above influenced our decisions regarding traffic
control and routing strategies. Obviously, buffer management,
line management, routing and traffic control are interdependent
issues.

7.3.4. Analytical results

Previous work on diffusion process models has been extended to
the case of general service times with multiple classes of
customers and FIFO service at each station [IRL78].

This model has been applied to the prediction of the performances of a 7 node CIGALE network assuming two classes of traffic (short and long packets). Results indicate that for this model, average queue lengths within nodes range from 0.2 to 3.6 packets. These results are in agreement with results obtained from early simulations.

A model of store-and-forward packet switching networks in which nodes are of limited capacity has been studied and a numerical solution technique is used to predict performances of a 7 node CIGALE network including 4.8 and 9.6 kbits/s half-duplex links [IRL75]. Results indicate that for 1000-bit packets, transit delays average 1 sec. Those analytical results have been compared to simulations.

It appears they are equivalent when exponential service times are assumed whereas analytical results are less accurate when other distributions (Erlang, hyperexponential) are considered.

7.4.Routing

Various types of routing algorithms have been proposed or implemented in the past. Theoretical and experimental work has been carried out in this area, more specifically for adaptive routing strategies. The main problems to be solved with such algorithms are stability, convergence and avoidance of loops.

7.4.1. Simulation

An initial design of routing mechanism for CIGALE was assessed through simulation. This mechanism, to be referred to in the following as the basic algorithm, had to be compared with another mechanism, which is based on rapid routing strategy and length-two loop-control [IRL76].

The rapid routing technique is intended to force a routing message to be generated by a node whenever a change occurs. Length-two loop-control is done by changing the routing message before it is sent to make it impossible for the node receiving the routing message to create a loop of length two. Whenever the node originating a routing packet has the link to the destination node as its current best route, then instead of sending its current cost for that destination, it sends a cost of infinity in order to prevent packets from travelling back and forth between the two nodes and never reach the destination. Both rapid routing and length-two-loop control techniques are described in further details in section 4.4.3.

7.4.2. Results

Detailed results may be found in [IRL76]. The most dramatic
result measured is in the case of rapid routing. In almost
every measurement taken, the rapid routing algorithm
outperformed the basic algorithm. This is independent of all
of the other variations tested. It is also interesting to note
that the results with rapid routing seem to be very stable. The
other variations had little effect on the results when rapid
routing was in use, while they had significant effect when the
basic algorithm was used.

The effect of changing the basic routing interval in
conjunction with rapid routing was surprising. Less frequent
routing messages were generally as good as, and sometimes
better than, the same situation with more frequent routing
messages.

When routing messages are sent too frequently, routing tends to
be too sensitive to transient conditions and the overhead is
higher. Under some circumstances, global performances are
degraded. For the basic algorithm, however, the expected
results were observed. With more frequent routing messages,
the algorithm reacted better. As could be expected, of course,
with more frequent routing messages, the overhead on the
network was increased. In the cases of 0.3 second interval,
during the tests with one and then two links broken, the
network became congested, losing a high proportion of packets.

The effect of length-two loop-control in conjunction with the
basic algorithm was surprising. There are cases where it caused
a significant improvement, and cases in which there was a
significant deterioration. The important difference between the
two occurrences is that the improvements occur when the network
becomes disconnected, while the deterioration occurs when the
network remains connected.

In conjunction with rapid routing, length-two loop-control
generally had no effect. However, in two cases some
improvements did occur while, on the other hand, in one case,
addition of length-two loop-control caused some packets to be
lost because the responsiveness of the algorithm to changes in
topology was diminished.

7.4.3. Conclusions

Primary simulation results indicate that the basic algorithm
works in principle. This was confirmed by another model
including random link breakdowns.

It is quite clear that the rapid routing strategy should be
used. It is more effective in reacting to changes in the
network topology, and requires a smaller proportion of the
network resources when no changes are occurring.

It would seem that there is no harm, and occasionally some
advantage, to setting to a very small value the rapid routing
message background frequency (i.e. the minimum frequency at
which routing packets are generated even when no change of
routing tables is observed, (see section 4.4.3). Further
analysis would probably be useful to determine the best rate,
but the slowest frequency tested (20.0 seconds) seems to be the
best based on the results presented here. Consequently, it was
decided to implement rapid routing in CIGALE. Length-two
loop-control is beneficial occasionally and harmful
occasionally, with more benefit than harm. However, there is no
strong motivation for using it. Further, the simulation did not
make any allowances for the increased processing time required
for this algorithm (it requires different routing packets to be
generated for each link from a node). This difference could be
of considerable importance if the node is processor bound
rather than I/O bound. Thus the decision was made to leave out
this kind of control in CIGALE.

7.5. Traffic control

7.5.1. Data on node congestion

The simulation model referenced in section 7.3 was used to
produce exact figures of network performances. The single most
important measure of network performance is the network
throughput rate. This rate is defined as the average amount of
traffic delivered at the destination hosts in unit time. It can
be measured either in number of packets or in total traffic
length, say in bytes.
As can be seen in figure 7.5.1.(1), the throughput rate reaches
a maximum for arrival rate equal to about 15 packets per
second, and then declines. This decline occurs mainly for the
reason that some of the node-to-node links reach high
utilization levels ; corresponding queues use up all available
storage in the packet node and incoming packets are dropped.
These packets are never delivered to their destination, thus
resulting in a flattening in throughput. In figure 7.5.1.(2) it
can be seen that no packet (out of 10,000 sent) are dropped for
arrival rates of less than 13.3 packets per second ; only about
0.3 % are dropped at this rate, but unacceptable drop rates are
observed for higher arrival rates.

Because of transient conditions, it may be necessary to drop
packets. However, each packet drop wastes network resources and
should be carefully controlled. Intuitively, it would have been
better to keep these dropped packets outside of the network.
Then, the problem to solve is how to decide at which moment a
packet should be allowed to enter the network. This is called
traffic control. Additional difficulty comes from the fact
that traffic control should be a distributed algorithm.

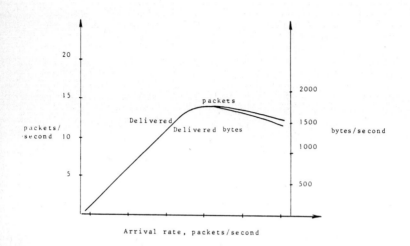

Figure 7.5.1. (1) Network throughput

Pioneering work in traffic control has been conducted at NPL ;
simulation of the "isarithmic" technique was most helpful in
understanding the real causes and the intimate mechanisms of
network congestion. Theoretical and experimental work was also
carried out for the ARPA network. However, reassembly and
sequencing problems are so intertwined with traffic control
that it is hard to sort out their respective influence on
throughput and delay.

7.5.2. Node congestion - a look behind

Congestion is often associated with buffer clogging as if
buffers were the sole cause of congestion. Actually, buffer
clogging is just a symptom, not a cause of congestion.

Indeed, with the assumption that both packet arrival and length
follow an exponential distribution, simple queueing theory
shows that the number of packets waiting for output increases
drastically when line load exceeds 70 %. As a result, more

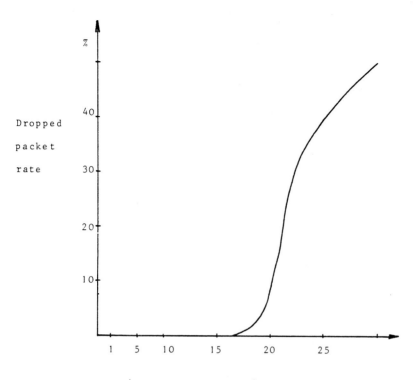

Figure 7.5.1.(2)- Dropped packets (as percent of total
number of packets generated)

buffer space is utilized for more time. It is certainly
desirable, from the standpoint of cost-effectiveness, to get a
high ratio of line utilization. But this conflicts with the
objective of shortest transit delay, since queueing and
buffering mean increased delay. Therefore, a compromise
appears to be necessary between line load and transit delay.

Transit delays are dependent on line speed, packet length,
queue length and number of hops, not to mention transmission
error rate. Clearly, queue length is not the only sensitive
factor in meeting delay requirements. Assuming that network
designers end up with some figures for average and maximum
queue length, it is possible to determine from analysis or
modelling the average and maximum line load, or vice versa.
Thus, buffer and line utilization are two facets of a single

problem : resource management.

Taking into account present terrestrial transmission technologies, it appears that line bandwidth is scarce, with increasing costs, while buffers may be provided in large enough sizes with declining costs. Thus, it is presumably more realistic to determine a bandwidth limit in the first place, and thereafter to derive buffer requirements. Putting more buffers than is actually necessary is a waste of resources, without any improvement in transit delay. Results presented in section 7.3.3 suggested that monitoring line load could be instrumental for a better control of local congestion spots. Two methods providing for that kind of monitoring are described below.

7.5.3. Isoflow traffic control

It is desirable to limit the amount of traffic admitted into the communication network to the extent that the busiest link is utilized below, say, 75 %. In deference to the isarithmic control policy the term "isoflow" control will be applied. The method involves installing a gating mechanism between each host and the network. This mechanism allows packets into the network with a certain preset frequency. This frequency is determined for each host based on the known characteristics of the traffic applied to the whole network, in particular, the geographical distribution of the traffic, and also the network topology and routing. The frequencies can be updated frome time to time to accomodate changing traffic characteristics during, for example, the daily operation of the network. The responsibility for allocating to users the transmission capacity allowed by the network is left to the host machine.

It is recognized that isoflow control may limit the utilization of the network transmission resources. It is meant to be a crude first level control policy with very little overhead. If and when a higher utilization of links is needed, the isoflow control could be supplemented with some kind of more selective traffic control mechanism. In this case the isoflow admission gates may be retuned for higher admission frequencies.

7.5.4. Channel Load Limiter

A detailed description of the Channel Load Limiter (CLL) mechanism is given in section 4.4.6. In short, CLL consists in controlling link loads and sending choke packets to those sources which contribute to congest a specific link. Choke packets are sent when a link is in warning state. Each time a source being in a listening period receives a choke packet, it should slow down its traffic for the destination indicated. Otherwise, it runs the risk of having to retransmit dropped packets.

Two important issues with CLL are the precise setting of
threshold values between normal, warning and alarm states and
the actual host reaction to choke packets.

7.5.4.1. Simulation context

The topology of the subnetwork simulated included seven packet
nodes interconnected by eight full-duplex links, using the MV8
protocol. Links were assumed to be error free. Each packet
node had room for up to twenty packets. Twenty six hosts were
connected to the subnetwork, each of which generated a specific
traffic pattern such that the nominal traffic entering the
subnetwork amounted to 41.2 packets/sec.

Several experiments have been conducted. They consisted in
doubling the nominal traffic rate uniformly for all hosts or in
increasing the packet rate from one host to a single
destination in order to saturate a specific link.

The reduction rule for the traffic issued by a host receiving a
choke packet has been chosen to be an arithmetic progression,
limited by a maximum reduction level, which is a system
parameter.

Also, in order to reduce possible oscillations in the
computation of the link load state variable, double thresholds
were introduced to change the value of these state variables.
A summary of the results presented in [IRL77a] is given below.

7.5.4.2. Results

Transit delays are reduced by the controls, except in some
cases where the overhead control traffic forces a slight delay
increase. Also, the controls reduce the utilization of
saturated links but sometimes not as much as desired.

Very few packets were observed as lost on storage overflow.
However, a percentage of generated traffic was not allowed to
enter the network because of host reaction to chokes. It was
also observed that too many packets were dropped in the "alarm"
state.

Clearly, the controls were overreacting with the parameter
values chosen for these simulation runs. Attempts to tune the
thresholds to reduce the alarms severity did not produce a
satisfactory improvement. Throughput increased significantly
only when the alarm state was completely suppressed. It is
thought at present that the alarm state should be removed. A
better way to protect the network from ill-behaved hosts could
be the tripping mechanism which works as follows : only two
possible states, normal and warning, are involved in the
propagation of the path load state ; if the path to a
particular destination remains in the warning state for a

predefined time interval, called the tripping period, any
packet entering the network for that destination is dropped ;
a choke packet is generated as usual in the warning state.

Another result was that the use of double thresholds in the
load state computation had secondary importance to the
effectiveness of traffic control. Therefore, a single
threshold is used in CIGALE.

It seems that the host reaction to choke packets should be
modified so that the traffic rate is reduced exponentially.
Also, the implementation could be simplified by having that
reduction happen globally, for all destinations. These issues,
as well as parameter tuning, are currently under investigation.

It is worth noticing that because of the simplicity of the CLL
scheme, it can be turned off in the whole network, or in a
subset of nodes. Therefore, it will be possible to introduce
and independently observe other control mechanisms. This is an
important degree of flexibility when several schemes are
combined in order to balance one another in various traffic
conditions.

7.6. Transport protocols

Communication networks exhibit specific properties like
transmission errors, losses or failures, and introduce variable
transit delays. Designing a reliable transport protocol for
such a hostile environment is not straightforward. A case study
is described, which shows how helpful heuristic techniques can
be in protocol verification. Another facet of the transport
protocol design issue is efficiency ; heuristic techniques are
used also to evaluate the performance of various flow control
mechanisms ; performance as seen by users of transport
protocols is evaluated and data regarding trade-off choices are
given.

7.6.1. Protocol verification

The initial design of the CYCLADES transport protocol included
three modes of operation : regular Letters, Letters on
connections (liaisons) and Letters on virtual channels (voies
virtuelles). Connections and virtual channels (VC's) are
opened and closed identically. Nevertheless, they provide for
different services. On VC's, Letters are sequentially numbered
by the transport station (TS), which provides sequential Letter
references further used for acknowledgment and error control.
Error and flow control are performed automatically on a Letter
basis ; the Letter size is not limited.

On connections, the Letter size is limited (255 octets) and
Letters are mutually independent. Letter references are given
by the user. Letters may be error-controlled or not. Flow
control is dynamic and works as follows : a credit must be
allocated to the sender for each Letter to be sent ; requests
must be made continuously by the sender according to the
current load ; credit requests are sent within normal user
Letters or within special "empty" packets (no text) ; according
to local availability, the receiver goes on returning credit
values to the sender.

To open a link (connection or VC), the command U-ETAB-LI must
be issued by the TS user.

Setting up a connection or a VC is done according to a
Demand - Response - Confirmation scheme along with negotiation
of parameters. A TS can go through seven internal states (see
Fig. 7.6.1.(1)) ; EA is the idle state ; EB, EC, ED and EE are
intermediate states, all protected by a time-out ; EF is the
active state allowing transmission and reception of Letters ;
EG is the resetting state during which a TS is "unavailable"
for a given user, while returning to state EA ; EG is also
controlled by a time-out. Service messages carry parameter
values. D-ETAB-LI, R-ETAB-LI and C-ETAB-LI are respectively:
demand message, response message and confirmation message.

On a connection or a VC, two addressing formats were
specified : 1) general address : to be used during the set-up
phase, 2) short address : to be used after completion of the
set-up phase (EF at both ends) and dynamically allocated. This
was intended to reduce transmission overhead.

Two different "reset" commands were also provided to TS users :
1) a close command (U-FERM-LI) using short addressing, 2) a
purge command (U-PURG-LI) using general addressing.

Although all this appeared as a reasonable initial design, it
was felt necessary to simulate the protocol before embarking
upon an implementation [LEL73, LEL77].

In order to discover possible inconsistencies or abnormal
conditions, user commands at both ends were issued at random
and the simulated packet network behaved like a real one, i.e.,
it introduced variable transmission delays and packet losses.

We actually verified that simulation was most helpful to trace
down design bugs and to understand some of the detailed
characteristics of distributed systems.

7.6.1.1. Opening and closing a link

a) One interesting situation was shown to occur because of the
existence of two different reset commands. Let us assume that
two stations A and B are exchanging Letters (state EF) and that

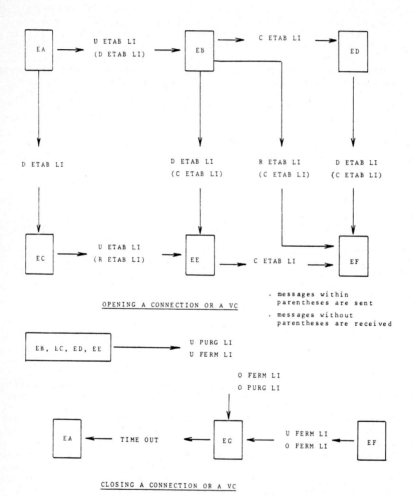

OPENING A CONNECTION OR A VC

. messages within
  parentheses are sent
. messages without
  parentheses are received

CLOSING A CONNECTION OR A VC

Figure 7.6.1.(1) - The TS automaton

user B wishes to close the link (U-FERM-LI). Let us assume now
that the corresponding message (O-FERM-LI) is lost within the
packet network. After a while, station B is reset to EA (normal
timer action) ; it is now impossible for station B either to
close the link in station A or to open the same link locally.

Indeed, any attempt (U-ETAB-LI) will be rejected after a while
because of lack of answer from station A. The reason for this
is that station A drops any incoming PURG message because, when
in state EF, the only reset message to be obeyed is a FERM-type
message. D-ETAB-LI requests are also discarded because of state
EF. Meanwhile, nothing prevents station A from continuing to
send and retransmit Letters to station B.

b) Losses, errors and variable transmission delays are the
three   facets   of   uncertainty.   Obviously,   from such
characteristics, it is easy to infer that desynchronization
between stations may occur. For example, let us assume that a
link is being opened and that the TS's at both ends are in
state EE : they have sent a C-ETAB-LI and they are expecting
reception of a distant C-ETAB-LI. If one of those messages is
lost, then only one TS moves to state EF and starts
transmitting Letters whereas the other one returns to state EA.
Requiring all service messages, like C-ETAB-LI, to be
acknowledged does not solve the problem because acknowledgments
may be lost ; for instance, in the above example, this would
only result in reversing the desynchronization.

Even simpler protocols suffer desynchronization. The current
CYCLADES protocol, described in section 3.2, has been
simulated, mainly for the purpose of performance evaluation
(see   section   7.6.2) ;   this   protocol is based upon a
Demand - Response scheme ; unfortunately, simplicity does not
prohibit the occurrence of undesirable situations as shown in
figure 7.6.1.(2).

For local reasons (malfunctioning, user mistakes, user
decisions, etc.) a CLOSE operation is initiated from station A
shortly after the OPEN operation. If the messages are received
in reversed order and if the OPEN is granted in station B, a
symmetrical OPEN message will be sent to station A ; when such
a message arrives during the "closing state" phase, it is
rejected, thus leading to a situation where the liaison is
closed for A and open for B.

If messages are acknowledged, then one might suggest that
non-acknowledged messages be retransmitted several times in
order to avoid such desynchronizations. This only reduces the
probability of occurrence of a desynchronization.

Conclusion

Simulation showed that it is impossible to devise a mechanism,
based on timers and retransmission, which is absolutely
reliable when opening or closing a link. Clearly, one may

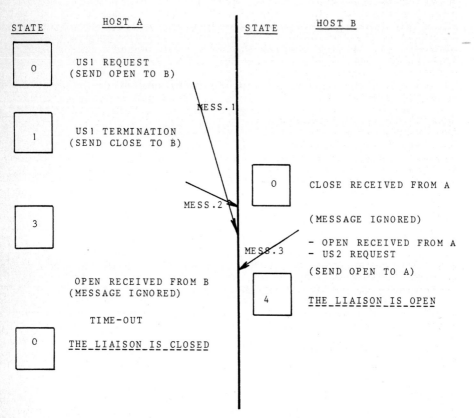

Figure 7.6.1.(2) - A case of desynchronization with
the ST2 protocol

devise more sophisticated protocols, e.g. three-way handshake
and sequence numbers [SUN75]. However, even with very complex
protocols, the probability of occurrence of a desynchronization
can never be null. Simulation also indicated that only one
"close" command should be used ; this was adopted for the
current CYCLADES transport protocol.

7.6.1.2. Flow control

The flow control scheme on connections has been described in
section 7.6.1. Simulation has revealed several cases of

desynchronization.   Desynchronization on connections

a) error-control off.

It is impossible for the sender to know whether or not its
requests for credit allocation are received by the receiver.
Also, it is possible for credit-allocation messages to be lost.
This applies to acknowledgments as they are not
error-controlled.

b) error-control on.

Several cases of desynchronization may exist. We give here only
two examples. When a Letter is timed out, it is retransmitted.
However, the integer indicating the number of credits to be
allocated may have changed in the meantime, because n new
Letters have been submitted by users. If the Letter was timed
out only because the acknowledgment was lost, this results in a
situation where the receiver rejects (but acknowledges) the
duplicate Letter, without taking into consideration the extra n
credit allocation requests.

Another flaw is that acknowledgments carry the identity of the
Letter being acknowledged with the number of Letters which were
received since the previous acknowledgment was sent. Mutual
agreement between the sender and the receiver cannot be
guaranteed because of race conditions and retransmissions.

Similar desynchronizations are known to be possible with the
Allocate mechanism on ARPANET connections. On the contrary,
simulation showed that the VC flow control scheme was
reliable ; the window technique takes its inspiration from this
scheme.

7.6.1.3. Conclusion

These results were obtained before connection or VC
implementation had begun ; they contributed to the decision to
revamp the transport protocol. A description of the current
CYCLADES protocol is given in section 3.2.

Obviously, the lack of a precisely defined reference system or
utilization of implicit time references lead definitely to
unrecoverable desynchronizations in distributed systems
[LEL77b]. The other reference which can be used is space, and
this is what has been adopted for VC´s ; a common measuring
unit is agreed upon by the two stations, thus allowing error
and flow control to be achieved by referring to a specific
location in the data stream. VC´s were the first transport
mechanism to include the so called "window scheme". Absolute
safety is possible for flow control assuming that uncertainty
is reduced at the packet network level : that is, if an upper
limit can be defined for packet transit delay, then the window
mechanism, using a cyclic numbering scheme for Letters, is

absolutely reliable.

Although desynchronizations have been shown to be possible when opening a communication link, hierarchical control provides for improved reliability at higher levels in the system, the highest one being the user level. Abnormal silence of a Transport Station may be noticed or systematically controlled by one of the higher system levels and clearing of the unsafe situation is then feasible. Theoretically , desynchronization at higher levels can occur, but it is always possible to devise mechanisms with a probability of undetected error as low as desirable, e.g. by using different or more expensive error-control schemes where needed.

7.6.2. Protocol evaluation

7.6.2.1. Flow control for transport protocols

Two protocols have been evaluated. These protocols are the CYCLADES protocol (CYP) and the Transmission Control Protocol (TCP), described in [ZIM75b] and [CER74a]. They both use a positive acknowledgment - retransmission scheme and the window technique. The main differences are in the areas of error and flow control.

1) Error control.

When fragmentation is on (Letters longer than one packet), CYP provides only for acknowledgments of complete Letters. With TCP, it is possible to return one acknowledgment either per Letter or per fragment. For the purpose of comparing buffer requirements, the latter option was used in our simulation of TCP. When a fragment is timed out, TCP provides for the retransmission of that fragment only. When a Letter is timed out, CYP requires this Letter and all subsequent Letters to be retransmitted.

2) Flow control.

Credit values are indicated in octets with TCP. CYP assumes an agreement between sender and receiver on a common Letter size at liaison set-up time ; then, credit values are indicated in terms of Letters.

Evaluation results

Identical environments have been simulated for CYP and TCP [LEG76a], [LEL76]. Letter lengths of 120 octets and 480 octets have been chosen to evaluate effects brought about by fragmentation. The virtual full-duplex link used by the communicating processes is symmetrical, i.e. processes behave identically. With regard to the packet network, an accurate

simulation was felt necessary : a three hop path has been
chosen with links operating at 19.2 kbits/s.

For medium size Letters (120 octets), the two protocols have
nearly identical performances. TCP achieves better throughput
than CYP when credit values made available by the receiver are
small and not exact multiples of the Letter length ; this is
due to the octet based flow control policy used in TCP. For
all other cases, CYP yields a slightly increased throughput
because of a smaller overhead incurred per packet.

For long Letters (480 octets), throughput with TCP is higher
than with CYP as long as credit values are kept small ; this
is due to the acknowledgment per fragment policy used in TCP ;
otherwise, CYP takes advantage again of a smaller overhead per
packet.

Simulation results for transmission delays indicate quite
similar performances for CYP and TCP.

It can be anticipated that better throughput would result from
more sophisticated buffer management policies, at least to the
extent that buffer space is in limited supply. There is one
thing which cannot be evaluated through simulation, that is
software complexity.

7.6.2.2. Performances as seen by transport network users

It may be questioned how costly it is to transmit a short
Letter (a few octets) in one packet ; this is the case for many
applications, like interactive ones. This mode of operation
probably induces a high overhead, thus reducing the available
bandwidth for the user ; on the other hand, it achieves fast
transmission. Are there conditions for which it should be
better, when possible, to multiplex several short Letters
within one packet ?

Simulation helped us to understand some trade-offs encompassing
several layers of protocols. As will appear in the following,
attempts to increase throughput at the transport level
introduce side-effects at the transmission level, which in turn
produce counteracting effects at the transport level, to the
point of finally degrading throughput.

The CYCLADES protocol has been simulated to compare multiplexed
and non-multiplexed options. The results presented in [LEL77]
indicate very clearly that the highest throughput for the user
(in terms of octets of text) is reached when short Letters are
sent as individual packets, for the most realistic credit
values at the receiving TS. This throughput may exceed by 25 %
that obtained when short Letters are multiplexed within a
single packet. This is due to the fact that multiplexing
Letters into packets leads to longer packets resulting in
longer transit delays.

For the same reason, acknowledgments being piggy-backed with the reverse traffic are slower to come back ; new credit values are carried with these acknowledgments. Thus, it may happen that the sending TS runs short of credits and must stop transmission. This results in reduced throughput.

Multiplexing is efficient only if a large number of credits is made available at the receiving station. As stations are supposed to handle many liaisons simultaneously, such luxurious values do not seem realistic. Thus, in practical cases, better delay and better throughput will be achieved at the user level if short Letters are sent as individual packets.

The threshold value is a function of the packet network load. Some network traffic (AT) interfering with the actual traffic to be measured was incorporated in the simulation. It can be seen in figure 7.6.2.(1) that multiplexing is more likely to be efficient as packet network traffic increases. For instance, the threshold value is 19 for AT = 0 (no packet network traffic); it is only 5 for AT = 10. The reason for this is that transit delays are longer when the traffic increases and, for a given amount of Letters, multiplexing reduces the number of packets to be transmitted compared to non-multiplexing.

When used, multiplexing brings a better use of bandwidth at the transmission level. However, it reduces user throughput for a given amount of buffer allocation. This is a typical example of conflicting optimization in hierarchical systems. These problems are discussed in [LEG78].

7.6.2.3. Influence of priority routing for acknowledgment packets

Considering that round-trip time is the limiting factor for user throughput when the multiplexed option is used, it may seem attractive to send back acknowledgments (and credit values) in special service packets only, provided that short packets are routed prior to any other packets inside the packet network ; internode protocols using such schemes have been presented and analyzed previously, (see section 7.2).

Three strategies have been simulated :

1) conventional strategy : acknowledgment packets are issued by a TS only if it is not possible to send a user Letter (either no Letter is available or credit value is null) ; priority is given to acknowledgment packets inside switching nodes,

2) for each Letter received by a TS, an acknowledgment packet is generated ; priority is given to acknowledgment packets inside nodes and at TS level,

3) only one packet is generated for all Letters multiplexed within one packet ; again, priority is given to acknowledgment

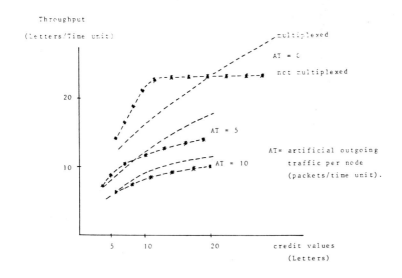

Throughput

(Letters/Time unit)

Figure 7.6.2.(1)- Threshold value as a function of the
subnetwork load

packets inside nodes and at TS level.

Simulation runs showed that, for these strategies, differences
in performances are small ; furthermore, smaller differences
correspond to smaller credit values which are realistic
situations [LEG76a]. Thus, we drew the conclusion that using
special acknowledgment packets and a priority routing mechanism
to return credits brings practically no advantage to the user.
Therefore, there is no need to change the current piggybacking
scheme used in CYCLADES.

As a general conclusion to this chapter, it can be said that
simulations were very helpful to understand the intimate
behaviour of specific mechanisms as well as their mutual
relationships. On the other hand, analytical models were most

interesting to predict general performances in specific environments.

CHAPTER 8

DISTRIBUTED SYSTEMS AND APPLICATIONS

8.1. General concepts

The notion of distributed system appears as an attempt to integrate the general CYCLADES objectives at the application level, i.e., heterogeneity, distribution of control and use of existing local systems [CHU77], [SEG78].

Every application (be it intended for single machines or networks) must take into account two classes of parameters : system environment (application-independent) and application-dependent requirements.

In other words, it is particularly important to define a level, which plays the role of an operating system in the network and takes into account the CYCLADES environment. This level, termed Logical Network Machine (LNM), provides the network application designer with a means of directly implementing distributed applications [CHU74].

Software engineering techniques argue for a precise layering of levels, in order to get an increasing degree of independence from the physical machine.

8.1.1. Logical Network Machine Functions

As illustrated in figure 8.1.1.(1), LNM functions are derived from concepts of heterogeneity and distribution when applied to data and programs [CHU75].

The problems posed by data distribution can be identified as retrieval, presentation and transfer. This is a direct consequence of accepting existing systems. In the usual sense, a task requires that associated data be linked to it prior to its execution. This linking process includes, as a minimum, retrieval (identification and addressing) and transfer.

In addition, if the data format conventions are not identical for the host containing the task and the host containing the associated data, presentation control (internal format conversion, record conversion, description conversion) may be necessary.

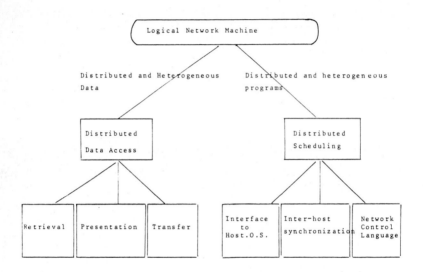

Figure 8.1.1.(1) - Logical Network Machine Functions

If we consider that a Network Task (i.e., one which is defined at the network level) may lead to the execution of local tasks (within single systems) on several and possibly dissimilar hosts, a problem of distributed scheduling arises.

An extended Remote Job Entry approach turns out to be inadequate because of the need for an overall control. In this matter, most existing Job Control Languages are so primitive that job control from a remote host becomes impossible. In addition, the heterogeneous nature of the hosts makes a network control strategy difficult.

Only the tasks running under an operating system may benefit directly from the services it offers. To make these services available to tasks running on a different host, these tasks must remain accessible from the network (using the transport station).

In order to reduce redundancy and complexity, all services should be presented in the same form, processing a unified set of network control primitives.

Each set of services located within a single host constitutes a component of the Logical Network Machine, termed a Network Control Sub-System (NCSS´s). These NCSS´s have to take care of inter-host synchronization and to translate network control primitives into local operating system primitives. The set of unified network control primitives constitutes a Network Control Language. In section 8.2, we describe an example of such a Network Control Language implemented in the CYCLADES network.

8.1.2. Architecture of a distributed network application

So far, the study has been restricted to the system environment. We shall now describe briefly how to develop Network Functional Sub-Systems (NFSS), which together with the LNM constitute a network distributed application. In fact, most of the additional problems encountered are specific to the type of application (nature of objects, naming, operating protocols, etc.).

The components of the various layers can be summarized as follows :

Transmission network + the set of transport stations = the transport facility.

Transport facility + the set of network control sub-systems = the logical network machine.

The logical network machine + a set of network functional sub-systems = a distributed application.

In section 8.3, we describe a particular type of distributed applications experimented in the CYCLADES project : the Distributed Database Management Systems.

8.2. Distributed Operating Systems

In this section, we describe an experimental study of a Logical Network Machine undertaken at Grenoble University. This research, undertaken within the framework of CYCLADES, is referred to as IGOR (Interpreteur General Oriente Reseau), [DNG76], [DNG78].

8.2.1. Introduction

Typical job control languages do not provide facilities for expressing the control of a task in a network environment. Of course they were designed for a single self-contained operating system. Thus, some new mechanisms had to be devised.

Instead of trying to expand deficient and dissimilar tools, it appeared more attractive to design a control language equipped with all facilities found to be desirable in a network environment.

Some debate took place about the superiority of an algorithmic approach vs. a more traditional control language approach. Eventually, the preference was given to an algorithmic language, where parameters may be evaluated dynamically as results of function execution.

The lack of theory and experience covering such network languages, and the highly interative mode of operation, favoured interpretive execution.

Although the primary objective of a common network control language is to provide facilities for task control and scheduling, it appeared very early that it contained as well all the basic facilities for expressing complete programs. From this observation, the language was designed to be usable as a regular general purpose programming language. However, a convenient human oriented interface would have been necessary to promote its use in programming applications. In practice, development efforts were focused on control aspects.

The remaining part of section 8.2 presents an overview of the structure of the NCSS (see section 8.1.1), a description of the language and examples of its applications.

8.2.2. NCSS Structure

The language mentioned in section 8.2.1 and termed Intermediate Language (IL) is processed by the NCSS in each host, [DUM74], [DUM74a].

The NCSS is structured as illustrated in figure 8.2.2.(1).
This structure is intended to minimize machine dependence.
Indeed, the Interpreter module may be written in any portable
language, including IL, because it does not make use of any
specific operating system implementations. However, it has to
interface somehow with the local operating system. To that
effect, a set of network wide primitives has been defined. They
are processed by a host dependent module, called SYNCOP (Syteme
Normalise de COmmunication de Processus), which takes care of
process, resource and time management according to the host
operating system facilities.

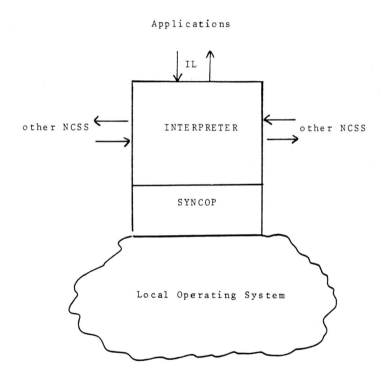

Figure 8.2.2.(1) - NCSS structure

8.2.3. The IL language

8.2.3.1. Introduction

Several reasons lead us to chose our definition of an intermediate interpreted language, [FAR74] : a) the heterogeneity of the networks calls for a single language able to run on any machine, b) the compactness of the algorithms written in IL minimizes the volume of information transferred on the network, and c) the interpretation, being flexible and modular, allows extensions to new functions and mechanisms.

One of the disadvantages of interpretation is its overhead in execution. Computer networks at the present time, however, are such that this handicap is masked by transmission delays.

8.2.3.2. Procedure oriented language

As languages such as Algol and PL/1, IL is based on the concept of procedure with the following characteristics :

- every procedure is declared within another procedure (termed "son of.."); the outermost procedure is son of an initialization procedure ;

- every procedure may have parameters and local variables.

However some restrictions have been introduced :

- a call to another procedure, to be processed on another host, is forbidden;

- the use of global variables is forbidden.

The procedure is thus considered as a basic entity by the interpreter.

An application is defined as a tree-structured set of procedures. The root procedure is initialized on a single host. Typically, the root procedure contains instructions to activate inner (son) procedures (ACTIVATE instruction). All procedures, at every level of activation, are executed in parallel on the different hosts.

The activation of a procedure indicates as a parameter the host on which execution is to take place. Any host may be selected, including the one executing the activating (father) procedure.

As will be explained later in section 8.2.4, procedures are provided with mechanisms for exchanging control information and data.

As a special case a procedure may be called as a subroutine, (CALL instruction), i.e., the father's execution is suspended

until control is returned, when the son´s execution is
completed. However, execution may proceed in parallel within
the called procedure and its sons.

8.2.3.3. Langage components

a) Variables and instructions

Besides conventional variables (e.g., logical, integer,
floating point) IL offers four special types of variables :
SON, EVENT, RENDEZ-VOUS and LIAISON. They are described in
section 8.2.4.3 along with the corresponding instructions.

b) Parameters

Every parameter belonging to a procedure must be declared by
address (only in CALL instructions), by name or by value.

c) MACRO instructions

This facility may be invoked anywhere. The corresponding set of
instructions (stored in a standard library) is simply copied
into the body of the calling procedure prior to its activation.

8.2.4. NCSS functions

8.2.4.1. Introduction

The table below summarizes the NCSS functions, their aims and
the corresponding IL instructions to be presented in more
detail in the following sections.

8.2.4.2. Procedure activation and termination

The code of a procedure is always executed in the context of a
process. A process is created each time a son procedure is
activated. An implicit liaison is then established between the
two processes executing the son and father procedures. As
mentioned earlier, the execution host is a parameter of the
ACTIVATE instruction. In the CYCLADES environment, it was
considered an advantage that the whole code of an application
be introduced in one place and then disseminated for
distributed execution. Therefore, the code of a procedure is
transferred from father to son on every activation.

When an application is stabilized, it is possible to optimize
execution by permanently storing procedure code where execution
is to occur. After that, only ACTIVATE instructions need be

Aims	NCSS functions	IL elements
Procedure activation and termination. control of execution	Process initiation and termination Implicit father-son liaison	SON variable ACTIVATE instruction Parameter passing
Information transfer	Inter process communications	LIAISON and RENDEZ-VOUS variables ; RESERVE, OPEN, READ, WRITE, CLOSE, FREE instructions
Control over parallelism between procedure	Interprocess Synchronization	EVENT variable ; WAIT, WAITM, POST, CHECK instructions
NCSS interface to existing programs	Execution of procedures written in other Languages than IL	See 8.2.4.6.

Figure 8.2.4.(1) - NCSS Functions

transferred from father to son.

There is but one exception to the aforementioned mechanism, that is the CALL instruction, which is equivalent to a conventional subroutine call. The CALL instruction is restricted to procedures executed on the same host and uses the same process for calling and called procedures.

The ACTIVATE instruction contains the following parameters :
- SON descriptor (state, implicit liaison),
- HOST identifier for execution,
- procedure identifier (IL code of the son procedure),
- parameter list.

A process is terminated at the end of the corresponding procedure. The implicit liaison between father and son is cleared as soon as either of them terminates. Other errors, such as network or host failures, may cause the liaison to be discontinued and an error handling routine to be activated on either side.

8.2.4.3. Information transfer

A liaison may be set up explicitly and dynamically between two son processes for exchanging information. Variables of type RENDEZ-VOUS and LIAISON are necessary to carry out this communication function.

RENDEZ-VOUS variable

This variable is located in the father procedure and is passed to the sons as a parameter. Only the sons may update it, while it may be read by father and sons. It controls the rendez-vous of the two son processes and it contains for each son the following information :
 . reservation event,
 . son name,
 . liaison opening event.

LIAISON variable

This variable is declared in the two sons procedures as local variables. It is the responsibility of each son to issue a RESERVE instruction that specifies its LIAISON variable and the common RENDEZ-VOUS variable declared in the father procedure ; the result being a resource reservation.

Then, each son procedure must issue an OPEN instruction for the liaison to become operational. This instruction puts the son process into a wait state until the opposite OPEN is executed.

This operation is protected by a time-out in order to perform
diagnostics and retries. Failures may result from such causes
as :
. no reservation made by the opposite son,
. abnormal delay,
. network disruption.

The other instructions concerning a liaison, READ, WRITE, CLOSE
(opposite to OPEN) and FREE (opposite to RESERVE) need no
further comment. Information on the liaison can be found in the
LIAISON variable which contains :

. the state of the liaison (e.g. death of opposite partner,
network failure, closing stage),
. liaison identifier,
. address of the RENDEZ-VOUS variable,
. addresses of error handling routines,
. addresses of users' procedures (e.g., compression and
decompression of information transferred on the liaison,
conversion, encryption).

Remarks :

Although the father's presence (i.e., access to father's
variables) is necessary to establish the liaison between two
sons, no additional instruction is required in its procedure.
Access to the RENDEZ-VOUS variable uses the implicit liaison.
The father and son procedures may be developed independently.

8.2.4.4. Synchronizations

Synchronizations are based upon the following elements :

. EVENT variables,
. WAIT, multiple WAIT, POST and CHECK instructions invoking
SYNCOP functions,
. Implicit liaisons between father and sons,
. Explicit liaison between two sons.

The example in section 8.2.6 illustrates this mechanism.

8.2.4.5. Development of procedures written in other languages
than IL

It may be desirable to use other languages ; an example is the
use of already existing procedures. This requires the following
adaptations :

. the writing of a prologue for passing parameters,
. the writing of an epilogue for returning the results.

8.2.5. Application to Network Command Language

As of today, we have not yet defined the structure of a
CYCLADES network control language. Some preliminary thoughts
favor the following characteristics :

. a high level language more attractive for a programmer than
a traditional job control language,
. availability in batch mode as well in interactive mode,
. an extensible structure.

The basic idea is that of a high level programming language,
usable as a network control language. PASCAL with appropriate
network extensions could be a reasonable candidate. Compilation
would produce IL, which could be transported and executed
anywhere on the network.

8.2.6. Applications to distributed data bases

8.2.6.1. Overview

The idea is to use IL as a general purpose programming
language. Generally, in a data base system, a user request is
compiled in two phases : generation of intermediate code and
generation of machine code. The data base system compilers may
be modified to generate directly IL code with a procedure
structure corresponding to the potential parallelism. On the
other hand data base systems would have to be designed or
modified to accept IL as input language.

8.2.6.2. Example

Let us take the network configuration shown in figure 8.2.6.(1)
and let us assume the following user request expressed in a
certain data manipulation language :

GIVE NAMES OF ALL PERSONS HAVING CARS WITH COLOUR = ´RED´ AND
ADDRESS = ´GRENOBLE´.

The request defines two criteria :
. red coloured car relating to the car data base,
. person living in Grenoble relating to the person data base.

The interest is to define a procedure representing each of
these criteria and have it run locally on the two hosts
concerned.

One solution consists in executing these two procedures
independently and collecting the results in host A. All people
owning red cars would be transferred from B to A and all those
living in Grenoble from C to A.

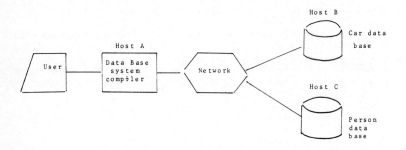

Figure 8.2.6.(1) - Distributed Data Base Applications

If an objective is to minimize the volume of network traffic, the best strategy is to start with the host where the volume of entities matching the criterion is minimum. In the above example, there are likely more people living in Grenoble than red cars. Therefore, the preferred solution is to establish directly a liaison between the two hosts B and C. A procedure in B looks for people owning a red car, sends their identification to a procedure in C, which transfers to A only those people belonging to the subset defined in B and living in Grenoble.

After activation of procedures in B and C, we have the structure shown in figure 8.2.6.(2).

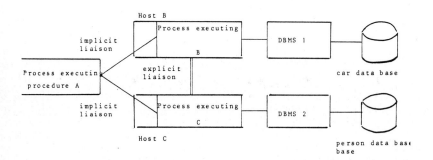

Figure 8.2.6.(2) - Procedure structure

Typical procedures corresponding to this example are given below. Since IL is similar to machine code, it would not be very illustrative to use it as it stands. Thus, an equivalent literary form is used instead ; it could be an external human oriented form of IL.

```
A : PROCEDURE (N) ;
    DCL N INTEGER BY ADDRESS ;
    DCL RV RENDEZ-VOUS ; DCL (SON1, SON2) SON ;
    DCL TAB (N) CHAR (20) ; DCL EVENTA EVENT ;

    B : PROCEDURE (PARAB) ;
        DCL PONTB LIAISON ; DCL I INTEGER ;
        DCL (COL, NAME) CHAR (20) ;
        DCL PARB RENDEZ-VOUS BY NAME ;
        RESERVE (PONTB) VIA PARB ; OPEN (PONTB) ;
        DO I = 1 TO N ;
            CALLEXT FINDCOLOUR (I, COL, NAME) ;
            /*call procedure FINDCOLOUR written in DB language
            to search the car data base and determine the cars
            and the red cars and the owners names */
            IF COL = 'RED' THEN WRITE (PONTB) NAME ;
        ENDDO ;
        WRITE (PONTB) 'STOP' ;
        CLOSE (PONTB) ;
    END B ;

    C : PROCEDURE (PARC, PARTAB, EVENTC) ;
        DCL PONTC LIAISON ;
        DCL J INTEGER ;
        DCL (RESULT, AD) CHAR (20) ;
        DCL PARC RENDEZ VOUS BY NAME ;
        DCL PARTAB ( ) CHAR (20) BY NAME ;
        DCL EVENTC EVENT BY NAME ;
        J = 1 ;
        RESERVE (PONTC) VIA PARC ;
        OPEN (PONTC) ;
        LOOP :
        READ (PONTC) RESULT ;
        /*wait if information not available*/
        IF RESULT = 'STOP' THEN GOTO NEXT ;
        CALLEXT FINDADDRESS (RESULT, AD) ;
        /*call procedure FINDADDRESS written in DB language
        to search the people base and determine the
        address of the persons whose name is in RESULT */
        IF AD = 'GRENOBLE' THEN DO ;
            PARTAB (J) = RESULT ;
            J = J + 1 ; ;
            ENDDO ;
        GOTO LOOP ;
        NEXT : POST (EVENTC) ; CLOSE (PONTC) ;
    END C ;
    ACTIVATE B (RV) HOST (HB) SON (SON1) ;
    ACTIVATE C (RV, TAB, EVENTA) HOST (HC) SON (SON2) ;
    WAIT (ENDTA) ;
    ...
END A ;
```

8.3. Distributed data bases

8.3.1. Introduction

Users requirements explain the success of Distributed Data Bases (DDB) concepts at a time when centralized systems and data bases show limitations and drawbacks. With respect to organizational approaches, users need new and adequate tools for data acquisition, storage, security, privacy and manipulation. Many organizations, and more particularly those that are geographically dispersed, consider centralized systems as inadequate for meeting their managerial and organizational objectives. Under these conditions, the emerging concepts should permit a true choice in order to : 1) reduce the risks of excessive centralization of programs and data, 2) select the most adequate solution for an application possibly involving different sub-systems, 3) make provision for the easy evolution of one sub-system without disturbing the rest of the information system, 4) ensure better service and performance, and 5) offer more flexibility in making data processing conform to organizational philosophies.

Distributed data bases are the point of convergence of networking and data base technologies, respectively representative of distribution and integration. This is due to the fast and often explosive evolution of these two domains over the past decade.

Indeed, as described in previous sections, basic techniques are being introduced in networking allowing for programs and data distribution amongst several interconnected systems. Alternatively, trends in Data Bases are towards a more conceptual and integrated data management in which users are presented with a global, coherent and unique collection of data [LEB76]. Distributed Data Bases are then the synthesis of two antinomic approaches in order to provide a unified handling of heterogeneous and distributed data [ADI78].

However, the problems to be solved are numerous and complex. Some of them have already been encountered either in conventional Data Base Management System design (models, concurrency, integrity) or in the network field (communication, protocols), but the association of these two domains leads to new problems.

To study this unexplored domain different approaches have been adopted in the CYCLADES project (see section 8.3.2). The results and the experience gained from these works led to the concept of general purpose Distributed Data Management Systems [ADI78]. They also served as a prelude to the SIRIUS project, a pilot project dedicated to DDB [IRI79].

8.3.2. A survey of DDB research in CYCLADES

As previously mentioned, research in Distributed Data Base Management (D-DBMS) has been undertaken from the beginning of CYCLADES. In this new field, few results were available at this time and it was not clear how to approach the problem. Thus, the objectives of CYCLADES research in Distributed Data bases have been to explore the domain step by step, to bring to light the most important problems and to propose unsophisticated solutions. Some of the studies undertaken to fit with these goals are described below. They illustrate the diversity of the different approaches.

8.3.2.1. The FRERES System

This research has been undertaken by IRISA (Institut de Recherche en Informatique et Systemes Aleatoires) at RENNES University [BOSC78].

a) Objectives

The context of this study has been determined by the following requirements :

- several files or data bases are managed on different computers;
- these computers are connected to the CYCLADES network;
- the data bases and the computers are heterogeneous, but these data bases are "semantically close", e.g., DB's of employees in a geographically distributed organization;
- all information about an "individual" (e.g. an employee) is stored in only one data base.

In addition, the study was "query processing" oriented, i.e. how to question a set of data bases distributed over a computer network. Thus, update and integrity problems were left out.

b) Principles

The collection of "semantically close" data bases is considered as a partitioned set of individuals (e.g., employers, students, cars) whose characteristics are given by a global view containing :

- informations about data localization,

- the description of an individual as a hierarchical structure (a tree) representing entities (records) and elementary attributes (fields). Each attribute is given a data type and a format.

The users access the data with a query language. This query
language permits us :

 - to define the part of the global data base involved in
 the query,

 - to specify criteria to select individuals,

 - to indicate the attributes to be extracted for the
 selected individuals.

The syntax of the query language is quite close to the SOCRATE
language.

The query language cannot be directly processed by each data
base management system existing on the different computers of
the network. Therefore some adaptation is required.

The choice made in the FRERES system is to translate this query
language into a pivot language independent of local systems.
The pivot language is used as a common language over the
network. This language has two sets of primitives : 1) data
manipulation primitives, 2) data access primitives.

Thus, the result of the translation phase is a set of programs
sent to the local systems where an "Adaptation Module"
interprets the pivot language primitives in term of local data
manipulation primitives.

c) System architecture

The FRERES system involves a set of subsystems distributed over
the computer network. Functionally there are two subsystems :
the Master Subsystem ans the Slave Subsystems, (see figure
8.3.2.(1)).

The Master Subsystem (MSS) handles user´s terminal, performs
the translation of queries into pivot language, maintains
communication and synchronization with Slave Subsystems on the
network and merges the answers provided by local systems.

The Slave Subsystems (SSS) translate pivot language primitives
into local ones. There is no direct communication between SSS.
They communicate only with the Master Subsystem.

Thus, MSS and SSS´s process two kinds of functions :

- distributed control functions such as communication and
synchronization. For subsequent reference, they shall be termed
"distributed subsequent reference they shall be termed
"distributed executive".

- distributed data management functions such as translation,
adaptation, or merging of results.

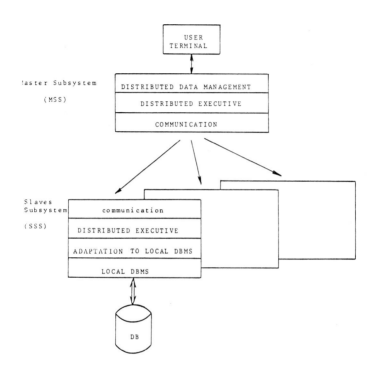

Figure 8.3.2.(1) - Architecture of the FRERES System

d) Implementations

The FRERES system has been implemented on the IRIS 80, a CII computer. The distributed control functions are written in assembly code. The distributed data management functions are written in COBOL and need 40 K words (32 bits) of core memory, which break down as follows :

    15 K words   syntactic analysis module
    16 K words   adaptation module
     6 K words   interpreter of access functions

      6 K words   results conversion module

Simplified applications have been set up on the FRERES system
and demonstrated, among others at the IFIP´77 Congress in
TORONTO (Canada).

8.3.2.2. Cooperation between homogeneous DBMS´s

This work has been undertaken by ECA-Automation, a French
software house [LEB73] [ECA75].

a) Objectives and principles

The first objective of the study was to experiment with the
possibilities of communications between several Data Base
Management Systems (DBMS). The problem was restricted to a
network of homogeneous DBMS´s (SOCRATE), which is implemented
on different computers (IRIS 80, IRIS 50, IBM 370).

The second objective was to define a "SOCRATE cooperation
protocol" as simple as possible, in order to minimize SOCRATE
modifications and to rapidly produce a prototype on the
CYCLADES network.

In the first step, several approaches have been investigated
and their costs evaluated. They are summarized in the
following :

- The distribution over the network of users, SOCRATE systems
and data, without any restriction of use, led to difficult
problems, specially those concerning the coherence of data.

- The communication between DBMS´s could be made at the file
level or at the virtual memory level, (which is a feature of
the SOCRATE system). In two cases, SOCRATE modifications were
too costly.

- A simpler (but less general) mode of communication was
possible : it was based on a "Remote Procedure Call"
principle. This solution described below, did not lead us to
modify in depth the SOCRATE systems, so the study was started
on this approach.

b) The Remote Procedure call

In SOCRATE a user program can access the data base by the means
of procedures written in the SOCRATE language. Buffers are
used to pass data between the main program and the called
procedures.

Communications between two Socrate Systems use an extension of
this principle. A program running in one SOCRATE may activate a
procedure in a remote computer and exchange data with it. Such
a communication needs a distributed system mechanism capable of

recognizing local requests for remote procedures, ensuring the transport of this request (and the answer) to the remote system, and activating the called procedure.

Thus, user programs can access data bases managed by interconnected SOCRATE systems through procedures written in the SOCRATE language (see figure 8.3.2.(2)) and activated by the distributed executive.

We can remark that this approach is also usable in a heterogeneous environment. Indeed to a certain extent, e.g., for a specific application, the intermediate procedure may even adapt to a different DBMS. The only requirement consists of a common protocol for the procedure call and the argument format.

c) User primitives

Primitives for accessing remote data bases are identical to those available in a local environment. These primitives are :

- LOGIN to a data base (local or remote),

- ALLOCATE BUFFER for exchanging parameters and data between user programs and procedures,

- EXECUTE PROCEDURE for starting the execution of a procedure (local or remote),

- LOGOUT of a data base.

d) Implementation

This system has been implemented on IRIS 50, a CII computer. The implementation included a demonstrative application concerning the management of students in three geographically separated Universities. The whole job took 6 man-months, illustrating the simplicity of this approach.

Three IRIS 50 were connected to CYCLADES. Each of them managed a student data base of one University, using the modified SOCRATE system.

The users, in this case people involved in administrati e tasks, were physically connected to their University computer. From their terminals, they were able :

- to retrieve student records, stored on any data base,

- to transfer the record of a given student from a remote data base to the local data base,

- to modify this record and to delete the remote record.

Thus, users did not see the whole data collection as a single data base. They had to deal with local and remote distinct data

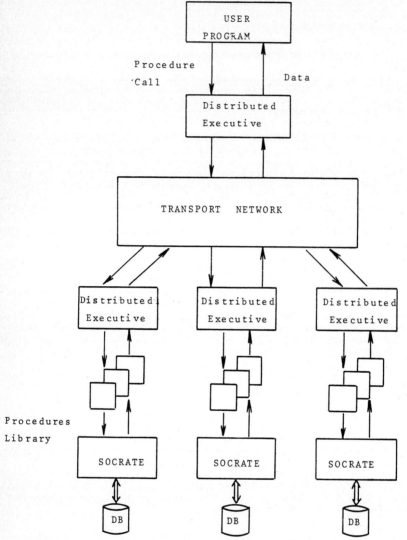

Figure 8.3.2.(2) - Architecture of the multi-SOCRATE Systems

bases. This approach is well adapted to applications where users work mainly with a local data base and occasionally with remote data bases. However, this technique implies the development of specific procedures for each new application.

8.3.2.3. Distributed SOCRATE

This work has been undertaken by the CII Scientific Center in GRENOBLE [CHU78].

a) Objectives and principles

In section 8.1 the concept of Logical Network Machine has been described. This concept has been applied to the SOCRATE data base management system in order to allow its distribution in the CYCLADES network.

A data base management system consists of three parts : the users (be they terminals or batch oriented), the data base management system internal functions and the physical data bases (collection of files, which are standard with respect to the operating system). Stated another way, we identify three major functional levels : terminal access method, logical access method and physical access method.

A distributed data base management system is then a data base management system for which one or more of the access methods have been distributed.

It is clear that such an approach, resulting in access distribution rather than data duplication, is opposed to the file transfer approach, which leads to multiple copies of the same data base.

We shall now examine the distribution process of two significant levels with respect to the concepts developed in section 8.1.

b) The physical access method

As explained earlier, this access method deals with physical data bases (i.e. sets of files in the usual sense) [CHU74a] [CHU74b]. As opposed to a file transfer solution, the approach consists of distributing access. We shall first establish the correspondence between the concepts developed in section 8.1 and the physical access method module.

A user (system or application program) is a process in the IGOR meaning of the term (see section 8.2). The associated algorithm consists of "threaded code" (IGOR instructions, e.g. IL instructions mixed with local code). The functional sub-systems are represented by physical access method modules.

The distributed executive takes care of :

- remote process creation/destruction,
- synchronization,
- interface with the different operating systems and the file management systems.

The distribution of the SOCRATE physical access method provides automatically a geographical distribution of physical data bases as well as the possibility of storing the data bases on heterogeneous hosts (see figure 8.3.2.(3)).

c) The logical access method

This level concerns the manipulation of structured data, possibly containing interrelationships, which must be maintained during update operations. It is very desirable to provide a certain independence from the data description language, so that the access method can be accessed by different (and heterogeneous) DBMS.

This level must be : a) independent of the user request language, b) independent of the physical data organization, and c) hopefully independent of the access path.

In order to allow different functional levels to reside on different hosts, it is necessary to define a special kind of interface between the levels. The interface cannot use local addressing since such a concept is not transportable from one computer to the other. Besides, the functional layering must be performed with a great care in order to minimize network traffic and response time. In particular, the updating of large tables should be avoided by two different levels, if these levels are to reside on different hosts.

It looks particularly interesting to provide a means of sharing a given access method between different and rather independent applications. This implies that some sort of a "login mechanism" must be present at the acccess method level and that higher levels introduce themselves to the acccess method using a contact/connection protocol.

d) Distribution and implementation

In SOCRATE the compilation of the user request language is performed in three phases : edition, pseudo-code generation and finally code generation.

The SOCRATE pseudo-code contains a set of logical access method primitives separated by branch operations. Fortunately, this level matches the requirements indicated for a minimum semantic level. The distribution must take place at this level.

It has been decided to adopt the IL as a vehicle for the operating protocol. This means either that SOCRATE pseudo-code be translated into IL or that the SOCRATE compiler be modified so that IL be directly generated.

The only remaining problem is site selection. First, we must adopt for the data bases a mode of designation, which is adapted to the network. The network data base name must contain in one way or another a site/host identification, which will be made available to the SOCRATE compiler.

Secondly, we must structure the generated IL into blocks,   each
of them corresponding to a given host. This structuring can be
performed according to different strategies : either   we   build
for   each   user   request   a   small   IL   block   to   be   executed
immediately, or we concatenate the blocks corresponding to   the
same   host before interpretation. In the latter case, IGOR must
provide two new pseudo-code   operations   in   order   to   achieve
synchronization :   pseudo   WAIT   (PSDWAIT)   and   pseudo   POST
(PSDPOST).

8.3.3. Conclusion

Following this early research work presented   in   the   previous
sections   it became possible to acquire a more general view and
to introduce the concept of general   purpose   distributed   data
management   systems.   This   is   the   objective   of   the SIRIUS
project. This project, started in June 1976, aims   to   federate
endeavours of research communities, users and manufacturers in
order to define   concepts,   to   experiment   techniques   and   to
evolve   a   methodology for distributed data bases. Thus, SIRIUS
can be   seen   as   a   new   step   in   the   study   of   distributed
information systems.

CHAPTER 9

STANDARDS

9.1. Standard usefulness

Standardization means agreement on reducing the number of ways
for doing a single thing. Diversity may be justified when it
results from substantially different constraints or objectives.
Nevertheless, it is fair to recognize that in the computing
field diversity is usually at the noise and nuisance level. A
substantial proportion of human skill and financial resources
is devoted to reinventing the wheel and converting from one
standard to another. Indeed, standards are like religions.
Various groups define their own and call the others heretical.
Politicking and propaganda take over, as standards affect
market boundaries and status symbol.

Thus, the term standard should not be taken at face value. In
real life there is always diversity. Standardization is only a
continuous trimming process, weeding out excesses of diversity.
The concentration of efforts on a limited number of methods has
a number of advantages. Techniques are better understood and
improvements are introduced earlier. Engineering and
maintenance costs as well as conversion problems are reduced.
Finally, there is more compatibility between products of
different suppliers.

There may be also constraints and counter-arguments. Suppliers
do not favour compatibility when they can control a captive
market. Past investment is a barrier to improvements, and
innovation is stifled. Thus standardization is a subtle game :
when and what to standardize ?

9.2. Areas for standardization

It may be observed that industry evolves by cycles. At some
point in time, over a period of 5 years, most large
organizations choose their options in a certain field. Present
day networks belong to a generation that sprang up between 1965
and 1970. A new cycle is occurring during 1975-1980, due to the
obsolescence of previous systems, and the maturation of new
manufacturer products. For standards to succeed the best period
is at the beginning of a cycle, when major changes are
acceptable.

As explained in section 2.1, computer networks tend to
heterogeneity. But a minimum of commonality is a prerequisite
to heterogeneity. This is where standardizaton becomes a
cornerstone for orderly evolution. Protocols are the only way
heterogeneous components can cooperate. The N square problem
must be cracked.

PTT´s are defining new standard interfaces for public packet
networks. In the near future this will just add to diversity,
as existing transmission services are to stay for several more
decades. But this is presumably a normal rejuvenation process
for keeping up with available technologies. On the other hand,
new transmission interfaces make nothing more compatible. They
are just other ways of carrying bits.

The real breakthrough in network standards is the emergence of
conventions introducing levels of commonality between data
processing equipment of various suppliers. In other words,
there appears now a real concern for agreement on protocols. If
this trend is not thwarted by powerful and conflicting
interests, standardization should become active in areas
identified earlier as the most vital layers of a distributed
resource sharing system, viz : a) Transport protocol,
b) Virtual terminal, c) Resource management (files,
peripherals), d) Data base access.

While it is often advocated to design systems top-down,
standardization progresses bottom-up. The reason is probably
that it is nearly impossible to reach an overall agreement on a
complete set of standards. Instead, standardization committees
start with the minimum acceptable by all parties, and that is
usually at a low level. The following sections give a brief
presentation of existing standards. As it was just said, they
relate to the lower levels of a network architecture.

9.3. Critical review of existing standards

9.3.1. Transmission interfaces

Interconnecting two pieces of equipment requires some wiring, physical connectors, and conventions on electrical characteristics. There are many independent industrial or military standards for short distance connections. Long distance connections are normally established through common carriers facilities. Thus, standards in this area are defined by a common carrier club, the CCITT (Comite Consultatif International Telegraphique et Telephonique), in which the European state monopolies, or PTT´s, exert a major influence.

In the following, the major international standards will be briefly introduced with comments on their area of applicability.

The following transmission interfaces are bit oriented, in the sense that they do not impose any character or block structure. Once a connection is established between two correspondents, they can exchange any sequence of bits of any length, at a predefined bit rate. Constraints imposed on acceptable bit patterns result only from the application of higher level conventions.

V 24

V24 is the electrical and mechanical interface between a data processing equipment, or terminal, and a modem. It operates at speeds up to 19.2 Kbits/s, and it is the most widely used interface for data transmission. It is data transparent, for point to point or multipoint circuits, but without switching capabilities.

Modems work by pairs. They translate digital signals into modulated voice frequencies carried through analog telephone circuits. Even though signals between modems are also standardized, speeds higher than 1200 bits/s usually require modems of the same make in order to operate in stable conditions.

V 35

V 35 is used with primary groups (48, 64 or 72 Kbits/s). Functionally, it is equivalent to V 24, but much less in use.

X.21

X.21 is an interface designed for public data networks using digital transmission [CCI76b]. In addition to electrical and mechanical characteristics, it includes a procedure for

establishing and closing switched digital circuits. There is no
upper limit on the bit speed.

X.21 is completely transparent to data and procedures. The
dialing phase is based on electrical signaling, rather than
formatted messages. This is a severe shortcoming due to an
early design, at a time where PTT's had not yet anticipated the
development of public packet switching networks.

The initial definition of X.21 dates from 1972. However, very
few public digital networks are operational (EDS is Germany and
quite recently the Nordic data network). Thus, the application
of X.21 has been lagging.

 X.21 bis

This variant allows access to leased digital circuits from
equipments using V24. It is an interim interface for easier
migration to X.21. The electrical and mechanical interface are
the same as V24, but signals are interpreted as X.21 functions
for data transfer only.

9.3.2. Transmission procedures

The term "transmission procedure", as used here, designates a
set of logical conventions between two correspondents for
exchanging messages (or blocks of information) in a reliable
manner. These conventions pertain to such matters as message
formats, numbering, initialization, error recovery, flow
control, dialogue, etc. They do not specify any electrical
characteristic.

Data link control procedures are used to transmit data over
point to point or multipoint circuits. They provide facilities
for error and flow control, as well as a number of additional
operational needs, such as initialization of the transmission,
dialogue control, diagnostics and status inquiry. Historically,
the term "procedure" has become customarily used for this low
level of end-to-end protocol.

 HDLC

The standardization of transmission procedures belongs to the
International Standard Organization (ISO), which is a
federation of national standardization bodies. Since 1967 ISO
has undertaken the definition of a standard procedure for
exchanging data blocks over a circuit. This effort was crowned
in 1976 with the adoption of a set of standards for various
configurations :

a) Point-to-point balanced mode, where both ends have equal
   capabilities,

b) Point-to-point unbalanced mode, where one end is a master
station (called a primary), and the other a slave (called a
secondary),
c) Multipoint mode, with one primary and several secondaries.

The generic term used to qualify these standards is HDLC (High
level Data Link Control). By the time it was adopted, many
higher levels protocols had sprung up, putting HDLC at a low
level.

The term HDLC is used to mean different levels of standards,
not always in a proper sense. It can apply to the framing of
the transmitted data blocks, to the data block format, or to
the procedure, as will be explained in the following. A pure
HDLC standard implementation should apply all these levels. In
practice, many implementations are hybrid, as they take only
some levels of HDLC.

Frame level

HDLC is intended for the transmission of data blocks, not
characters. Due to technical constraints associated with
signal processing, it is necessary to introduce clear
separations between noise and meaningful signal. This is called
framing. Separators are special sequences, which occur at the
beginning and at the end of an information block, in order to
indicate unambiguously where the meaningful bits are located
[ISO76].

In the HDLC standard, the special bit sequence used as a
separator is called a flag. Its representation is : 01111110.

Confusion would definitely arise when transmitting data
containing some bit pattern identical to a flag. This is
prevented with an additional convention called "bit stuffing",
which preserves data transparency. Whenever five consecutive
ones occur in transmitting data, the transmitter inserts an
extraneous zero. Conversely, a receiver drops a zero following
five consecutive ones. Thus, there cannot be any confusion
between flags and data.

A sequence : <flag> <data> <flag> is called a frame.

The generation of flags, the bit stuffing, and their
recognition are usually done in hardware as part of an I/O
adapter.

Format level

Data in between flags are formatted as shown in figure 9.3.(1).
Field A (8 bits) designates the address of the sending or
receiving secondary. Field C (8 bits) contains control
information. Field TEXT, if present, contains any bit

sequence. Field FCS (16 bits) is a frame checking sequence, i.e. a cyclical checksum insuring with a high probabilitv the bit integrity of the whole frame. The computation and checking of FCS is usually performed in hardware.

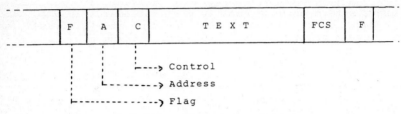

Figure 9.3.(1) - HDLC frame format

Procedure level

Historically, the term procedure has been used to designate the set of rules followed by a transmitter and a receiver for exchanging data over a circuit. More recently, the term protocol was coined to designate similar rules in a more general context. These rules include error detection and recovery by retransmission.

The structure of HDLC procedures is based on commands and responses, i.e. coded messages exchanged between a primary and one or several secondaries [ISO77]. Field C in the frame format contains the coding of commands and responses.

Frames transmitted may be numbered, or unnumbered. Numbered frames, as their name implies, carry a number increasing sequentially. This is used by the receiver to detect missing or duplicate frames. Acknowledgements are numbers, indicating that all frames sent with a lower number have been received correctly. The numbering cycle runs modulo 8, but it may be extended to 128. Unnumbered frames are used for additional functions, such as resetting, initialization, or signaling.

HDLC procedures are usually implemented in software, or micro-programs. There are some expectations that a chip will appear on the market.

HDLC framing, format and procedure may be applied independently. E.g. HDLC formatted blocks may be framed with the character sequences used over the last decade in conjunction with BSC procedures, while the procedure used could be specific. Thus, the expression "We are using HDLC" calls for more lengthy explanations.

X.25

The X.25 standard was worked out in a hurry in 1976, shortly after European PTT's recognized the potential of packet switching. It provides three levels of functions [CCI77].

Level 1 - The electrical and mechanical characteristics of the
interface between the user equipment (or DTE) and the network
(or DCE) conform to X.21 or X.21 bis. However, it is restricted
to leased circuits. Thus, the switching capabilities of X.21
are unused.

Level 2 - The data link control procedure is a specific subset
of HDLC, called LAP-B. It performs error and flow control over
the physical circuit between user and network. This HDLC
subset belongs to the class of "balanced" procedures, i.e. user
and network have symmetric functions, and handle traffic
two-way simultaneously.

Level 3 - This level is also called the packet level, and it is
often what people have in mind when they refer to X.25. In line
with other CCITT standards, X.25 defines only the conventions
between user system and public network, not between two users
systems.   The rationale is that CCITT´s mandate covers only
public networks, and their interface to users, while user to
user conventions are left to ISO.

This approach could work if two conditions were met : 1) the
proper operation of an X.25 interface should not depend on the
options taken by the other correspondent, and 2) X.25 should be
transparent to user to user conventions. Neither condition is
met.

The only packet network interface that does not mingle with
user to user conventions is a datagram service interface.
However, back in 1976, priority was put on the definition of a
VC interface. It also turned out that a VC oriented packet
interface required a minimum of user to user conventions.   This
built-in contradiction has not been solved, and probably never
will. Most carriers (e.g. Bell Canada, TELENET, NTT) assumed
that some X.25 functions had to be implemented in providing for
user to user functions, but the French PTT wanted to be more
restrictive. Thus, the X.25 wording left the matter open to
either interpretation.

The major bone of contention was whether flow control
information sent by a user at one end of a VC had to be
delivered to the user at the other end, and simultaneously be
interpreted as acknowledging previously received packets (as in
HDLC). Thus, some X.25 implementations, rather than the X.25
standard, provide for user to user error and flow control
functions, within a single network boundary.

Since common carriers and PTT´s went on and implemented X.25
networks in their own way, a revised version of the standard
was agreed in 1980, with one more control bit (the D-bit),
indicating that flow control information is carried from user
to user [CCI80]. Nevertheless, this function remains a carrier
option.   Thus, the matter is far from being settled. The only

change is that users computers will be able to sense the D-bit (after 1982).

In addition to this major dilemma, X.25 caters for numerous national and user options. This market oriented approach fits the needs of large organizations, which can select their own X.25 for private networks (closed user groups). On the other hand, it is unlikely that any two users could communicate in a meaningful fashion, unless they have carefully chosen a common set of options, in taking into account the way carriers have implemented them. As with high speed modems, the best way to insure compatibility is to take X.25 implementations of the same make.

Datagram

A universal datagram interface would only require the definition of a datagram format, a numbering plan, and a few diagnostic packets formats. After X.25 was standardized, it was contended that another public data network interface would generate more burden than benefit, if it departed substantially from X.25. Thus, the datagram standard agreed by the CCITT in 1980 is an extension of X.25 [CCI80]. It uses nearly identical packet formats, and the same level-3 procedure. However, it is not necessary to open a VC in order to transmit datagrams.

This approach favours large users and manufacturers, who can afford integrated implementations. Low cost terminals, which would benefit the most in using only datagrams, are penalized by an overly complex interface piling up functions that they do not need [POU761].

An interface properly designed for simple terminals, using only HDLC, has been under discussion for several years within CCITT and ISO [POU77], but its standization does not progress too fast.

9.3.3. Asynchronous character oriented interfaces

S 15

S 15 is the telex interface, working at 6.6 characters/s, with a 5-bit character, and without parity bit. No improvements are to be expected, but telex tariffs are more attractive than telephone tariffs.

X.4 - X.20

X.20 is an asynchronous interface to switched digital networks [CCI77a]. Asynchronous terminals transmit characters (5 to 8 bits) framed with start and stop signals. X.4 defines the bit speed, the format and the framing of characters. The procedure

for establishing and closing switched circuits is X.20.   Since
X.20   and   X.21 are functionally equivalent, two terminals, one
using X.20 and the other using X.21, may call   each   other   and
exchange   information,   provided   that it contains multiples of
the character size.

ASCII terminal interface to packet networks (PAD)

The major attraction of public packet networks is that   tariffs
are   lower   than   those   of switched or leased circuits for low
speed transmission.   Therefore, standards have been defined for
the attachment of asynchronous terminals,   up   to   300   bits/s.
The interface to virtual circuit packet networks is X.28.

The   attachment   of   an   ASCII   terminal   to   a virtual circuit
requires a terminal handler,   which   converts   an   asynchronous
character   stream   into   X.25   packets,   and   vice versa.   The
terminal handler, called a PAD (Packet Assembler   Disassembler)
is   part   of   public   packet   networks.   In   order   to adapt to
different terminal characteristics, parameters may   be   set   by
the   person   using   the   terminal.   The   definition   of these
parameters are in X.3. The command language   available   to   the
user   for   parameter   setting, virtual circuit establishment and
packet transmission is defined in X.28, (figure 9.3.(2)).

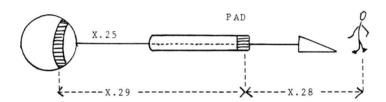

Figure 9.3.(2) - Remote terminal handler

An   ASCII   terminal   is   usually   in   conversation   with   an
interactive   system   on   a computer attached through X.25. This
latter standard is insufficient,   because   more   functions   are
required   to   interact   with   a   PAD, for parameter setting and
reading, and the identification of   the   human   user   requests.
They reflect in terms of packets the functions available to the
terminal user. The corresponding standard is X.29.

X.3,   X.28   and   X.29   should   be viewed as the components of a
single package (called the   PAD).   It   has   been   designed   to
dovetail with X.25, and cannot be used independently. This is a
definite   violation   of the principle of layer independence. On
the   other   hand,   the   PAD   does   not   fit   into   the   network
architecture   proposed   by ISO, since it provides no end-to-end
protocol.   Physical terminal characteristics (except bit speed,

line length and carriage return delay) have to be dealt with on
the user application side. Thus, terminal virtualization is
close to nil.

Other limitations restrict the interest for the PAD :

a) The transmission mode is only asynchronous at a maximum
speed of 300 bits/s, using the ASCII code (the same as ISO
IA5). This speed is too slow for interactive applications, and
there is no protection against transmission errors.

b) The setting of the PAD parameters is cumbersome, prone to
errors, and it can be done independently by the human user, the
application program, or any common carrier network involved,
without mutual signaling or interlocking. This is a sure way to
create confusion.

c) Since packet networks operators charge traffic by the packet
(full or empty), there is a financial incentive to favour line
oriented dialogues. This is totally dissuasive and unfit to
sophisticated human oriented and context sensisitive
interfaces.

d) There is not even the crudest editing capability, such as
erase character, or line, or word. (Actually, the 1980 revision
introduces those facilities as carrier options).

To compensate for these deficiencies, some common carriers
(NTT, Bell Canada, TELENET) have introduced their own version
of the PAD, with extended non standard facilities, and specific
product oriented terminal handlers (mostly IBM compatible). It
is already apparent that in this area public networks standards
have gone awry.

9.3.4. Inter-networking standards

This area is still underdeveloped. The world of public
transmission facilities is roughly split into three major
techniques : telephony, digital circuit and virtual circuit.
All three are circuit oriented. Thus, it appears tempting to
build data paths out of segments based on different techniques,
when the need arises. This is not implemented presently.

Telephone access to a virtual circuit network is the most
common inter-network facility. The user must dial a phone
number giving him a connnection to an asynchronous port on a
PAD. Thereafter, he may establish a virtual circuit by typing a
command on his keyboard. However, there is no dial out
facility to go from a virtual circuit into the switched
telephone system.

In anticipation of a futuristic world where every subscriber of
any network could connect to any other subscriber of another
network, a standard numbering plan has been standardized by the

CCITT as X.121 [CCI78a]. It provides for the numbering of national data networks, with a hierarchical name space. Potentially, there is provision for dialing out into the telephone or Telex networks to reach a called subscriber.

After X.25 was defined, it turned out that another interface was desirable to interconnect X.25 networks. This additional interface, called X.75, is only applied between public networks [CCI78]. It is not available to private networks, which would like to interconnect with public ones.

X.75 specifies how packets are presented at an inter-network boundary. Since X.25 is a menu rather than a specification, each network is responsible to map its own options into X.75 terms. There is much similarity between X.75 and X.25. On one hand, X.75 does not offer options related to a subscriber interface. On the other hand, networks exchange additional information related to billing and routing.

9.4. Future standards

ISO has undertaken an ambitious program to standardize an architecture for Open System Interconnection (OSI). This work is carried out within TC 97/SC 16. The goal is to define a set of layers, with their associated protocols, so as to make possible the interconnection of heterogeneous systems, without resorting to ad-hoc adaptations.

The proposed model comprises 7 layers. The top layer (7) is defined as being the user application. Below it are 6 functional layers :

6 - Presentation. Pertaining to the handling of data structures.
5 - Session. In charge of the management of the dialogue between user applications.
4 - Transport. To present a unified and reliable service for transporting data.
3 - Network. Routing and signaling, such as the packet level of X.25
2 - Procedure. Management of a physical link to a transmission network.
1 - Physical and electrical interface.

9.5 Proposed standards

In anticipation of the ISO work, a number of professional organizations put forth proposals. The best known forum in which network experts work out some degree of international consensus is represented by IFIP working groups within the Technical Committee on Data Communications, (TC.6).

The working group WG 6.1 has proposed the following standards : a) a datagram format [IFI74], [IFI76], b) a transport protocol [CER76], c) a virtual terminal protocol [IFI78], and d) several drafts have been published for a file transfer protocol [GIE78].

These proposals are backed by experiments in inter-networking, which establish their feasibility and provide some insight into performance parameters.

9.6. Conclusions

The making of standards is a long and arduous process. When a standard is expressed as a 100 pages document in natural language, there is some legitimate doubt that it can ever be interpreted in only one unambiguous way. Nevertheless, this is presently the state of the art in standard engineering. A number of researchers are attempting to work out practical methods to describe standards in a formal language, which would be unambiguous and which could be submitted to automated validation tools [BOC75].

Assuming that such efforts could succeed, it could be envisioned to produce from the formal definition of an interface, or procedure, a reference implementation, for test and validation purposes. Unless progress is made in this direction, the definition of coming network standards may become entangled in continuous misunderstandings. Another approach could be considered, however. It would consist in agreeing on a reference implementation made available, or validated, by an international standard bureau.

CHAPTER   10

AFTERWORD

Here I will attempt to summarize the major contributions
of   the   Cyclades   project,   as   seen   by   an   outside   but
not-quite-unbiased observer. They are as follows.

First, the datagram subnetwork. The use of a subnetwork,
whose sole function is to move datagrams from source to
destination, was a novel and useful contribution. In   light of
the decision by the CCITT to follow the opposite road - X.25
subnetworks with the notion of virtual circuits embedded in the
design - a number of advantages of the CIGALE approach are
apparent. The design and construction of the subnetwork is
simpler, hosts are easily able to have multiple ports,   the
construction of inter-network gateways is simpler and the
performance of interworked subnetworks is   improved, owing to
tha absence of concatenated virtual circuits. The last points
will become increasingly important as   interworking of public
data   networks   with   local   area   networks and with each other
proliferates in the next few years.

Second, the use of a single address space in CIGALE to
represent both ports and network services. This provided a
clean, simple representation which deserves to be imitated. The
related ideas of CIGALE services as a distributed machine
followed naturally, and were equally helpful as unifying ideas
to allow a single mechanism to serve several purposes.

Thirdly, the contributions to protocol design. Current
transport protocols and proposed international standards derive
many of their ideas and features directly from the original
design of the Cyclades transport station. Many ideas of current
VTPs and FTPs also can be traced to early Cyclades proposals.

Fourth, contributions to the early experimentations in
routing, flow control and congestion control, such as the
channel load limiter. (I am happy to record here that members
of the University of Waterloo Computer Communications Networks
Group helped with all of these topics !).

Fifth, insight into the principles of host software design
for networking. The investigations by the Cyclades team
provided one of the bases for the ideas of Open System
Interconnection.

Finally, I feel that the non-technical contributions of
Cyclades were among its most important ones. Unusual
organizational principles such as the use of the circuit rider
to carry news and gossip among centers, the use of borrowed
staff as vehicles for technology transfer, the emphasis on a
very skinny chain of command - these amply proved their worth.
As well, the Cyclades project provided some of our most
penetrating and useful insights into the sociology of
networking and the impact it has on the humans which it is
intended to serve.

Eric Manning
Waterloo, Ontario, Canada
January 1982

CYCLADES - REFERENCES

[ABR70]
N. Abramson - The Aloha system : Another alternative for computer communications, Proc. AFIPS-FJCC´70, (Nov. 1970), pp. 695-702

[ADI78]
M. Adiba, J.C. Chupin, R. Demolombe, G. Gardarin, J. Le Bihan - Issues in distributed data base management systems : a technical overview, Proc. 4th. Internat. Conf. on VLDB, Berlin, (Sep. 1978), pp. 89-110

[ADI78a]
M. Adiba, J.Y. Caleca, C. Euzet - A distributed data base system using logical relational machines, Proc. 4th. Internat. Conf. on VLDB, Berlin, (Sep. 1978), pp. 450-461

[ALA74]
G. Alarcia, S. Herrera - C.T.N.E´s Packet Switching Network, Proc. ICCC´74, Stockholm, (Aug. 1974), pp. 163-170

[AND78]
E. Andre, P. Decitre - On providing distributed application programmers with control over synchronization, Proc. Comp. Network Protocols Symp., Liege, (Feb. 1978), pp. D1.1-D1.6

[ANS76]
J.P. Ansart - Systeme interactif dans un environnement reseau : connexion d´une machine a memoire virtuelle "IBM 360/67" au Reseau CYCLADES, These Univ. USMG, Grenoble, Doc. Cyclades SCH 578, (Feb. 1976), pp. 223

[ARP73]
ARPANET - TELNET protocol specification, Doc. ARPA NIC-18639, (Aug. 1973), pp. 19

[BAL71]
R.M. Balzer - PORTS : A method for dynamic inter-program communication and job control, Proc. AFIPS-SJCC´71, Atlantic City, (May 1971), pp. 485-489

[BAN79]
J.S. Banino, C. Kaiser, H. Zimmermann - Synchronization for distributed systems using a single broadcast channel, 1st Internat. Conf. on Distrib. Comp. Systems, Huntsville, (Oct. 1979), pp. 330-338

[BAR64]
P. Baran - On distributed communications, Rand Series Reports, Rand Corp., Santa Monica, (Aug. 1964), pp.

[BBN72]
BBN - Interface Message Processor, BBN Report 1822, (Dec. 1972), pp. 141

[BEN77]
M. Bennett - A week of CYCLADES data as seen by an IRIS 80, CII-HB C.S.Grenoble Internal Report, (Nov. 1977), pp. 22

[BOC75]
G. Bochman - Logical verification and implementation of protocols, Proc. 4th. Data Comm. Symp., Quebec City, (Oct. 1975), pp. 7.15-7.20

[BOS78]
P. Bosc, A. Chauffaut - Le systeme Freres : Contribution a la cooperation de bases existantes, interrogation de fichiers repartis, Doc. Cyclades SCH-I-041, (Aug. 1978), pp. 171

[BRB70]
D.L.A. Barber, D.W. Davies - The NPL Data Network, Proc. Conf. on Lab. Automation, Novosibirsk, (Oct. 1970), pp. 14

[BRB72]
D.L.A. Barber - The European Computer Network project, Proc. ICCC´72, Washington D.C., (Oct. 1972), pp. 192-200

[BRB74]
D.L.A. Barber - Progress with the European Informatics Network, Proc. ICCC´74, Stockholm, (Aug. 1974.), pp. 215-220

[BRB76]
D.L.A. Barber - A European Informatics Network : achievement and prospects, Proc. ICCC´76, Toronto, (Aug. 1976), pp. 44-50.

[BRE75]
J. Bremer, A. Danthine - Communication protocols in a network
context, Proc. ACM Interprocess Comm. Workshop, Santa Monica,
(Mar. 1975), pp. 87-92

[BRT69]
K.A. Bartlett, R.A. Scantlebury, P.T. Wilkinson - A note on
reliable full-duplex transmission over half-duplex links, CACM
Vol. 12, No. 5, (May 1969), pp. 260-261

[CAR70]
C.S. Carr, S.D. Crocker, V.G. Cerf - Host-Host communication
protocol in the ARPA network, Proc. AFIPS-SJCC´70, Atlantic
City, (May 1970), pp. 589-597

[CAS76]
P.M. Cashin -   DATAPAC network protocols, Proc. ICCC´76,
Toronto, (Aug. 1976), pp. 150-155

[CCI77]
CCITT - Recommendation X.25 : Interface between DTE and DCE for
terminals operating in the packet mode on Public Data Networks,
Orange Book, Vol. VIII-2, (1977), pp. 70-108

[CCI77a]
CCITT - Recommendation X.20 : Interface between DTE and DCE for
start-stop transmission services on Public Data Networks,
Orange Book, Vol. VIII-2, (1977), pp. 25-35

[CCI77b]
CCITT - Recommendation X.21 : General purpose interface between
DTE and DCE for synchronous operation on Public Data Networks,
Orange Book, Vol. VIII-2, (1977), pp. 38-56

[CCI77c]
CCITT - Provisional recommendation X.28 : DTE/DCE interface for
a start-stop DTE accessing the PAD in a Public Data Network
situated in the same country, ITU, Geneva, (1977), pp. 50-73

[CCI77d]
CCITT - Provisional recommendation X.29 : Procedures for the
exchange of control information and user data between a packet
mode DTE and a PAD, ITU, Geneva, (1977), pp. 74-84

[CCI77e]
CCITT   -   Provisional   recommendation   X.3 :   Packet
Assembly/Disassembly facility (PAD) in a Public Data Network,
ITU, Geneva, (1977), pp. 2-7

[CCI78]
CCITT - Recommendation X.75 : Terminal and transit call control
procedures and data transfer system on international circuits
between packet-switched data networks, SG VII, Temp. Doc.
132-E, (Apr. 1978), pp.

[CCI78a]
CCITT - Recommendation X.121 : International numbering plan for
public data networks, SG VIII, Temp. Doc. 186-E, (Apr. 1978),
pp.

[CCI80]
CCITT - Draft Revised CCITT Recommendation X.25, ACM Comp.
Comm. Rev., Vol. 10, No. 1-2, (Jan.-Apr. 1980), pp. 56-129

[CER74]
V.G. Cerf,   R.E. Kahn   -   A   protocol for packet network
intercommunication, IEEE Trans. on Comm., Vol. COM-22, No. 5,
(May 1974), pp. 637-648

[CER75]
V.G. Cerf, A. Curran - The work of IFIP Working Group 6.1., ACM
Comp. Comm. Rev., Vol. 5, No. 2, (Apr. 1975), pp. 18-21

[CER75a]
V.G. Cerf - An assessment of ARPANET protocols, INFOTECH State
of the Art Report, No. 24, Network Systems and Software,
(1975), pp. 461-478

[CER76]
V.G. Cerf,   A. McKenzie,   R. Scantlebury,   H. Zimmermannn   -
Proposal for an international end-to-end protocol, ACM Comp.
Comm. Rev., Vol. 6, No. 3, (Jan. 1976), pp. 63-89

[CER78]
V.G. Cerf,   P. Kirstein   -   Issues   in   Packet   Network
Interconnection, Proc. IEEE, Vol. 66, No. 11, (Nov. 1978),
pp. 1386-1408

[CHA76]
J.F. Chambon, J. Le Bihan - Architecture d´un frontal en environnement informatique : application au reseau CYCLADES, These Ecole Nat. Sup. des Mines de St. Etienne, Doc. Cyclades SCH 589, (), pp. 230

[CHU74]
J.C. Chupin - Control concepts of a logical network machine for data banks, Proc. IFIP´74 Congress, Stockholm, (Aug. 1974), pp. 291-295

[CHU74a]
J.C. Chupin, J. Seguin - Objectifs et definition d´une methode d´acces direct reseau (MADRE), Doc. Cyclades DAT 505, (Apr. 1974), pp. 26

[CHU74b]
J.C. Chupin, J. Seguin - Specifications de realisation d´une methode d´acces direct reseau (MADRE), Doc. Cyclades DAT 506, (Apr. 1974), pp. 40

[CHU75]
J.C. Chupin - Systemes de gestion de bases de donnees reparties (SGBDR), Doc. Cyclades DAT 509, (Feb. 1975), pp. 13

[CHU77]
J.C. Chupin - Repartition d´applications et de base de donnees sur un reseau general d´ordinateurs, These Univ. USMG, Grenoble, Doc. Cyclades DAT 521, (Oct. 1977), pp. 235

[CHU78]
J.C. Chupin - Etude et realisation d´un Socrate reparti sur CYCLADES : implementation de MARS, Doc. Cyclades SCH-I-057, (Oct. 1978), pp. 115

[CII72]
CII-HB - Moniteurs SIRIS7/SIRIS8, CII-HB Doc. 56-58, (1972), pp.

[CII76]
CII-HB - STRATEGE sous SIRIS7/SIRIS8, CII-HB Doc. 4410 E3, (Nov. 1976), pp. 305

[CII77]
CII-HB - SOCRATE/II : manuel d´utilisation, CII-HB Doc. 4742, (Feb. 77), pp. 190

[CMT75]
D. Comte - Techniques de communication et de synchronisation
entre programmes repartis sur le reseau CYCLADES, These Univ.
P. Sabatier, Toulouse, Doc. Cyclades XEC 501, (Jan. 1975),
pp. 185

[COC75]
B. Cochi, G. Tellier - Simulation du routage adaptatif dans le
reseau CIGALE, Doc. Cyclades MOD 519, (Nov. 1975), pp. 85

[COL71]
G.D. Cole - Computer network measurements : techniques and
experiments, PhD. Thesis UCLA, Los Angeles, (Oct. 1971),
pp. 350

[COM75]
M. Combes, P. Maximovitch - Manuel d´utilisation du
concentrateur CYCLADES, Doc. Cyclades MIT 616, (Dec. 1975),
pp. 31

[COT78]
I.W. Cotton - Computer Network Interconnection, Computer
Networks, Vol. 2, No. 1, (Feb. 1978), pp. 25-34

[CRO72]
S.D. Crocker, J.F. Heafner, R.M. Metcalfe, J.B. Postel -
Function-oriented protocols for the ARPA computer network,
Proc. AFIPS-SJCC´72, Atlantic City, (May 1972), pp. 271-280

[CRW75]
W.R. Crowther, F.E. Heart, A.A. McKenzie, J.M. McQuillan,
D.C. Walden - Issues in packet switching network design, Proc.
AFIPS-NCC´75, Anaheim, (Jun. 1975), pp. 161-175

[DAN75]
A. Danthine, E. Eschenauer - Simulation de procedures de
transmission dans CIGALE, Doc. Cyclades MOD 512, (Jul. 1975),
pp. 15

[DAN75a]
A. Danthine, E. Eschenauer - Influence on the node behaviour of
the node-to-node protocol, Proc. 4th. Data Comm. Symp., Quebec
City, (Oct. 1975), pp. 7.1-7.8

CYCLADES - REFERENCES   359

[DAN75b]
A. Danthine, J. Bremer - Communication protocols in a network
environment, Proc. ACM Interprocess Comm. Workshop, Santa
Monica, (Mar. 1975), pp.

[DAN78]
A. Danthine, J. Bremer - Specification and Verification of
end-to-end protocols, Proc. ICCC´78, Kyoto, (Sep. 1978),
pp. 811-816

[DAV67]
D.W. Davies, K.A. Bartlett, R.A. Scantlebury, P.T. Wilkinson -
A digital communication network for computers giving rapid
response at remote terminals, Proc. ACM Symp. on Operating
System Principles, Gatlinburg, (Oct. 1967.), pp.

[DAV68]
D.W. Davies - The principles of a data communication network
for computers and remote peripherals, Proc. IFIP´68 Congress,
Edinburgh, (Aug. 1968), pp. 709-714

[DAV71]
D.W. Davies - The control of congestion in packet switching
networks, Proc. 2nd. Symp. on Problems of Optimization of Data
Comm. Systems, Palo Alto, (Oct. 1971), pp. 46-50

[DAV74]
D.W. Davies - Translation of four papers on CYCLADES from the
AFCET´73 Congress held in Rennes, NPL Com. Sci. Report, TM 84,
(Mar. 1974), pp. 65

[DAV76]
D.W. Davies - Some possible features of a datagram service,
IFIP W.G. 6.1., INWG Note No. 112, (Jan. 1976), pp. 11

[DAY77]
J. Day, G. Grossman - An RJE protocol for a resource sharing
network, Doc. ARPA NIC-38316, (Mar. 1977), pp. 26

[DAY80]
J. Day - Terminal protocols, IEEE Trans. on Comm., Vol. COM-28,
No. 4, (Apr. 1980), pp. 585-593

[DEC77]
P. Decitre - Acces depuis PL1 a la station de transport ST2
sous SIRIS 8, Doc. Cyclades UTI 501, (Aug. 1977), pp. 37

[DEN73]
F. Denjean - Procedures d'exploitation d'une liaison entre un
noeud CYCLADES et un participant avec la procedure IBM-BSC,
Doc. Cyclades TRA 519, (Sep. 1973), pp. 14

[DEN75]
F. Denjean - Connexion de terminaux a un reseau de commutation
de   paquets,   Journees   Internat.   d'Etudes   sur   les
Mini-ordinateurs et la Transmission de Donnees, Liege,
(Jan. 1975), pp. 27.1-27.4

[DEN75a]
F. Denjean - Terminaux connectables au concentrateur CYCLADES,
Doc. Cyclades TER 512.1, (Mar. 1975), pp. 14

[DEP76]
M. Deparis, A. Duenki, M. Gien, J. Laws, G. Le Moli, K. Weaving
- The implementation of an end-to-end protocol by EIN centres :
a survey and comparison, Proc. ICCC'76, Toronto, (Aug. 1976),
pp. 351-360

[DES72]
R. Despres - A packet switching network with graceful saturated
operation,   Proc.   ICCC'72,   Washington D.C.,   (Oct. 1972),
pp. 345-351

[DGQ77]
K. Dang-Quoc - CYCLADES in 77 : Organization, Tools   and
Services, Doc. Cyclades EXP 507, (Jun. 1977), pp. 9

[DIC79]
V. Diciccio, C. Sunshine, J. Field, E. Manning - Alternatives
for Interconnection of Public Packet Switching Data Networks,
Proc. 6th. Data Comm. Symp., Pacific Grove, (Nov. 1979),
pp. 120-125

[DNG76]
Ng. Dang, G. Sergeant - System and portable language intended
for distributed and heterogeneous network applications, Doc.
Cyclades LAN 512, (Dec. 1976), pp. 21

[DNG77]
Ng. Dang, V. Quint - The CICG approach of the IBM 360's
connection to the EIN network : problems and solutions, Doc.
Cyclades SCH 049, (Jun. 1977), pp. 22

[DNG78]
Ng. Dang - Systeme et langage portables pour le traitement des
applications reparties, These Univ. USMG, Grenoble, Doc.
Cyclades LAN 513, (Mar. 1978), pp. 124

[DUM74]
J. Du Masle, M. Farza, G. Sergeant - Proposed organisation of
an interpreter intended for the implementation of high level
procedures on a computer network, Proc. IFIP Working Conf. on
Command Languages, Lund, (Aug. 1974), pp. 7

[DUM74a]
J. Du Masle, M. Farza, G. Sergeant - Specifications de
definition de l'interpreteur reseau et du langage LI-IGOR, Doc.
Cyclades LAN 510, (May 1974), pp. 95

[ECA75]
ECA Automation - SOCRATE/CYCLADES : Manuel d'operation et
d'utilisation, Doc. Cyclades APP-I-004, (May 1975), pp. 24

[EIN76]
EIN - An end-to-end protocol for EIN, EIN Report 76/002,
(Jan. 1976), pp. 22

[EIN77]
EIN - Proposal for a scroll mode Virtual Terminal Protocol, ACM
Comp. Comm. Rev., Vol. 7, No. 3, (Jul. 1977), pp. 23-55

[ELI73]
M. Elie, H. Zimmermann - Vers une approche systematique des
protocoles sur un reseau d'ordinateurs : application au reseau
CYCLADES, Proc. AFCET'73 Congress, Rennes, (May 1973),
pp. 267-283

[ELI75]
M. Elie, H. Zimmermann - Transport protocol : standard
end-to-end protocol for heterogeneous computer networks, IFIP
W.G. 6.1., INWG Note No. 61, (May 1975), pp. 33

[EUR79]
EURONET - Data Entry Virtual Terminal protocol for Euronet,
EEC/DGXIII Doc. WGS/165, (Mar. 1979), pp. 58

[EYR77]
F. Eyries, M. Gien - On line performance measurement in the
CYCLADES computer network, Proc. EUROCON´77, Venice,
(May 1977), pp. 3.1.7.1-3.1.7.6

[FAB76]
G. Fabre, J.P. Le Guigner, G. Le Lann - Presentation et
evaluation de procedures de controle de lignes de transmission,
Doc. Cyclades MOD 093, (Feb. 1976), pp. 35

[FAR74]
M. Farza, G. Sergeant - Machine interpretative pour la mise en
oeuvre d´un langage de commande sur le reseau CYCLADES, These
Univ. P. Sabatier, Toulouse, Doc. Cyclades LAN 511,
(Oct. 1974), pp. 231

[FAY74]
G. Fayolle, E. Gelenbe, J. Labetoulle, D. Bastin - The
stability problem of broadcast packet switching computer
networks, Proc. Internat. Workshop on Comp. Architect. and Net.
Modelling and Evaluation, IRIA, Rocquencourt, North-Holland
Pub. Co., (Aug. 1974), pp. 135-140

[FAY75]
G. Fayolle - Etude du comportement d´un canal radio partage
entre plusieurs utilisateurs, These Univ. Paris VI, Doc.
Cyclades MOD 522, (Oct. 1975), pp. 96

[FOU76]
R. Fournier - Le traitement par lots dans un reseau heterogene,
implementation du serveur OS/MVT sur IBM 360/67 pour le reseau
CYCLADES, These Univ. USMG, Grenoble, Doc. Cyclades SCH 592,
(Dec. 1976), pp. 167

[FOU78]
R. Fournier, J. Seguin - Le teletraitement et les reseaux
d´ordinateurs, Doc. Cyclades GAL 529, (Jan. 1978), pp. 54

[FRA70]
H. Frank, I. Frisch, W. Chou - Topological considerations in
the design of the ARPA computer network, Proc. AFIPS-SJCC´70,
Atlantic City, (May 1970), pp. 581-587

[FRA72]
H. Frank, R. Kahn, L. Kleinrock - Computer communication
network design : experience with theory and practice, Proc.
AFIPS-SJCC´72, Atlantic City, (May 1972), pp. 255-270

[FUL72]
G.L. Fultz - Adaptive routing techniques for message switching
computer communication networks, PhD. Thesis UCLA, Los Angeles,
(Jul. 1972), pp. 418

[GAB71]
H. Gabler - The German EDS Network, Proc. 2nd. Symp. on
Problems in the Optimization of Data Comm. Systems, Palo Alto,
(Oct. 1971), pp. 80-85

[GAR75]
C. Garcia, R. Gardien, A. Marchand, M. Martin, H. Zimmermann -
Specifications de realisation de la station de transport ST2
portable, Doc. Cyclades SCH 536.2, (May 1975), pp. 84

[GEL75]
E. Gelenbe - Exact and approximate solution to probabilistic
models of computer system behaviour, Doc. Cyclades MOD 509,
(Apr. 1975), pp. 39

[GEL77]
E. Gelenbe, J.-L. Grange, P. Mussard - Performance limits of
the TMM Protocol : Modelling and Measurement, Doc. Cyclades
MOD 535, (Apr. 1977), pp. 17

[GEL78]
E. Gelenbe, J. Labetoulle, G. Pujolle - Performance evaluation
of the protocol HDLC, Proc. Comp. Network Protocols Symp.,
Liege, (Feb. 1978), pp. G3.1-G3.5

[GER73]
M. Gerla - The design of store-and-forward networks   for
computer   communications,   PhD. Thesis UCLA, Los Angeles,
(Jan. 1973), pp. 300

[GIE72]
M. Gien, J. Seguin - Langage de macro Fanny et portabilite,
Rapport projet CRIC, Doc. Cyclades LAN 014, (Jan. 1972), pp. 61

[GIE75]
M. Gien, J. Laws, R. Scantlebury - Interconnection of
packet-switched networks : theory and practice, Proc.
EUROCOMP'75, London, (Sep. 1975), pp. 241-260

[GIE77]
M. Gien - Proposal for a standard File Transfer Protocol (FTP),
Doc. Cyclades DAT 519, (May 1977), pp. 48

[GIE77a]
M. Gien - Network Interconnection and Protocol Conversion,
Proc. COMNET´77, Budapest, (Oct. 1977), pp. 39-57

[GIE77b]
M. Gien - Protocole de Transfert de Fichiers (PTF), Doc.
Cyclades IFR 512, (Jun. 1977), pp. 44

[GIE78]
M. Gien - A File Transfer Protocol (FTP), Proc. Comp. Network
Protocols Symp., Liege, (Feb. 1978), pp. D5.1-D5.7

[GIE78a]
M. Gien, J.-L. Grange - Performance evaluations in CYCLADES,
Proc. ICCC´78, Kyoto, (Sep. 1978), pp. 23-32

[GIE79]
M. Gien - Introduction aux reseaux locaux, Doc. Cyclades
RES 1.501, (Apr. 1979), pp. 11

[GIE79a]
M. Gien, H. Zimmermann - Design Principles for Network
Interconnection, Proc. 6th. Data Comm. Symp., Pacific Grove,
(Nov. 1979), pp. 109-119

[GLO73]
J. Glories - The SITA story, SITA monograph 4, (May 1973),
pp. 26

[GRA74]
J.-L. Grange - Specifications du routage adaptatif dans CIGALE,
Doc. Cyclades MIT 576, (Dec. 1974), pp. 64

[GRA75]
J.-L. Grange - Organisation generale du software CIGALE, Doc.
Cyclades MIT 520.1, (Aug. 1975), pp. 10

[GRA75a]
J.-L. Grange - Specifications des mecanismes systeme de CIGALE,
Doc. Cyclades MIT 521.1, (Aug. 1975), pp. 16

[GRA75b]
J.-L. Grange, M. Jastrabsky - Exploitation du reseau CIGALE,
Proc. Convention Informatique'75, Paris, (Sep. 1975), pp. 19

[GRA75c]
J.-L. Grange - CIGALE implementation, tools and techniques,
Doc. Cyclades MIT 602, (Sep. 1975), pp. 10

[GRA76]
J.-L. Grange - CIGALE, the packet switching subnetwork of
CYCLADES, Journees d'Informatique Medicale, Toulouse, Doc.
Cyclades MIT 617, (Mar. 1976), pp. 9

[GRA76a]
J.-L. Grange - L'experience d'un reseau de commutation de
paquets : CIGALE, de la conception a l'exploitation, Proc.
AFCET'76 Congress, Gif-sur-Yvette, (Nov. 1976), pp. 891-900

[GRA76b]
J.-L. Grange - Test et maintenance d'un logiciel de commutation
de paquets : l'experience CIGALE, Doc. Cyclades RES 510,
(May 1976), pp. 8

[GRA76c]
J.-L. Grange, P. Maximovitch - Mesures de delais de propagation
en ligne sur le reseau CIGALE, Doc. Cyclades MES 514,
(Mar. 1976), pp. 7

[GRA77]
J.-L. Grange - Operating the CIGALE packet switching network :
concepts, techniques and results, Proc. EUROCON'77, Venice,
(May 1977), pp. 3.1.6.1.-3.1.6.6

[GRA77a]
J.-L. Grange, H. Zimmermann - Les reseaux a commutation de
paquets : principes et exemples, Symp. Granit, Rennes, Doc.
Cyclades RES 517, (Jun. 1977), pp. 13

[GRA78]
J.-L. Grange, P. Mussard - Performance measurements of line
control protocols in the CIGALE network, Proc. Comp. Network
Protocols Symp., Liege, (Feb. 1978), pp. G2.1-G2.13

[GRA78a]
J.-L. Grange, M. Irland - Thirty nine steps to a computer
network, Proc. ICCC'78, Kyoto, (Sep. 1978), pp. 763-769

[GRA79]
J.-L. Grange - The transition from Informatique to Telematique,
Doc. Cyclades GAL 1501, (Mar. 1979), pp. 4

[GRA79a]
J.-L. Grange - Traffic control in a packet switching network,
Doc. Cyclades SCH 618, (Nov. 1979), pp. 19

[GRA79b]
J.-L. Grange, M. Gien (Ed.) - Flow Control in Computer
Networks, Proc. Intern. Symp. on Flow Control in Comp.
Networks, Versailles, North-Holland Pub. Co., (Feb. 1979),
pp. 429

[GRA80]
J.-L. Grange, J.C. Majithia - Investigation of a two-level
congestion control mechanism for a packet switched network,
Doc. Cyclades MOD 555, (May 1980), pp. 49

[GRD77]
G. Gardarin, J. Le Bihan - An approach towards a virtual data
base protocol for computer networks, Proc. AICA'77 Congress,
Pisa, (Oct. 1977), pp. 17

[GRO79]
G. Grossman, A. Hinchley , C.A. Sunshine - Issues in
International Public Data Networking, Computer Networks,
Vol. 3, No. 4, (Sep. 1979), pp. 259-266

[HEA70]
F.E. Heart, R.E. Kahn, S.M. Ornstein, W.R. Crowther,
D.C. Walden - The interface message processor for the ARPA
computer network, Proc. AFIPS-SJCC'70, Atlantic City,
(May 1970), pp. 551-567

[HEA73]
F.E. Heart, S.M. Ornstein, W.R. Crowther, W.B. Barker - A new
minicomputer multiprocessor for the ARPA network, Proc.
AFIPS-NCC'73, New-York, (Jun. 1973), pp. 529-537

[HIG75]
P.L. Higginson, A.J. Hinchley - The problems of linking several
networks with a gateway computer, Proc. EUROCOMP'75, London,
(Sep. 1975), pp. 452-466

[HLP77]
High Level Protocol Group - A network independent file transfer
protocol, IFIP W.G. 6.1., INWG Protocol Note No. 86,
(Dec. 1977), pp. 97

[HOU78]
J. Houbard - Des ordinateurs pour communiquer, Industries et
Techniques, No. 365, (Mar. 1978), pp. 20-26

[IFI74]
IFIP W.G. 6.1. - Experiment in internetworking : Basic message
format, IFIP W.G. 6.1., INWG Protocol Note No. 1, (Nov. 1974),
pp. 14

[IFI75]
IFIP W.G. 6.1. - Data communications standards, IFIP W.G. 6.1.,
INWG Note No. 84, (May 1975), pp. 15

[IFI76]
IFIP W.G. 6.1. - Basic message format for inter-network
communication, Doc. ISO/TC97/SC6 N1281, (Apr 1976), pp. 7

[IFI78]
IFIP W.G. 6.1. - Proposal for a standard Virtual Terminal
Protocol, ISO/TC97/SC16 N23, (Feb. 1978), pp. 56

[IFR78]
INFOREP - Protocoles d'Appareil Virtuel pour les classes de
terminaux utilises par les applications de teletraitement par
lots., Doc. Cyclades IFR 515.2, (May 1978), pp. 40

[IRI75]
IRIA - Brochure CYCLADES, Doc. Cyclades GAL 525, French,
(Sep. 1975), pp. 30

[IRI75a]
IRIA - Brochure CYCLADES, Doc. Cyclades GAL 526, English,
(Sep. 1975), pp. 30

[IRI75b]
IRIA - Brochure CYCLADES, Doc. Cyclades GAL 527, Spanish,
(Sep. 1975), pp. 30

[IRI76]
IRIA - Report on European User Workshop on end-to-end
protocols, Doc. Cyclades GAL 010, (Mar. 1976), pp. 41

[IRI76a]
IRIA - Rapport du Workshop Modelisation et Simulation de
Reseaux d´Ordinateurs, Doc. Cyclades MOD 521, (Feb. 1976),
pp. 221

[IRI76b]
IRIA - Workshop on protection and security in data networks,
Doc. Cyclades SEC 021, (Jun. 1976), pp. 83

[IRI77]
IRIA - Catalogue des services reseau, Doc. Cyclades EXP 504,
(Jan. 1977), pp. 98

[IRI79]
IRIA - SIRIUS, Bulletin de Liaison de la Recherche en
Informatique et Automatique, No. 57, IRIA Ed., (Oct. 1979),
pp. 59

[IRL75]
M. Irland - Queueing analysis of a buffer allocation scheme for
a packet switch, Proc. IEEE-NTC´75, New Orleans, (Dec. 1975),
pp. 24.8-24.13

[IRL75a]
M. Irland - Simulation of CIGALE : report on assumptions and
results, Univ. of Waterloo, Doc. Cyclades MOD 506, (Jan. 1975),
pp. 54

[IRL75b]
M. Irland - Simulation of CIGALE 1975 : Progress report, phase
1, Univ. of Waterloo, Doc. Cyclades MOD 511, (Jul. 1975),
pp. 27

[IRL75c]
M. Irland - Simulation of CIGALE 1974, Proc. 4th. Data Comm.
Symp., Quebec City, (Oct. 1975), pp. 5.13-5.19

[IRL75d]
M. Irland - Reflections on simulating CIGALE at the University
of Waterloo, Doc. Cyclades MOD 518, (Dec. 1975), pp. 19

[IRL76]
M. Irland, J. McDonald - Simulation of route propagation
mechanism in CIGALE, Univ. of Waterloo, Doc. Cyclades MOD 524,
(May 1976), pp. 27

[IRL76a]
M. Irland, N. Cohen - Simulation of switch-switch protocol
(MV8) in CIGALE, Univ. of Waterloo, Doc. Cyclades MOD 527,
(Aug. 1976), pp. 33

[IRL77]
M. Irland - Analysis and simulation of congestion in
packet-switched networks, PhD. Thesis Univ. of Waterloo, Doc.
Cyclades MOD 099, (Apr. 1977), pp. 221

[IRL77a]
M. Irland, N. Cohen - Simulation of congestion controls in
CIGALE, Univ. of Waterloo, Doc. Cyclades MOD 537, (Jul. 1977),
pp. 33

[IRL78]
M. Irland - Buffer management in a packet switch, IEEE Trans.
on Comm., Vol. COM-26, No. 3, (Mar. 1978), pp. 328-337

[ISO76]
ISO - High level Data Link Control : frame structure, IS 3309,
(1976), pp. 6

[ISO77]
ISO - High level Data Link Control : elements of procedures,
IS 4335, (1977), pp. 40

[ISO79]
ISO - Reference Model of Open Systems Interconnection, Doc.
ISO/TC97/SC16 N227, (Jun. 1979), pp. 181

[KAH71]
R.E. Kahn, W.R. Crowther - A study of the ARPA network design
and performance, BBN Report 2161, (Aug. 1971), pp. 32

[KAH72]
R.E. Kahn, W.R. Crowther - Flow control in a resource-sharing
computer network, IEEE Trans. on Comm., Vol. COM-20, No. 3,
(Jun. 1972), pp. 539-546

[KAM76]
F. Kamoun - Design considerations for large computer communication networks, PhD. Thesis UCLA, Los Angeles, UCLA-ENG-7642, (Apr. 1976), pp. 388

[KAM80]
F. Kamoun, J.-L. Grange, A. Belguith - Congestion control with a buffer management strategy based on traffic priorities, Proc. ICCC'80, Atlanta, (Oct. 1980), pp. 30

[KLE70]
L. Kleinrock - Analytic and simulation methods in computer network design, Proc. AFIPS-SJCC'70, Atlantic City, (May 1970), pp. 569-579

[KLE73]
L. Kleinrock, S. Lam - Packet switching in a slotted satellite channel, Proc. AFIPS-NCC'73, New-York, (Jun. 1973), pp. 703-710

[KLE76]
L. Kleinrock - Queuing Systems, Wiley Pub., New-York, (1976), pp.

[KUO74]
F.F. Kuo - Political and economic issues for internetwork connections, Proc. ICCC'74, Stockholm, (Aug. 1974), pp. 389-391

[LAB76]
J. Labetoulle, G. Pujolle - A study of queueing networks with deterministic service and applications to computer networks, Doc. Cyclades MOD 076, (Mar. 1976), pp. 11

[LEB73]
J. Le Bihan - Specifications d'une communication entre des systemes SOCRATE heterogenes sur le reseau CYCLADES, Doc. Cyclades SCH-I-001, (Apr. 1973), pp. 28

[LEB75]
J. Le Bihan - A survey of problems in distributed data bases, IIASA Workshop on Data Comm., Doc. Cyclades DAT 510, (Sep. 1975), pp. 7

[LEB76]
J. Le Bihan - La repartition des donnees dans les reseaux informatiques, Proc. AFCET'76 Congress, Gif-sur-Yvette, (Nov. 1976), pp. 55-65

[LEB76a]
J. Le Bihan   -   Manuel   de   raccordement   d´equipements
informatiques au reseau CYCLADES, Doc. Cyclades EXP 502.1,
(Feb. 1976), pp. 14

[LEB80]
J. Le Bihan, C. Esculier, G. Le Lann, W. Litwin, G. Gardarin,
S. Sedillot, L. Treille - SIRIUS : a french nation-wide project
on distributed data bases, Doc. Cyclades GAL-I-035, (1980),
pp. 26

[LEG76]
H. Le Goff - Etude generale et evalution de protocoles de
transport dans les reseaux informatiques, These Univ. Rennes,
Doc. Cyclades SCH 588, (Apr. 1976), pp. 149

[LEG78]
H. Le Goff,   G. Le Lann   -   Trade-off simulation, Computer
Networks and Simulation, S. Schoemaker Ed., North-Holland Pub.
Co., (1978), pp. 155-167

[LEH76]
A. Lehon, G. Le Lann, R. Negaret - Distribution of access and
data in large data bases, Doc. Cyclades DAT 517, (Mar. 1976),
pp. 20

[LEL73]
G. Le Lann - La simulation et le projet CYCLADES, Proc.
AFCET´73 Congress, Rennes, (Nov. 1973), pp. 297-306

[LEL76]
G. Le Lann, H. Le Goff - Advances in performance evaluation of
conmunication protocols, Proc. ICCC´76, Toronto, (Aug. 1976),
pp. 361-366

[LEL77]
G. Le Lann   -   Introduction   a   l´analyse   des   systemes
multireferentiels, These Univ. Rennes, Doc. Cyclades CTR-I-004,
(May 1977), pp. 202

[LEL77a]
G. Le Lann - Distributed systems : towards a formal approach,
Proc. IFIP´77 Congress, Toronto, (Aug. 1977), pp. 155-160

372   CYCLADES - REFERENCES

[LEL78]
G. Le Lann - Some fundamental issues in distributed processing,
Doc. Cyclades CTR-I-011, (Jun. 1978), pp. 7

[LEL78a]
G. Le Lann - An overview of distributed control techniques,
Doc. Cyclades CTR-I-012, (Jun. 1978), pp. 17

[LEL78b]
G. Le Lann - Algorithms for distributed data-sharing systems
which use tickets, Proc. 3rd. Berkeley Workshop on Distributed
Data Management and Comp. Networks, (Aug. 1978), pp. 259-272

[LEL78c]
G. Le Lann - Pseudo-dynamic resource allocation in distributed
databases, Proc. ICCC'78, Kyoto, (Sep. 1978), pp. 245-251

[LEL78d]
G. Le Lann - Distributed interprocess communication and
signalling, Atlanta Workshop on Highly Distributed Systems,
Doc. Cyclades SYN-I-004, (Nov. 1978), pp. 18

[LEL78e]
G. Le Lann, H. Le Goff - Verification and evaluation of
communication protocols, Computer Networks, Vol. 2, No. 1,
(Feb. 1978), pp. 50-69

[LEL79]
G. Le Lann - Le controle dans les systemes informatiques
repartis : nature du probleme et quelques solutions, Doc.
Cyclades CTR-I-005, (Jan. 1979), pp. 21

[LEL79a]
G. Le Lann - Consistency and concurrency in distributed
database systems, EEC Advanced Course on Distributed Data
Bases, Sheffield, (Jul. 1979), pp. 29

[LEM73]
G. Le Moli - A theory of colloquies, Proc. 1st. European
Workshop on Comp. Networks, Arles, IRIA Ed., (May 1973),
pp. 153-173

[LIT78]
W. Litwin - Virtual hashing : a dynamically changing hashing,
Proc. 4th. Internat. Conf. on VLDB, Berlin, (Sep. 1978),
pp. 517-523

[LIT79]
W. Litwin - Linear virtual hashing : a new tool for files and
tables implementation, Doc. Cyclades MAP-I-008, (Jun. 1979),
pp. 24

[LLO75]
D. Lloyd, P.T. Kirstein - Alternative approaches to the
interconnection of computer networks, Proc. EUROCOMP´75,
London, (Sep. 1975), pp. 499-518

1 1 .if par
[MAJ78]
J.C. Majithia, M. Irland, C. O´Donnell - Further investigations
concerning congestion control in CIGALE, Univ. of Waterloo,
Doc. Cyclades MOD 542, (Mar. 1978), pp. 28

[MAJ78a]
J. Majithia, M. Irland, C. O´Donnell - Simulation of CIGALE
1978 : investigation of congestion control and host reaction
mechanisms,   Univ.   of   Waterloo,   Doc. Cyclades MOD 549,
(Nov. 1978), pp. 36

[MAJ79]
J.C. Majithia, M. Irland, J.-L. Grange, N. Cohen, C. O´Donnell
- Experiments in congestion control techniques, Proc. Internat.
Symp.   on   Flow   Control   in Comp. Networks, Versailles,
North-Holland Pub. Co., (Feb. 1979), pp. 211-234

[MAN74]
E. Manning - A homogeneous network for data sharing, Proc.
Internat. Workshop on Comp. Architect. and Network Modelling
and Evaluation, IRIA, Rocquencourt, North-Holland Pub. Co.,
(Aug. 1974), pp. 345-353

[MAR78]
I. Margitics - Final report of scholarship on the CYCLADES
computer network, Doc. Cyclades GAL 530, (Sep. 1978), pp. 18

[MCD70]
M.H. Mac Dougall   -   Computer   system   simulation :   an
introduction, ACM Computing Surveys, No. 2-3, (Sep. 1970),
pp. 191-209

[MCK72]
A.A. McKenzie, B.P. Cosell, J.M. McQuillan, M.J. Thrope - The network control center for the ARPA network, Proc. ICCC'72, Washington D.C., (Oct. 1972), pp. 185-191

[MCQ72]
J.M. McQuillan, W.R. Crowther, B.P. Cosell, D.C. Walden, F.E. Heart - Improvements in the design and performance of the ARPA network, Proc. AFIPS-FJCC'72, (Nov. 1972), pp. 741-754

[MCQ74]
J.M. McQuillan - Adaptive routing algorithms for distributed computer networks, PhD. Thesis Harvard Univ., BBN Report No. 2831, (May 1974), pp. 490

[MET73]
R.M. Metcalfe - Packet Communication, PhD. Thesis Harvard Univ., (Dec. 1973), pp.

[MET76]
R.M. Metcalfe, D.R. Boggs - Ethernet : distributed packet switching for local computer networks, CACM, Vol. 19, No. 7, (Jul. 1976), pp. 395-404

[NAF75]
N. Naffah - Presentation du systeme TIPAC, Doc. Cyclades TER 524, (Nov. 1975), pp. 15

[NAF75a]
N. Naffah - Etude de la gestion des terminaux dans un reseau general informatique et developpement d'un systeme microprogramme pour la connexion directe d'un terminal intelligent sur le reseau CYCLADES, These Univ. Paris VI, Doc. Cyclades TER 542, (Dec. 1975), pp. 237

[NAF76]
N. Naffah - Protocole d'appareil virtuel type ecran, Doc. Cyclades IFR 503.2, (Oct. 1976), pp. 61

[NAF76a]
N. Naffah - Multiplexeur miroprogramme de Liaisons Virtuelles (MLV), Doc. Cyclades MPX 502.1, (Nov. 1976), pp. 23

[NAF76b]
N. Naffah - Implementation of host protocols in an intelligent
terminal connected to the CYCLADES computer network, MIMI´76,
Zurich, Doc. Cyclades TER 535.1, (Jun. 1976), pp. 4

[NAF77]
N. Naffah - Impact des microprocesseurs sur les reseaux
informatiques, Doc. Cyclades SCH 599, (May 1977), pp. 11

[NAF77a]
N. Naffah - Le concept de l´appareil virtuel et ses
implications sur l´industrie des terminaux, Proc. AFCET´77
Congress, Versailles, (Nov. 1977), pp. 422-433

[NAF77b]
N. Naffah - Utilisation des microprocesseurs pour
l´interconnexion des ordinateurs a un reseau informatique,
Proc. Convention Informatique´77, Paris, (Sep. 1977), pp. 40-44

[NAF77c]
N. Naffah - Data Entry Virtual Terminal mapping study for
EURONET, Doc. Cyclades TER 546, (Oct. 1977), pp. 180

[NAF78]
N. Naffah - TIPAC : An approach to the intelligent terminal
interconnection to packet switched networks, Proc. Comp.
Network Protocols Symp., Liege, (Feb. 1978), pp. E4.1-E4.6

[NAF78a]
N. Naffah - High level protocol for alphanumeric data entry
terminals, Computer Networks, Vol. 2, No. 2, (May 1978),
pp. 84-94

[NAF78b]
N. Naffah - Diagnostics and Supervision in informatics
networks., Proc. EUROCOMP´78, London, (May 1978), pp. 647-658

[NAF78c]
N. Naffah, H. Zimmermann - Protocol converters and user
interface in the CYCLADES network, Proc. 3rd. Berkeley Workshop
on Distributed Data Management and Comp. Networks, (Aug. 1978),
pp. 36-53

[NEI73]
N. Neigus - File Transfer Protocol, Doc. ARPA NIC-17759,
(Jul. 1973), pp. 50

[NIV77]
B. Nivelet - CYCLADES : Banc d´essai de l´Informatique
Repartie, Doc. Cyclades RES 519, (Jul. 1977), pp. 4

[NIV78]
B. Nivelet - The relations between client and supplier : a
requirement for clarification, Proc. EUROCOMP´78, London,
(May 1978), pp. 821-829

[NPL76]
NPL - Second European User´s Workshop on network protocols,
Doc. Cyclades GAL 017, (Nov. 1976), pp. 87

[ORN72]
S.M. Ornstein,   F.E. Heart,   W.R. Crowther,   H.K. Rising,
S.B. Russell, A. Michel - The terminal IMP for the ARPA
computer network, Proc. AFIPS-SJCC´72, Atlantic City,
(May 1972), pp. 243-254

[PAY75]
R.C. Payne - A brief description of CIGALE´S MV8, Univ. of
Waterloo, Doc. Cyclades MIT 136, (Aug. 1975), pp. 3

[POS71]
J.B. Postel - Official initial connection protocol, Doc. ARPA
NIC-7101, (Jun. 1971), pp. 5

[POU72]
L. Pouzin - Rapport d´analyse du projet CYCLADES, Doc. Cyclades
GAL 510, (Jun. 1972), pp. 250

[POU73]
L. Pouzin, J.-L. Grange - CIGALE, la machine de commutation de
paquets du reseau CYCLADES, Proc. AFCET´73 Congress, Rennes,
(Nov. 1973), pp. 249-263

[POU73a]

L. Pouzin - Architectures et varietes de reseaux, Proc.
AFCET´73 Congress, Rennes, (Nov. 1973), pp. III-XXX

[POU73b]
L. Pouzin - Network architectures, SITA 1st. Technical Conf.,
Paris, Doc. Cyclades RES 504.1, (Nov. 1973), pp. 13-15

[POU73c]
L. Pouzin - Presentation and major design aspects of the
CYCLADES computer network, Proc. 3rd. Data Comm. Symp., Tampa,
(Nov. 1973), pp. 80-87

[POU73d]
L. Pouzin - Interconnection of packet switching networks, Doc.
Cyclades SCH 513.1, (Oct. 1973), pp. 19

[POU73e]
L. Pouzin - Network architectures and components, Proc. 1st.
European Workshop on Comp. Networks, Arles, IRIA Ed.,
(May 1973), pp. 227-265

[POU73f]
L. Pouzin - Network protocols, NATO Adv. Study Institute on
Comp. Comm. Networks, Univ. of Sussex, Brighton, Noord hoff
Ed., (Sep. 1973), pp. 231-255

[POU73g]
L. Pouzin - Efficiency of full-duplex synchronous data link
procedures, Doc. Cyclades TRA 510, (Jun. 1973), pp. 9

[POU73i]
L. Pouzin - Les choix de CIGALE, Proc. AFCET´73 Congress,
Rennes, (Nov. 1973), pp. 265-274

[POU74]
L. Pouzin - The economics of computer networks : the CYCLADES
case, Proc. Symp. on Economics of Informatics, Mainz,
North-Holland Pub. Co., (Sep. 1974), pp. 79-88

[POU74a]
L. Pouzin, H. Zimmermann - Presentation du reseau CYCLADES :
introduction generale aux reseaux et a CYCLADES, Doc. Cyclades
GAL 514, (Feb. 1974), pp. 10

[POU74b]
L. Pouzin - Informatique et Telecommunications, Revue Avenirs,
ONISEP, No. 258, Doc. Cyclades GAL 516.1, (Nov. 1974),
pp. 23-25

[POU74c]
L. Pouzin - Revised CIGALE header, Doc. Cyclades MIT 571,
(Apr. 1974), pp. 2

[POU74d]
L. Pouzin - CIGALE, the packet switching machine of the
CYCLADES computer network, Proc. IFIP´74 Congress, Stockholm,
(Aug. 1974), pp. 155-159

[POU74e]
L. Pouzin - Le reseau CYCLADES, Journal Le Monde, Doc. Cyclades
RES 501, (Sep. 1974), pp. 27

[POU74f]
L. Pouzin - Interconnection of packet switching networks, 7th.
Hawaian Internat. Conf. on System Sciences, Doc. Cyclades
SCH 525, (Jan. 1974), pp. 2

[POU74g]
L. Pouzin - A proposal for interconnecting packet switching
networks, Proc. EUROCOMP´74, London, (May 1974), pp. 1023-1036

[POU74h]
L. Pouzin - Data communications for computers, Doc. Cyclades
TRA 517, (Apr. 1974), pp. 3

[POU74i]
L. Pouzin   -   Structure   d´une   procedure de transmission
point-a-point, Doc. Cyclades TRA 520, (Dec. 1974), pp. 11

[POU75]
L. Pouzin - Le   reseau   CYCLADES,   Revue   l´Informatique,
(Mar. 1975), pp. 12-15

[POU75a]
L. Pouzin - The communications network snarl, Datamation,
(Dec. 1975), pp. 70-72

[POU75b]
L. Pouzin - Congestion control based on channnel load, Doc.
Cyclades MIT 600, (Aug. 1975), pp. 5

[POU75c]
L. Pouzin - An integrated approach to network protocols, Proc.
AFIPS-NCC´75, Anaheim, (May 1975), pp. 701-707

[POU75d]
L. Pouzin - The CYCLADES network : Present state and development trends, Proc. IEEE-NBS Symp. on Comp. Networks Trends and Applications, Gaithersburg, (Jun. 1975), pp. 8-13

[POU75e]
L. Pouzin - Une methodologie pour la normalisation des reseaux de commutation de paquets, Doc. Cyclades SCH 543, (Jan. 1975), pp. 12

[POU75f]
L. Pouzin - Standards in data communications and computer networks, Proc. 4th. Data Comm. Symp., Quebec City, (Oct. 1975), pp. 2.8-2.12

[POU75g]
L. Pouzin - Logique d'adaptation a un reseau de commutation de paquets, Doc. Cyclades SCH 557, (Apr. 1975), pp. 26

[POU75h]
L. Pouzin - Virtual call issues in network architectures, Proc. EUROCOMP'75, London, (Sep. 1975), pp. 603-618

[POU75i]
L. Pouzin - Les reseaux : concepts et structures, Journees INFOREP, St. Maximin, Doc. Cyclades SCH 577, (Dec. 1975), pp. 101

[POU75j]
L. Pouzin - Network design philosophies, INFOTECH State of the Art Report, No. 24, Network Systems and Software, (1975), pp. 134-156

[POU76]
L. Pouzin - Flow control in data networks : methods and tools, Proc. ICCC'76, Toronto, (Aug. 1976), pp. 467-474

[POU76a]
L. Pouzin - Reseaux informatiques, Bulletin de Liaison de la Recherche en Informatique et Automatique, No. 26, IRIA Ed., (May 1976), pp. 2-3

[POU76b]
L. Pouzin - The network business : monopolies and
entrepreneurs, Proc. ICCC´76, Toronto, (Aug. 1976), pp. 563-567

[POU76c]
L. Pouzin - An introduction to data networks, Doc. Cyclades
GAL 521, (Jun. 1976), pp. 9

[POU76d]
L. Pouzin - Distributed congestion control in a packet
network : the channel load limiter, Proc. 6th. Congress
Gesellschaft fur Informatics, Stuttgart, (Sep. 1976), pp. 16-21

[POU76e]
L. Pouzin - The CYCLADES network development, Doc. Cyclades
RES 511, (Jun. 1976), pp. 9

[POU76f]
L. Pouzin - Virtual Circuits v.s. Datagrams : technical and
political problems, Proc. AFIPS-NCC´76, New-York, (Jun. 1976),
pp. 483-494

[POU76g]
L. Pouzin - Acces aux ordinateurs et aux terminaux d´un reseau
informatique heterogene, Doc. Cyclades SCH 581, (Mar. 1976),
pp. 11

[POU76h]
L. Pouzin - Names and objects in heterogeneous computer
networks, Proc. 1st. Conf. on the European Coop. in
Informatics, Amsterdam, (Aug. 1976), pp. 1-11

[POU76i]
L. Pouzin - Standards in data networks, Doc. Cyclades SCH 586,
(Jun. 1976), pp. 11

[POU76j]
L. Pouzin - Connexion de terminaux en mode caractere aux
reseaux publics de donnees : presentation simple du PAD, Doc.
Cyclades TER 539.1, (Nov. 1976), pp. 7

[POU76k]
L. Pouzin - Basic elements of a Network Data Link Control
procedure (NDLC), ACM Comp. Comm. Rev., Vol. 5, No. 1,
(Jan. 1975), pp. 6-23

[POU761]
L. Pouzin - The case for a revision of X.25,   ACM Comp.   Comm.
Rev., Vol. 6, No. 3, (Jul. 1976), pp. 17-20

[POU76m]
L. Pouzin - Application of HDLC to the multiplexing of data
links, Doc. Cyclades TRA 531, (Nov. 1976), pp. 11

[POU76n]
L. Pouzin - Pour une revision de X.25, Doc. Cyclades TRA 528.1,
(Jun. 1976), pp. 4

[POU77]
L. Pouzin - A restructuring of X.25 into HDLC, ACM Comp.   Comm.
Rev., Vol. 7, No. 1, (Jan. 1977), pp. 9-28

[POU77a]
L. Pouzin - Interconnection of virtual circuits and datagrams,
Doc. Cyclades SCH 603, (Feb. 1977), pp. 7

[POU77b]
L. Pouzin - Reseaux de paquets : questions et options, Doc.
Cyclades SCH 611, (Mar. 1977), pp. 7

[POU77c]
L. Pouzin - Les reseaux informatiques, Proc. Electronique+5,
Paris, (Apr. 1977), pp. 7

[POU77d]
L. Pouzin - Existing and future networks, SEAS Technical
meeting, Baden-Wien,   Doc. Cyclades RES 518, (Apr. 1977),
pp. 181-198

[POU77e]
L. Pouzin - The pop art of public data networks, Proc. On Line
Conf. on Comp. Networks, London, (May 1977), pp. 16

[POU77f]
L. Pouzin - Packets networks : issues and choices, Proc.
IFIP´77 Congress, Toronto, (Aug. 1977), pp. 515-521

[POU77g]
L. Pouzin - Network Interconnection, INFOTECH Report on Future
Networks, Vol. 2, (Nov. 1977), pp. 239-254

382   CYCLADES - REFERENCES

[POU78]
L. Pouzin - Les Projets Pilotes, Bulletin de Liaison de la Recherche en Informatique et Automatique, No. 46, IRIA Ed., (Jun. 1978), pp. 2-6

[POU78a]
L. Pouzin, H. Zimmermann - A tutorial on protocols, Proc. IEEE, Vol. 66, No. 11, (Nov. 1978), pp. 1346-1370

[POU79]
L. Pouzin - Recent developments in data networks, INFOTECH State fo the Art Conference on Convergence, (Aug. 1979), pp. 26

[POU80]
L. Pouzin - Internetworking, Computer Communications : State of the Art and Direction of the Future, Prentice-Hall Pub., (1980), pp.

[PRI72]
W.L. Price - Survey of NPL simulation studies of data networks, NPL Com. Sci. Report, No. 60, (Nov. 1972), pp. 21

[PRI73]
W.L. Price - Simulation of packet-switching networks controlled on isarithmic principles, Proc. 3rd. Data Comm. Symp., Tampa, (Nov. 1973), pp. 44-49

[PRI74]
W.L. Price - Simulation studies of an isarithmically controlled store and forward data communication network, Proc. IFIP'74 Congress, Stockholm, (Aug. 1974), pp. 151-154

[PUJ76]
G. Pujolle - Ergodicity conditions and congestion control in computer networks, Doc. Cyclades MOD 090, (Oct. 1976), pp. 33

[PUJ78]
G. Pujolle - Analysis of flow control in switched data network by a unified model, Proc. ICCC'78, Kyoto, (Sep. 1978), pp. 123-128

[PUJ78a]
G. Pujolle - The influence of protocols on the stability conditions in packet-switching networks, Doc. Cyclades MOD 547, (May 1978), pp. 26

[QUI76]
V. Quint - Complement de specifications pour l'utilisation du
protocole appareil virtuel, Doc. Cyclades TER 540.1,
(May 1977), pp. 8

[QUI78]
V. Quint - Convertisseur d'interface CYCLADES-HASP :
specifications de realisation, Doc. Cyclades SCH 614,
(Apr. 1978), pp. 11

[QUI78a]
V. Quint - Terminal lourd pour le reseau CYCLADES :
specifications de realisation, Doc. Cyclades SCH 615,
(Apr. 1978), pp. 15

[QUI78b]
V. Quint - Deux utiisations particulieres du Protocole
d'Appareil Virtuel, Doc. Cyclades TER 589, (Jun. 1978), pp. 9

[RAS75]
J. Rascol - Acces a la ST2-SIRIS8 par boites aux lettres en
mode non bloquant : notice d'utilisation, Doc. Cyclades
SCH 561, (Jun. 1975), pp. 25

[ROB70]
L.G. Roberts, B.D. Wessler - Computer network development to
achieve resource sharing, Proc. AFIPS-SJCC'70, Atlantic City,
(May 1970), pp. 543-549

[ROB72]
L.G. Roberts - Extensions of packet communication technology to
a hand held personal terminal, Proc. AFIPS-SJCC'72, Atlantic
City, (May 1972), pp. 295-298

[SCA68]
R.A. Scantlebury, P.T. Wilkinson, K.A. Bartlett - The design of
a message switching centre for a digital communication network,
Proc. IFIP'68 Congress, Edinburgh, (Aug. 1968), pp. 723-727

[SCA69]
R.A. Scantlebury - A model for the local area of a data
communication network : objectives and hardware organization,
Proc. ACM Symp. on Problems in the Optimization of Data Comm.
Systems, Pine Mountain, (Oct. 1969), pp. 17

[SCA71]
R.A. Scantlebury, P.T. Wilkinson - The design of a switching
system to allow remote access to computer services by other
computers and terminal devices, Proc. 2nd. Symp. on Problems in
the Optimization of Data Comm. Systems, Palo Alto, (Oct. 1971),
pp. 160-167

[SCH75]
P. Schicker, A. Duenki, W. Baechi - Bulk transfer function,
Doc. ETH EIN/ZHR/75/20, Zurich, (Sep. 1975), pp. 24

[SED76]
S.Sedillot - Caracteristiques generales du reseau EIN, Doc.
Cyclades EIN 501, (May 1976), pp. 6

[SEG75]
J. Seguin, G. Sergeant - SYNCOP, systeme normalise de
commutation de processus, Doc. Cyclades XEC 010, (Sept. 1975),
pp. 74

[SEG78]
J. Seguin - Traitement distribue d'informations reparties dans
les reseaux d'ordinateurs, These Univ. USMG, Grenoble, Doc.
Cyclades DAT 524, (Mar. 1978), pp. 185

[SHE75]
C.D. Shepard - An overview of computer network security, Doc.
Cyclades SEC 002, (Nov. 1975), pp. 23

[SUN75]
C.A. Sunshine - Interprocess communication protocols for
computer networks, PhD. Thesis Stanford Univ., DSL Technical
Report, No. 105, (Dec. 1975), pp. 258

[SUN76]
C.A. Sunshine - Survey of communication protocol verification
techniques, Proc. IEEE-NBS Symp. on Comp. Networks,
Gaithersburg, (Nov. 1976), pp. 24-26

[SUN77]
C.A. Sunshine - Interconnection of computer networks, Computer
Networks, Vol. 1, No. 3, (Jan. 1977), pp. 175-195

[TEN74]
P.A. Tenkhoff - The INFONET remote teleprocessing communication
network : design, performanceand operation, Proc. ICCC´74,
Stockholm, (Aug. 1974), pp. 401-412

[THO73]
R.H. Thomas - A resource sharing executive for the ARPANET,
Proc. AFIPS-NCC´73, New-York, (Jun. 1973), pp. 155-163

[TOM74]
R.S. Tomlinson - Selecting sequence numbers, IFIP W.G. 6.1.,
INWG Protocol Note No. 2, (Aug. 1974), pp. 11

[TYM71]
L.R. Tymes - TYMNET : A terminal oriented communication
network, Proc. AFIPS-SJCC´71, Atlantic City, (May 1971),
pp. 211-216

[VER78]
C. Vernier, A. Vichy - Manuel simplifie d´utilisation de
l´editeur de texte et de Gutenberg, Doc. Cyclades UTI 502,
(Nov. 1978), pp. 16

[WAL75]
D.C. Walden, R.D. Rettberg - Gateway design for computer
network interconnection, Proc. EUROCOMP´75, London,
(Sep. 1975), pp. 113-128

[WEB77]
S. Weber - Concentrateur CYCLADES : manuel de reference, Doc.
Cyclades EXP 506, (Apr. 1977), pp. 30

[WEB77a]
S. Weber - Concentrateur CYCLADES : introduction aux concepts
et a l´usage, Doc. Cyclades EXP 506, (May 1977), pp. 52

[WOO75]
D.C. Wood - Measurement of user traffic characteristics on
ARPANET, Proc. 4th. Data Comm. Symp., Quebec City, (Oct. 1975),
pp. 9-2

[ZEI71]
J.F. Zeigler - Nodal blocking in large networks, PhD. Thesis
UCLA, Los Angeles, (Oct. 1971), pp. 152

[ZIM73]
H. Zimmermann - Protocols, Formalization, Hierarchy, Proc. 1st.
European Workshop on Comp. Networks, Arles, IRIA Ed.,
(May 1973), pp. 267-283

[ZIM74]
H. Zimmermann - A brief survey of the CYCLADES computer
network, Proc. EUROCON'74, Amsterdam, (Apr. 1974), pp. D.1-D.4

[ZIM74a]
H. Zimmermann - Communications protocols and network
implementation, Doc. Cyclades SCH 522, (May 1974), pp. 9

[ZIM74b]
H. Zimmermann - Protocoles de communication, Doc. Cyclades
SCH 530, (Jun. 1974), pp. 11

[ZIM74c]
H. Zimmermann - Standard transport protocol : design and
implementation, Proc. European Workshop on Distributed Comp.
Systems, Darmstadt, (Oct. 1974), pp. 9

[ZIM75]
H. Zimmermann - The CYCLADES end-to-end protocol, Proc. 4th.
Data Comm. Symp., Quebec City, (Oct. 1975), pp. 7.21-7.26

[ZIM75a]
H. Zimmermann - Insertion d'une station de transport dans un
systeme d'exploitation, Doc. Cyclades SCH 546, (Jan. 1975),
pp. 8

[ZIM75c]
H. Zimmermann - Protocole de communication inter-ordinateurs :
une experience de realisation portable, Proc. Convention
Informatique'75, Paris, (Sep. 1975), pp. 3

[ZIM75d]
H. Zimmermann - Le protocole appareil virtuel dans CYCLADES,
Journees Internat. d'Etudes sur les Mini-ordinateurs et la
Transmission de Donnees, Liege, (Jan. 1975), pp. 16.1-16.4

[ZIM75e]
H. Zimmermann - Terminal access in the CYCLADES computer
network, Proc. ICS'75, Juan les Pins, North-Holland Pub. Co.,
(Jun. 1975), pp. 97-99

[ZIM76]
H. Zimmermann - Reseaux informatiques et normalisation, Proc.
AFCET´76 Congress, Gif-sur-Yvette, (Nov. 1976), pp. 901-909

[ZIM76a]
H. Zimmermann - High level protocols standardisation :
technical and political issues, Proc. ICCC´76, Toronto,
(Aug. 1976), pp. 373-376

[ZIM76b]
H. Zimmermann - Proposal for a Virtual Terminal Protocol (VTP),
Doc. Cyclades TER 533.1, (Jul. 1976), pp. 20

[ZIM77]
H. Zimmermann - The CYCLADES experience : results and impacts,
Proc. IFIP´77 Congress, Toronto, (Aug. 1977), pp. 465-469

[ZIM78]
H. Zimmermann, N. Naffah - On Open Systems Architecture, Proc.
ICCC´78, Kyoto, (Sep. 1978), pp. 669-674